JOHN PAUL II
AND THE NEW EVANGELIZATION

JOHN PAUL II AND THE NEW EVANGELIZATION

How You Can Bring the Good News to Others

Bishop William Houck • Fr. Avery Dulles • Ralph Martin
Fr. Tom Forrest • Bishop Samuel Jacobs • Fr. Kenneth Boyack
Fr. Kilian McDonnell • Archbishop Gabriel Gonsum Ganaka
Rev. Vinson Synan • Susan Blum • Peter Herbeck
Leonard Sullivan • Fr. Bruce Nieli • Sr. Linda Koontz
Frank and Gerry Padilla • Frank Mercadante
Michael Timmis • Pepe Alonso • Fr. Marc Montminy
David Thorp • Ernesto Elizondo
Fr. Peter Hocken • Charles Colson

Edited by
Ralph Martin and Peter Williamson

IGNATIUS PRESS   SAN FRANCISCO

Cover design: Roxanne Mei Lum
Cover photograph: CNS/Arturo Mari

ISBN 0–89870–536–3
Library of Congress catalogue number 94–79294
Printed in the United States of America

CONTENTS

ABBREVIATIONS

AA	Vatican II, Decree on the Apostolate of Lay People *Apostolicam Actuositatem*, November 18, 1965.
AG	Vatican II, Decree on the Church's Missionary Activity *Ad Gentes Divinitus*, December 7, 1965
CT	Pope John Paul II, *Catechesi Tradendae (Catechesis in Our Time)*, October 16, 1979
EN	Pope Paul VI, *Evangelii Nuntiandi (Evangelization in the Modern World)*, December 8, 1975
GMD	United States Bishops, *Go and Make Disciples: A National Plan and Strategy for Catholic Evangelization in the United States*, November 18, 1992
LG	Vatican II, Dogmatic Constitution on the Church *Lumen Gentium*, November 21, 1965
NPPHM	United States Bishops, *National Pastoral Plan for the Hispanic Ministry*, November 1987.
RH	Pope John Paul II, *Redemptor Hominis (Redeemer of Man)*, March 4, 1979
RM	Pope John Paul II, *Redemptoris Missio (The Mission of the Redeemer)*, December 7, 1990
SC	Vatican II, Constitution on the Sacred Liturgy *Sacrosanctum Concilium*, December 4, 1963
UR	Vatican II, Decree on Ecumenism *Unitatis Redintegratio*, November 21, 1964

CONTRIBUTORS

Jose (Pepe) Alonso is Mission Director of Kerygma in Miami, Florida, which promotes the evangelization of Hispanics in the United States. Mr. Alonso, a Catholic layman, has been active in the evangelization of Hispanics for nearly twenty years.

Dr. Susan Blum is Executive Director of Isaiah Ministries, which promotes renewal and evangelization through parish missions, and Vice President of the National Council for Catholic Evangelization. Her publications include *The Ministry of Evangelization* and *Text, Study Guide, and Implementation Process for Go and Make Disciples.*

Fr. Kenneth Boyack, C.S.P., is Director of the Paulist National Evangelization Organization and consultant to the Catholic Bishops' Committee on Evangelization. Fr. Boyack has authored or edited several books on evangelization including most recently, with Rev. Frank DeSiano, C.S.P., *Creating the Evangelizing Parish.*

Charles Colson is the founder of Prison Fellowship, a ministry to prisoners in the United States and around the world. His many publications include *Born Again, The Body,* and *The God of Stones and Spiders.*

Fr. Avery Dulles, S.J., is the Lawrence J. McGinley Professor of Religion and Society at Fordham University and is a member of the International Theological Commission. Fr. Dulles has published sixteen books including *Models of the Church, The Reshaping of Catholicism,* and *The Craft of Theology: From Symbol to System.*

Ernesto Elizondo is National Coordinator of SINE in the United States. SINE promotes the implementation of a model for parish transformation and evangelization. Mr. Elizondo has a national ministry of promoting Catholic evangelization, especially among Hispanics.

Fr. Tom Forrest, C.Ss.R., is Executive Director of Evangelization 2000, a global effort to promote the Decade of Evangelization in response to the call of Pope John Paul II for a "new evangelization".

Archbishop Gabriel Gonsum Ganaka is the Ordinary of the Catholic Archdiocese of Jos, Nigeria. Archbishop Ganaka also serves as the President of the Council of Bishops' Synods of Africa and Madagascar.

Peter Herbeck is Mission Director for Renewal Ministries and a member of the Leadership Team of The Word of God, an ecumenical charismatic Christian community in Ann Arbor, Michigan. Mr. Herbeck has most recently been involved in coordinating lay Catholic evangelization ministry in Eastern Europe.

Fr. Peter Hocken is an ecumenical theologian residing in the Mother of God Community in Gaithersburg, Maryland. Fr. Hocken has participated in numerous ecumenical endeavors, including the editorial board of *One in Christ,* the Catholic Ecumenical Commission for England and Wales, participation in official consultations on New Religious Movements, and the Society for Pentecostal Studies.

Bishop William R. Houck is the Ordinary of the Catholic Diocese of Jackson, Mississippi. Bishop Houck served as Chairman of the United States Bishops' Committee on Evangelization from 1985–1993.

Bishop Samuel Jacobs is the Ordinary of the Catholic Diocese of Alexandria, Louisiana. Bishop Jacobs is Chairman of the Bishops' Ad Hoc Committee on Charismatic Renewal and serves as Chairman of the Board of Renewal Ministries.

Sr. Linda Koontz, S.N.J.M., is Director of the Spirit of the Lord International Mission located in El Paso, Texas. Sr. Linda ministers to the physical and spiritual needs of the poor of Juarez, Mexico.

Fr. Kilian McDonnell, O.S.B., is Director of the Institute for Ecumenical and Cultural Research and Professor of Theology at

Saint John's University in Collegeville, Minnesota. His recent publications include *Christian Initiation and Baptism in the Holy Spirit* (coauthored with George Montague, S.M.).

Ralph Martin is President of Renewal Ministries and host of the television series *The Choices We Face*. His books include *Hungry for God* and *The Catholic Church at the End of an Age: What Is the Spirit Saying?* Mr. Martin served as chairman of the conference "John Paul II and the New Evangelization" and is the coeditor of this volume.

Frank Mercadante is Executive Director of Cultivation Ministries, of St. Charles, Illinois, which promotes the development of parish youth ministry through training and consultation. Mr. Mercadante has been involved in youth evangelization for more than a dozen years and has written an extensive youth ministry training manual for student leaders and adult youth workers.

Fr. Marc Montminy is Pastor of Ste. Marie's Catholic Church in Manchester, New Hampshire, a parish that has experienced a dramatic renewal over the last five years. Fr. Montminy has promoted spiritual renewal in the diocese of Manchester for a number of years and is the founder of Joseph House, a contemplative retreat center.

Fr. Bruce Nieli, C.S.P., is Director for Evangelization of the National Conference of Catholic Bishops. Besides coordinating the activities of the NCCB Committee on Evangelization, Fr. Nieli travels throughout the United States speaking and giving workshops and retreats.

Frank Padilla is International Mission Director of Couples for Christ. Frank and his wife, Gerry, have been leaders in that movement since it began in 1981. Couples for Christ now numbers over one hundred thousand active members in fifteen different countries and nearly doubles in number every year.

Leonard Sullivan is the current Master of the Westminister Catholic Evidence Guild in London, England. He has been involved in Catholic street evangelism for decades.

Dr. Vinson Synan is Dean of Theology at Regent University in Virginia Beach, Virginia, and has been a regular participant in the Vatican-Pentecostal dialogues. Dr. Synan's books include *The Holiness-Pentecostal Movement in the U.S., Launching the Decade of Evangelization,* and *The Spirit Said "Grow".*

David Thorp is Director of Evangelization for the Archdiocese of Boston. He conducts workshops and retreats on evangelization and spiritual growth throughout the United States and Canada.

Michael Timmis is co-owner, Vice Chairman, and General Counsel for Talon, Inc., a privately held company employing six thousand people. Besides his business responsibilities, Mr. Timmis is extremely active in evangelization and civic affairs.

Peter Williamson was Program Coordinator of the conference "John Paul II and the New Evangelization" and is the coeditor of this volume. Mr. Williamson divides his energies between graduate studies in theology and evangelization in the United States and in Eastern Europe.

PREFACE

Soon after I began to notice the frequency with which Pope John Paul II wrote and spoke on the theme of evangelization, I came across an article by Fr. Avery Dulles, S.J., pointing out the same development. As he says in the chapter he has written for this volume, "The evangelical shift brought about by Vatican II, Paul VI, and the present pope is one of the most dramatic developments in modern Catholicism."

A development this important needed to be explored in a serious way, not with regard merely to its theological significance but also to its practical implementation. While on a trip to New York shortly afterward, my wife, Anne, and I had lunch with Fr. Dulles. Out of that conversation was born a conference on the subject of the new evangelization and its implementation, which Fr. Dulles agreed to keynote.

That conference was held in May 1994 near Ann Arbor, Michigan. It surpassed our expectations in every way: in those who agreed to contribute; in those who came (participants represented fifteen different countries); and in the subsequent quality and usefulness of the theological, spiritual, and pastoral results.

Drawing from the contributors to that conference, Peter Williamson, the program coordinator of the conference, and I have assembled in written form the excellent presentations. Some are more scholarly, some more popular, but all provide an important contribution in illuminating the nature, significance, and practical implications of the call for a "new evangelization".

The pages that follow represent an immense amount of theological insight, spiritual sensitivity, and pastoral experience. We believe this volume will serve as an important resource for the years ahead as the new evangelization unfolds. At the end of some of the chapters, we have provided the phone number and address of the particular organization with which that contributor is associated. We encourage you to contact them for further input as your own response to this important call takes shape.

RALPH MARTIN
Ann Arbor, Michigan
July 25, 1994

INTRODUCTION

Bishop William Houck

When I was a youngster growing up in Alabama, the prevailing attitude about evangelization relegated it to "the business of father and sister". Thus, my own desire to spread the gospel led me to St. Mary's Seminary in Baltimore, where I studied theology from 1947 to 1951.

Being one of the native vocations for the mission diocese of Mobile, I had been advised by my bishop to prepare myself for doing mission work in the diocese. I prepared in part by joining the Catholic Evidence Guild at the seminary and by doing street preaching in downtown Baltimore. One afternoon when a large crowd had gathered on the street corner, a woman asked, "Where are you guys from?" I told her we were students from St. Mary's Seminary and members of the Catholic Evidence Guild. She responded in a surprised tone of voice, "You mean you're *Catholic?*" I answered in the affirmative.

"*Roman* Catholic?" Again I said yes. I do not know if I ever fully convinced her or not, but she went on to exclaim, "I don't believe it! We *Catholics* don't do this kind of thing! *Protestants* do street preaching!"

Many in the Church still hold the same view of evangelization—even nineteen years after the magnificent document of Pope Paul VI, *Evangelii Nuntiandi (On Evangelization in the Modern World)*. Thankfully, we now see a growing awareness of this fundamental mission given to every believer. The call for a new evangelization was set in motion by the Second Vatican Council. The dogmatic constitution on the church *Lumen Gentium* calls all laity to holiness and to responsibility for the mission of the Church: "The obligation of spreading the faith is imposed on every disciple of Christ, according to his ability" (LG, no. 17).

Lumen Gentium clearly states the task of the laity:

> The laity are gathered together in the People of God and make up the Body of Christ under one Head. Whoever they are, they are called upon, as living members, to expend all their energy for the growth of the Church and its continuous sanctification....
>
> Through their baptism and confirmation, all are commissioned to that apostolate *by the Lord himself* [ital. added]. Moreover, through the sacraments, especially the Holy Eucharist, there is communicated and nourished that charity toward God and man which is the soul of the entire apostolate. The laity are called in a special way to make the Church present and operative in those places and circumstances where only through them can she become the salt of the earth. Thus, every layman, by virtue of the very gifts bestowed upon him, is at the same time a witness and a living instrument of the mission of the Church herself, "according to the measure of Christ's bestowal" (Eph 4:7) (LG, no. 33).

God's compassionate love came into our world in a unique way: through the gift of his only Son. The Father's love was made visible through the love and obedience of Jesus Christ, our Savior, by his life, death, and Resurrection. In his last words before his glorious return to "the right hand of the Father", Christ commissioned the apostles to proclaim the good news to all creation: "You will receive power when the Holy Spirit comes down on you; then you are to be my witnesses in Jerusalem, throughout Judea and Samaria, yes, even to the ends of the earth!" (Acts 1:8).

This mission of proclaiming the good news of salvation to all the world is indeed the very reason for the Church. Pope Paul VI identifies it as "the essential mission of the Church" (EN, no. 14). If we believe that to be true, then we must pursue ways of being more open to the power of the Holy Spirit in fulfilling this mission.

How can we more generously respond to the call of our Holy Father for new and creative and splendid approaches to the task of evangelization? Jesus said to his disciples, "I am the Way, and the

Truth, and the Life" (Jn 14:6). If we are to proclaim that truth to others, we must first deeply and sincerely believe what he is saying to us. Once we ourselves become convinced that God loves us and begin to respond to his love, we enter into the prerequisite phase of evangelization: our own personal, ongoing conversion.

Pope Paul VI said, "The Church is an evangelizer, but she begins by being evangelized herself" (EN, no. 15). When we begin to live as if we really believe in Jesus, when our faith begins to influence every aspect of our lives, we cannot help but share that "good news" with others. We also bring this awareness, this understanding, this conviction to the whole Church, that evangelization is a natural and unavoidable activity of all baptized Christians who truly believe in Jesus Christ, his message, and his values.

Pope John Paul II urges, pleads, challenges, and invites us to a new evangelization, "new in expression, new in fervor, and new in methods". We cannot sit back and "let George or Martha do it". We must convince ourselves and others that the first means of evangelization is the "witness of an authentically Christian life".

Jesus came to bring new life into the world, to help all of us put on that new person "created in God's image, whose justice and holiness are born of truth" (Eph 4:24). Our mission today is to put on that new person, with a new mentality, joyfully living and freely sharing the gift of faith and the good news of salvation in Jesus Christ.

The American bishops have recently issued the clear and challenging document, *Go and Make Disciples: A National Plan and Strategy for Catholic Evangelization* (GMD). The three goals outlined in this statement offer a balanced understanding of what Catholics mean by evangelization:

I. To bring about in all Catholics such an enthusiasm for their faith that in living their faith in Jesus, they freely share it with others.

II. To invite all people in the United States, whatever their social or cultural background, to hear the message of salvation in Jesus Christ, so they may come to join us in the fullness of the Catholic faith.

III. To foster gospel values in our society, promoting the dignity of the human person, the importance of the family, and the common good of our society, so that our nation may continue to be transformed by the saving power of Jesus Christ.

Evangelization means living and sharing this great gift of faith with enthusiasm. It means truly accepting Jesus Christ and sharing him with others—sharing his life, his love, his truth, his goodness, his values, his compassion, his integrity. As we foster a deepening conversion to Christ in our own lives, we can joyfully promote a new mentality, an openness, a desire, a willingness to bring to all the world what we Catholic followers of Jesus Christ have to offer.

We have all seen the spiritual hunger among many people in our society. All people want to experience "the good life". God wants to use us to make that colloquial expression become splendidly fulfilled through helping others know and accept Jesus as "the Way, the Truth, and the Life". Catholic evangelization means "bringing the good news of Jesus into every human situation and seeking to convert individuals and society by the divine power of the gospel itself. Its essence is the proclamation of salvation in Jesus Christ and the response of a person in faith, both being the work of the Spirit of God" (GMD, p. 2).

We should be joyful and proud of our privilege and responsibility to be Catholic evangelizers. Our bishops call us "to reexamine our hearts and recommit our wills to the pursuit of evangelization". Our hope and vision is "to make evangelization a natural and normal part of Catholic life and to give evangelizers the tools and support they need to carry out this ministry today" (GMD, p. 10).

What a privilege to be living in a time when we can vividly experience the impact of the Holy Spirit acting in the Church, generating enthusiasm and a new mentality for even the word *evangelization,* but more especially for the *meaning* and *activity* of evangelization. What a joy to be alive in the decade of the nineties, the last decade of this second Christian millennium, when we can help all members of the Church to respond to our Holy Father's call to a new evangelization.

We are not about developing a *program* that ends in the year 2000. Rather we are about developing a new way of thinking, an enthusiasm that continues and grows. We are about deepening our realization of who we are as Catholics, of our commission by the Lord Jesus, and of the power of the Holy Spirit that enables us to live and share our faith.

At the Fourth World Youth Day in 1989, Pope John Paul II defined the whole Church as missionary and evangelistic:

> To be Christians means to be missionaries, to be apostles. It is not enough to discover Christ—you must bring him to others! . . . You must have the courage to speak about Christ, to bear witness to your faith through a lifestyle inspired by the gospel. The harvest is great indeed for evangelization and so many workers are needed. Christ trusts you and counts on your collaboration.

Our Holy Father speaks that same message to us today. Let us pray that the Holy Spirit will increase our awareness, deepen our commitment, and extend the participation of all Catholic people in the ongoing, essential mission of the Church. It is our prayer that this book will help you to achieve these goals.

PART ONE

Catching the Vision

I

JOHN PAUL II AND
THE NEW EVANGELIZATION
—WHAT DOES IT MEAN?[1]

Fr. Avery Dulles, S.J.

Can the Roman Catholic Church be evangelical? Is Catholicism a religion centered on the gospel? Half a century ago some Catholics, and practically all Evangelicals, would have said no. Protestant churches, it was thought, could be churches of proclamation and evangelization, but the Catholic Church was a church of liturgy and law, centered on tradition, hierarchy, and sacraments. In other words, Protestants were viewed as specializing in the word of God and the gospel; Catholics, in the law of God and the sacraments.

This contrast was never anything but a caricature. Luther and Calvin placed high value on the sacraments and the law of God. The Council of Trent, conversely, taught that the whole point of the Catholic system was to transmit the gospel of Jesus Christ in its purity and completeness. The gospel, it was recognized, is the supreme norm for all Christian belief and practice.

For a variety of reasons, this evangelical perspective was obscured during the sixteenth century. Christianity in Europe became rather static, according to the principle that the religion of the sovereign was the religion of the people. Western Europe was carved up into Protestant states and Catholic states, where the faith of the citizens

---

[1] The present paper is an adaptation and updating of my article "John Paul II and the New Evangelization", *America* 166 (February 1, 1992):52–59, 69–72.

was determined more by political and sociological factors than by personal conviction. As far as Europe was concerned, the era of evangelization was closed.

The recently discovered territories in the Americas, Africa, and Asia did of course become objects of a new missionary thrust, but even there the focus was not so much on spreading the gospel as on extending the churches of the mother countries. The missionary task was almost totally in the hands of clergy and religious, who worked in close collaboration with the princes and governors of the colonial powers.

Several historical developments have gradually resuscitated the idea of evangelization. The progressive secularization of European and American culture, in the course of the last three centuries, prevented the churches from relying as they previously had on political and sociological factors to maintain the faith. In the new pluralistic situation, faith increasingly became a matter of personal decision in response to the testimony of convinced believers.

In order to win or maintain adherents, Christianity had to be proclaimed once more, as it had been in New Testament times, as a joyful message centered on Jesus Christ. Beginning in the eighteenth century, England and the United States witnessed several Protestant evangelical revivals. In the twentieth century, Catholicism has undergone an analogous evangelical renewal, partly occasioned by the dechristianization of formerly Catholic countries and greatly assisted by the ecumenical and biblical movements.

Vatican II marks an important stage in this recovery. A simple word-count indicates the profound shift in focus. Vatican I, which met in 1869–1870, used the term "gospel" (*evangelium*) only once[2] and never used the terms "evangelize" and "evangelization". Less than a century later, Vatican II mentioned the "gospel" 157 times, used the verb "evangelize" eighteen times and the noun "evangelization" thirty-one times. When it spoke of evangelization, Vatican II generally meant the proclamation of the basic Christian message of salvation through Jesus Christ.

---

[2] Dogmatic constitution *Pastor Aeternus,* chap. 1 (DS 3053). The reference here is to the written Gospels, not to the gospel message.

In the Wake of Vatican II

Building on the work of the Council, Paul VI dedicated his pontificate to the task of evangelization. His choice of the name Paul signified his intention to take the Apostle of the Gentiles as the model for his papal ministry. In 1967, he renamed the Congregation for the Propagation of the Faith the Congregation for the Evangelization of Peoples. At his burial in 1978, an open book of the Gospels was laid on his coffin, a fitting symbol of his ministry.

Often called the "pilgrim pope", Paul VI was the first pontiff in history to make apostolic journeys to other continents—first to the Holy Land (1964), then to India (1964), next to New York (1965), later to Portugal, Istanbul, and Ephesus (1967), to Colombia (1968), and to Geneva and Uganda (1969). Finally, in 1970, he undertook a long journey including Tehran, East Pakistan, the Philippines, West Samoa, Australia, Indonesia, Hong Kong, and Sri Lanka.

Wishing to engage the entire Church more decisively in the dissemination of the gospel, Paul VI chose as the theme of the Synod of Bishops in 1974 "the evangelization of the modern world". That synod provided him with materials for his great apostolic exhortation on evangelization, *Evangelii Nuntiandi*.[3] Here he described evangelization as the deepest identity of the Church, which exists in order to evangelize (no. 14). While proposing a broad and inclusive concept, the pope made it clear that there can be no evangelization without explicit proclamation of Jesus as Lord (no. 22). It cannot be reduced to any sociopolitical project of development and liberation (nos. 31–33).

John Paul II has carried this evangelical shift yet a stage farther. Summarizing the main orientation of his pontificate, he declared in Mexico City on May 6, 1990: "The Lord and master of history and of our destinies, has wished my pontificate to be that of a pilgrim pope of evangelization, walking down the roads of the

[3] English trans., *On Evangelization in the Modern World* (Washington, D.C.: United States Catholic Conference, 1975); hereafter abbreviated EN.

world, bringing to all peoples the message of salvation."[4] Shortly after his election as pope, John Paul attended in 1979 the Puebla conference of Latin American bishops on "Evangelization at Present and in the Future of Latin America". Since assuming the papal office, he has made sixty-one foreign trips, including ten to Africa.

Beginning in 1983, the pope has issued repeated calls for a "new evangelization". Evangelization, he insists, cannot be new in its content, since its theme is always the one gospel given in Jesus Christ. If it arose from ourselves and our situation, he says, "it would not be 'gospel' but mere human invention, and there would be no salvation in it."[5] Evangelization, however, can and should be new in its ardor, its methods, and its expression.[6] It must be heralded with new energy and in a style and language adapted to the people of our day.

In one of his major encyclicals, *Redemptoris Missio* (1990), John Paul declared: "I sense that the moment has come to commit all of the Church's energies to a new evangelization and to the mission *ad gentes.* No believer in Christ, no institution of the Church, can avoid this supreme duty: to proclaim Christ to all peoples" (no. 3).[7] In this encyclical (no. 86) and in many of his addresses, the present pope links the new effort of evangelization with the preparation for the third millennium of Christianity. We should view the decade of the 1990s, he says, as an extended Advent season in preparation for the great jubilee of the Incarnation.

---

[4] Arrival speech in Mexico City, May 6, 1990; *L'Osservatore Romano* (English ed.), May 7, 1990, pp. 1 and 12.

[5] Opening Address, Santo Domingo, October 12, 1992, no. 6; English trans. in Alfred T. Hennelly, ed., *Santo Domingo and Beyond* (Maryknoll, N.Y.: Orbis Books, 1993), pp. 41–60, at 44–45.

[6] "The Task of the Latin American Bishop", Address to CELAM, March 9, 1983; English trans. in *Origins* 12 (March 24, 1983): 659–62, at 661.

[7] English title, "The Mission of the Redeemer". For text, see *Origins* 20 (January 31, 1991): 541–68. Numbers in parentheses refer to paragraphs of this document, hereafter abbreviated RM.

Characteristics of the New Evangelization

John Paul II has not sought to prescribe in detail the methods and modalities of the new evangelization, which will inevitably take on distinct hues in different situations. He is content to provide the stimulus for local initiatives. But from a variety of papal statements, it is possible to sketch the basic lineaments of the program.

Like any evangelistic outreach, the "new evangelization" must be centered on the person of Jesus Christ and on the one and eternal gospel. Within this stable framework, the new evangelization has at least four characteristics that set it off from the evangelistic efforts of previous centuries.

1. *The participation of every Christian.* No longer reserved to clerics and religious with a special missionary vocation, evangelization is now seen as the responsibility of the whole Church. Vatican II had already taught that since the Church is missionary by her very nature, evangelization is the duty of every Christian (LG, nos. 16–17; AG, nos. 23, 35). Elaborating on this point, Paul VI in *Evangelii Nuntiandi* described the distinct contributions expected of the pope, bishops, priests, religious, and laity (nos. 66–73).

John Paul II makes similar distinctions. Bishops, he says, "are the pillars on which rest the work and the responsibility of evangelization, which has as its purpose the building up of the Body of Christ."[8] Priests, he holds, are by vocation "responsible for awakening the missionary consciousness of the faithful".[9] Members of religious orders and congregations can play a special role because their total gift of self through the vows of poverty, chastity, and obedience gives dramatic testimony to the values of the kingdom of God (RM, no. 69).

Since the beginning of his pontificate, the present pope has

[8] Address to Italian Bishops' Conference, May 18, 1989; *L'Osservatore Romano* (English ed.), June 5, 1989, pp. 7 and 16, at 16.

[9] Message for World Mission Day, October 21, 1990; *L'Osservatore Romano* (English ed.), June 11, 1990, p. 9.

emphasized the participation of all Christians, whether clerical or lay, in the prophetic office of Christ. In his apostolic exhortation on the laity in 1988,[10] he strongly accented the duty of lay Christians to make their daily conduct a shining and convincing testimony to the gospel (nos. 34, 51). It is their special responsibility, he said, to demonstrate how Christian faith constitutes the only fully valid response to the problems and hopes that life poses to every person and society (no. 34). In talks to special groups, such as families, women, students, children, the sick, and the disabled, the pope illustrates how the special gifts of each class can contribute to the total effort.

2. *Distinct from foreign missions.* In a period when it could be taken for granted that the Western world was solidly Christian, Europe and America were no longer regarded as suitable targets for evangelization. They were considered to have passed beyond that stage to the phase of pastoral care. Since the legal and social pressures in favor of religious conformity have been relaxed, it has become apparent that many Christians, including Catholics, were never effectively evangelized. Baptized in infancy, they have never made a living personal commitment to Christ and the gospel. As adolescents or adults, many drift away from the faith.

Evangelization, in fact, must be directed to the Church herself. Paul VI stated this quite bluntly: "The Church is an evangelizer, but she begins by being evangelized herself. She . . . needs to listen unceasingly to what she must believe, to her reasons for hoping, to the new commandment of love" (EN, no. 15). The members of the Church themselves are tempted by the idols of the prevailing culture.

Different strategies are required for dealing with different populations. In large parts of Europe and the Americas, fresh proclamation is urgently needed to fill in what can only be described as a growing religious vacuum. A new paganism,

---

[10] *Christifideles Laici,* December 30, 1988; text in *Origins* 18 (February 9, 1989): 561–95.

marked by phenomena such as astrology and earth-worship, is rampant. Large numbers of young people, especially in the inner cities, are simply ignorant of Christianity, as are multitudes of immigrants and refugees coming from non-Christian parts of the world. These groups stand in need of *primary evangelization,* that is to say, a first proclamation of the Christian message.

Quite different are the needs of people who were once superficially instructed in their religion but have lost a living sense of the faith and are alienated from the Church. They require *reevangelization,* rather than primary evangelization (RM, no. 33), in order to fan the embers of their dying faith into flame. They must be socialized, perhaps for the first time, in welcoming communities of vibrant faith.

3. *Directed to cultures.* Whereas evangelization had usually been studied in terms of individual conversion, Paul VI in *Evangelii Nuntiandi* observed that cultures themselves need to be regenerated by contact with the gospel (no. 20). Convinced of the unbreakable links between faith and culture, John Paul II established the Pontifical Council for Culture in 1982. The new evangelization, he declares, must strive to make human cultures harmonious with Christian values and open to the gospel message.[11]

This is not a matter of dominating cultures but rather of serving them. As the present pope puts it in his encyclical *Centesimus Annus* (1991), evangelization "plays a role in the culture of various nations, sustaining culture in its progress toward truth and assisting in the work of its purification and enrichment" (no. 50).[12] Where the prevailing culture remains closed and hostile, faith cannot fully express itself, nor can the culture achieve its full potential.

[11] Opening Address at Santo Domingo, 1992, no. 22; see also RM, nos. 52–54.
[12] English trans. in *Origins* 21 (May 16, 1991): 19.

In his visit to Los Angeles in 1987, John Paul II raised some challenging questions about the influence of the gospel upon the music, poetry, drama, painting, and sculpture of the United States today. He asked whether all these art forms were sufficiently imbued by the Christian spirit. To bring about this needed development, he added, is primarily the task of the Christian laity.[13]

4. *Envisaging comprehensive Christianization.* The initial proclamation of the basic Christian message is an indispensable first step, but it is only the beginning of a lifelong process. Paul VI set forth a rich and multifaceted program of evangelization in *Evangelii Nuntiandi.*

John Paul II repeatedly defines full evangelization as involving catechetical instruction, moral doctrine, and the social teaching of the Church. Personal transformation requires instruction in sound doctrine, participation in sacramental worship, and the acquisition of a mature ethical and social conscience. A total evangelization, he says, "will penetrate deeply into the social and cultural reality, including the economic and political order.... Such a total evangelization will naturally have its highest point in an intense liturgical life that will make parishes living ecclesial communities."[14] Evangelization in its completeness should lead to what John Paul II, following Paul VI, frequently calls "a civilization of love".

Obstacles to Implementation

The evangelical shift brought about by Vatican II, Paul VI, and the present pope is one of the most dramatic developments in modern Catholicism. Partly for that reason, it encounters incomprehension and resistance among some Catholics, who seem deaf to the new summons. Numerous obstacles must be overcome.

[13] *Origins* 17 (October 1, 1987): 263.
[14] Ad Limina visit of Puerto Rican bishops, October 27, 1988; *L'Osservatore Romano* (English ed.), December 5, 1988, pp. 7 and 14, at 14.

In countries such as our own, terms such as "evangelization" and "evangelism" have a Protestant ring. They appear to be the chosen trademarks of revivalist and fundamentalist sects, some of which are virulently anti-Catholic. Catholics distrust the biblicism, the individualism, the emotionalism, and the aggressive proselytization of certain Protestant evangelistic preachers. Many are further repelled by recent disclosures concerning the private lives of prominent televangelists.

Vatican II, moreover, has put Catholics on guard against anything smacking of triumphalism. Attempting to be modest and self-critical, many tend to gaze inward, asking themselves what still needs to be reformed in their own Church. Diffident about current Catholic doctrine and practices, they often fail to proclaim their faith with confidence. Influenced by the American tradition that religion is a purely private matter, they hesitate to bring pressure on anyone to undergo a deep conversion of mind and heart. Individuals, they assume, should make up their own minds in perfect freedom.

These concerns are not unfounded. Catholics should not be expected to admire or imitate every feature of Protestant evangelistic preaching. They must adopt an authentically Catholic style of evangelization and avoid obnoxious proselytization. But there are many excellent features in Evangelicalism that Catholics would do well to emulate.

In their call for a new evangelization, the recent popes, following the directives of Vatican II, have given the needed impetus. They have, I submit, correctly identified God's call to the Church in our day and have hit upon a suitable remedy for the Church's present ills.

Excessive preoccupation with inner-church issues has led to conflict and polarization in the Catholic community itself. We Catholics need to recapture the sense of having a message that is urgently needed for the redemption of the world. If some of us are weak and vacillating in our faith, this is partly due to our reluctance to share it. Once we grasp the universal validity and significance of the good news, we gain a new appreciation for the privilege of being its bearers. John Paul II puts it very concisely: "Faith is strengthened when it is given to others" (RM, no. 2).

The Ecumenical Dimension

The task of evangelization is complicated by persisting divisions among Christians, but even divided Christians may have much in common. Vatican II called attention to the widespread agreement regarding the central doctrines of the Trinity and the Incarnation, which are preeminent in the "hierarchy" of truths (UR, no. 11).

It should, therefore, be possible for Christians to unite in confessing before the whole world their faith in the triune God and in Christ as Son (UR, no. 12). In their missionary activity, Catholics and other Christians, according to the Council, should be able to join their voices in "a common profession of faith in God and in Jesus Christ". The name of Christ, their common Lord, should draw Christians ever closer together (AG, no. 15).

Tensions undeniably exist between Catholics and certain Evangelical Protestants who refuse to look upon Catholics as Christians and who deny the validity of baptism unless it is administered to believers who claim an inner assurance of having been personally saved. In spite of grave disagreements such as these, which need not be disguised, Catholics and Evangelicals have an important core of shared convictions.

More than most other Christians, Evangelicals are committed to the divine inspiration of Holy Scripture and to the articles of the Apostles' Creed. They unhesitatingly affirm the divinity of Christ, his virginal conception, his atoning death, and his bodily Resurrection. They, like Catholics, expect the return of the Lord in glory at the end of time.

In addition to these theological convictions, Evangelicals accept a strict moral code favoring chastity, parenthood, and family stability. Together with Catholics, they oppose radical programs of euthanasia, eugenics, and population control that would exploit the aged, the handicapped, and the unborn. These and other important convergences are spelled out in greater detail in a recent declaration on *Evangelicals and Catholics Together.* [15] A significant ecumenical realignment seems to be occurring in this country, enabling Evangelicals and Catholics to collaborate in defending the Christian heritage of our nation.

I have previously maintained, and continue to maintain, that Catholics and Evangelicals can greatly assist one another. Evangelicals can help Catholics to focus on the central Christian message, to achieve a deep personal relationship with Christ as Savior, to form warm and welcoming communities, and to proclaim the gospel without embarrassment.

Catholics, conversely, can help Evangelicals to overcome their own imbalances—to avoid a narrow biblicism, to escape from fundamentalistic literalism, to appreciate the value of tradition, and to cultivate a richer sacramental life, a livelier sense of worldwide community, and a keener realization of sociopolitical responsibility. A new ecumenism of convergence and mutual enrichment between Catholics and Evangelicals holds rich potential for the future of Christianity.

The Church's True Treasure

Many of us acknowledge in theory that we should be evangelizers, but we feel unable to measure up to the demands. We may have tried to bring others to the faith and resoundingly failed. Conscious of scandals within our own Church, and of the defection of some Catholics, we may feel humbled by the Church's present difficulties.

Why do people not see the truth of Catholicism? Are not its two-thousand-year history, its worldwide expansion, its inner unity, and its fruitfulness in good works a sufficient demonstration? How can people fail to be impressed by the stability of its structures, the profundity of its theology, the genius of its artists, the splendor of its cathedrals, and the beguiling beauty of its liturgies and music?

[15] Text in *First Things,* 43 (May 1994): 15–22.

While these features are humanly impressive, we must confess that if this were all the Church had to offer, she would be weighed in the scales and found wanting. People turn to the Church, if at all, for other motives. The true treasure of the Church is not what she possesses and produces but the Lord who possesses her and enlivens her with his Holy Spirit.

St. Paul reminds us that in Jesus Christ are all the treasures of wisdom and knowledge (Col 2:3); that he is our wisdom, justice, holiness, and redemption (1 Cor 1:30). To evangelize, therefore, is to preach the "unfathomable riches of Christ" (Eph 3:8).[16] In the words of Paul VI, "he indeed is the hope of the human race, its one supreme teacher and shepherd, our bread of life, our High Priest and our victim, the one mediator between God and men, the savior of this world and king of the eternal world to come."[17]

The Church, therefore, has one inescapable task: to lift up Christ. When she seeks to lift herself up, the Church becomes weak, but when she acknowledges her own weakness and proclaims her Lord, she is strong. Moses in the desert lifted up the bronze serpent, and all who looked upon it were healed. Applying this incident to himself, Jesus said that the Son of Man must be lifted up in order for believers to have life in him (Jn 3:14). "And I, he said, when I am lifted up, will draw all things to myself" (Jn 12:32).

The Church is privileged to lift high the Cross and let the light of Christ shine upon the whole world. Effective evangelization, according to the present pope, consists precisely in this. "The new evangelization", he says, "begins with the clear and emphatic proclamation of the gospel, which is directed to every person. Therefore it is necessary to awaken again in believers a full relationship with Christ, mankind's only Savior. Only from a personal relationship with Jesus can an effective evangelization develop."[18]

---

[16] Quoted by John Paul II in Opening Address at Santo Domingo, 1992, no. 6.

[17] Paul VI, "Opening of the Second Session of the Ecumenical Council", *The Pope Speaks* 9 (1963): 125–41, at 130.

[18] Ad Limina visit of Bishops of Southern Germany, December 4, 1992; *L'Osservatore Romano* (English ed.), December 23/30, 1992, pp. 5–6, at 5.

Here, precisely, lies a major difficulty. Caught up in a merely sociological or traditional type of Catholicism, too many Catholics of our day seem never to have met the Lord. They know a certain amount about him from the teaching of the Church, but they lack direct, personal familiarity. They have never realized that the deepest identity of the Church is to proclaim the gospel.

Many who shift their membership to Evangelicalism do so because Catholicism did not seem to offer them a real encounter with Christ. If they only understood who it is that is really speaking when the gospel is proclaimed from the pulpit, or who comes to them in Holy Communion, or who forgives their sins through the ministry of the priest in sacramental absolution, they could hardly feel as they do.

When Catholic priests address their congregations as if religion were simply a matter of legalistic conformity, they fail in their primary task of preaching the gospel. As often as parishioners go to Mass and receive the sacraments without inner devotion, as a matter of mere obedience or custom, they belie the central meaning of their actions. Deprived of any close relationship to the Lord, they become easy prey to sectarian preachers who give evidence of a joyful encounter with the Word of Life.

When our Lord ascended into heaven, he did not leave us orphans. Christ continues to be present through the Holy Spirit in word and sacrament. He is present in those who minister in his name; he is present in the hearts and minds of all who believe in him. Drawing near to us in so many ways, Jesus seeks to enter into the sanctuary of every Christian heart. If we grant him that entrance, he will be a living, energetic reality and will take over the direction of our lives.

Cardinal Newman, in his *Grammar of Assent,* asked himself how Christianity so quickly became the dominant faith of the Roman Empire. After surveying scores of texts from the early Church, he concluded that there was only one true explanation. The thought and image of Christ was the vivifying idea that made Christians so steadfast in their confession of the faith, so zealous in their practice of mutual love, and so ardent in their hope of eternal life.

The power of the Church today continues to rest on the living presence of the Lord, imprinted on the consciousness of the faithful. Everything in the life and worship of the Church should be aimed at sharpening that consciousness.

In the final analysis, it is not we ourselves who evangelize. The principal agent of evangelization, according to Paul VI, is the Holy Spirit, the divine witness par excellence. "It is not by chance", he wrote, "that the great inauguration of evangelization took place on the morning of Pentecost, under the inspiration of the Spirit" (EN, no. 75).

John Paul II agrees. "Missionary dynamism", he says, "is not born of the will of those who decide to become propagators of the faith. It is born of the Spirit, who moves the Church to expand, as it progresses in faith through God's love."[19] The Holy Spirit imparts the wisdom to seek out new and effective methods, the discretion to speak the appropriate words, and the courage to bear witness with power.

Through the highest leadership of the Church, we have received a call that is clearly inspired by the Holy Spirit. On hearing the call we may be tempted to respond, as Peter once did, "Master, we have worked hard all night and have caught nothing" (Lk 5:5). John Paul II meets this temptation by reminding us that evangelization does not rest on purely human logic. "Faced with the immensity of the tasks, we must repeat Peter's act of faith and trust in the Master: 'At your command I will lower the nets' (Lk 5:6)."[20]

The success of our efforts will not, of course, depend entirely on ourselves. Our hearers must accept the grace to respond. The word of God sometimes falls on rocky soil, as Jesus himself experienced, but the possibility of failure and rejection cannot excuse us from our duty to bear witness. When the acceptable time arrives, the Lord is capable of bringing forth a harvest out of all proportion to our labor and talents.

[19] To Italian bishops on liturgical course, February 12, 1988; *L'Osservatore Romano* (English ed.), March 14, 1988, p. 5.
[20] Ad Limina visit of Polish Episcopal Conference, January 12, 1993; *L'Osservatore Romano* (English ed.), February 3, 1993, pp. 5–6, at 6.

If we faithfully take up our task, in a spirit of prayerful confidence, we can firmly hope that the Church may be approaching a new springtime. We may yet be privileged to witness a new Catholic moment, a new Pentecost, the rebirth of a fresh and dynamic Catholicism.

2

WHAT IS OUR MESSAGE?

Ralph Martin

Recently someone asked me why many Southern Baptists were so eager to share the good news with others, in comparison to the average Catholic's total disinterest. Several reasons came to mind. The chief one is that most Baptists have a clear understanding of the heart of the gospel message: that we are *saved by grace through faith.* Igniting this head knowledge is a personal appreciation for what Jesus has done for them. They also grasp the eternal consequences of faith, that there really is a heaven and a hell.

Unfortunately, I cannot say the same for most Catholics. Despite all the years of religious education and catechesis, there seem to be some astounding gaps in our grasp of the gospel message—at least enough to dampen our enthusiasm for sharing the good news. Dr. Peter Kreeft, a professor of philosophy at Boston College, has made similar observations through contact with his predominantly Catholic students. "The life of God comes into us by faith, through us by hope, and out of us by the works of love. . . . But many Catholics still have not learned this thoroughly Catholic and biblical doctrine. They think we're saved by good intentions, or being nice, or sincere, or trying a little harder, or doing a sufficient number of good deeds."[1]

Over the last twenty-five years, Dr. Kreeft has asked hundreds of his students this pointed question: "If you should die tonight

---

[1] Peter Kreeft, "Luther, Faith, and Good Works", *National Catholic Register,* November 10, 1991, p. 8.

and God asks you why he should let you into heaven, what would you answer?" His findings? "The vast majority of them simply don't know the right answer to this, the most important of all questions, the very essence of Christianity. They usually don't even mention Jesus!"[2]

In our efforts toward evangelization, we must be clear on the content and substance of the gospel message, or else the means chosen and the results obtained will be quite ambiguous. While programs, plans, and processes of evangelization are important, clarity of content is indispensable. What has been *revealed* to us about what it means to be a Christian? What is the *truth* which God wants us to communicate to others? In short, what is the gospel message?

Saved by Grace

The Scriptures frequently summarize the most foundational elements of the gospel message. John 3:16 presents one such statement: "Yes, God so loved the world that he gave his only Son, that whoever believes in him may not die but may have eternal life." Ephesians 1:7–8 is another: "It is in Christ and through his blood that we have been redeemed and our sins forgiven, so immeasurably generous is God's favor to us."

When we read these brief summaries of the good news, we are struck by the overwhelming love, mercy, and generosity at the heart of the plan of salvation. The most foundational element of the gospel is not *our love for God,* but *his love for us* (1 Jn 4:9–10). Just as his love initiated creation, his love initiates the chance for a renewal of creation. Scripture characterizes God's love and mercy as great, immeasurably generous, rich, kind, and lavished upon us (see Eph 1:7–8, 2:1–10; Titus 3:3–8).

This saving gift of God's Son is totally undeserved and unmerited on our part. It is purely and entirely by God's free choice, by his

---

[2] Peter Kreeft, "Protestants Bring Personal Touch to the Life of Faith", *National Catholic Register* April 24, 1994, pp. 1 and 7.

favor, by his grace, that Jesus is given to us. "I repeat, it is owing to his favor that salvation is yours through faith. This is not your own doing, it is God's gift; neither is it a reward for anything you have accomplished, so let no one pride himself on it" (Eph 2:8–9).

What we deserve by nature is God's wrath, to die because of our sin. Apart from Christ, we would be "slaves of our passions and of pleasures of various kinds", locked hopelessly in "malice and envy, hateful ourselves and hating one another" (Titus 3:3). We would be under the sway of "the present age and . . . the prince of the air", "following every whim and fancy" (Eph 2:1–3).

God freely decided to give the human race another chance. And he chose a means designed to kill the root of pride at the origin of sin: Satan's lie that "you shall be as gods." At the heart of redemption is a profound act of humility, the self-offering of the Son of God as a sacrifice for us, and it must be met by an act of humility on our part, the acknowledgment of sin and the surrender of faith. We need humbly to receive rather than self-righteously to achieve salvation, so that pride can be broken, so that no human being can boast of anything except the Cross of Christ (1 Cor 1:27–31).

Saved through Faith

We also read in these scriptural summaries how we *receive* this great gift of God's saving love, his only Son, Jesus: we are *saved by grace through faith.* "Whoever believes in him may not die, but may have eternal life." (Jn 3:16) The baptism of new birth and renewal by the Holy Spirit both presuppose faith, which itself comes as a gift God offers to all people.

Faith normally comes from hearing the truth of the gospel preached, seeing or hearing about signs and evidence that confirm its truth, and a direct working of the Holy Spirit in the soul (Rom 10:8–15; 2 Cor 3:16–18; Jn 14:10–11; 1 Th 5:9). Faith itself, and the conversion that flows from it, are themselves gifts of God's grace and favor, the unmerited working of his Spirit. As John Paul II put it in *Redemptoris Missio:*

> The proclamation of the Word of God has Christian conversion as its aim: a complete and sincere adherence to Christ and his gospel through faith. Conversion is a gift of God, a work of the blessed Trinity. It is the Spirit who opens people's hearts so that they can believe in Christ and "confess him" (cf. 1 Cor 12:3); of those who draw near to him through faith Jesus says, "No one can come to me unless the Father who sent me draws him" (Jn 6:44) (no. 46).

What then is faith? Faith is a way of knowing and seeing with our spiritual eyes invisible realities that are infinitely more important than the realities we can see with our biological eyes. "Faith is confident assurance concerning what we hope for, and conviction about things we do not see. Because of faith the men of old were approved by God. Through faith we perceive that the worlds were created by the word of God, and that what is visible came into being through the invisible" (Heb 11:1–3).

Scripture invests the concept of faith with several different meanings. The "deposit of faith" (2 Tim 1:13–14, 2:2; Jude 3) refers to that body of truths revealed by God. This primary meaning of faith as a *knowledge of truth* is the one we have in mind when we talk about passing on "the faith" or teaching "the faith". Obviously, as essential as this kind of faith is, it is not enough. "Even the demons believe" (James 2:19) but lack both obedience and trust.

Scripture also speaks of *"the obedience of faith"* (Rom 1:5, 16:26). Faith in this sense means knowledge of truth that contains an implicit or explicit call to obedience. A well-known formulation of this concept would be "faith without works is dead" (James 2:17). An aim and fruit of the gospel is a particular kind of human behavior that accords with the truth. Jesus said, "If you live according to my teaching, you are truly my disciples; then you will know the truth, and the truth will set you free" (Jn 8:31–32).

As we obey the truth that is revealed to us, we will understand still more of that truth and experience still more of its fruits in our lives. Real change becomes possible through the power of the gospel. Even years of habit, addictions, and the influence of a pagan world can be overcome by a living relationship with God.

Yet this obedience, this sign of authentic saving faith, this manifestation of faith working through love, this growth in moral perfection, prayer, a life of love, fidelity, and service, is itself brought about and perfected through the grace of God. Ephesians 2:10 tells us that "we are truly his handiwork, created in Christ Jesus to lead the life of good deeds which God prepared for us in advance." We are once again humbled. The paths that we walk and the daily circumstances of our lives have been given to us for our transformation, that we may learn to serve and love God and others.

Even though salvation is a gift received through faith, Scripture exhorts us to "work out your own salvation with fear and trembling; for God is at work in you both to will and to work for his good pleasure" (Phil 2:12–13). God's grace is at work to enable us to will and to do what he is calling us to do. He not only calls us to the obedience of faith but also enables us to obey. What grace!

Faith as *trust* is the third and perhaps most common use of this word in Scripture. "Blest is she who trusted that the Lord's words to her would be fulfilled" (Lk 1:45). The basic thrust of Jesus' whole message is to trust in him and in the Father. He tells us to stop worrying about what we are to eat or drink and instead to seek out his kingship over us. The rest will follow in turn (Lk 12:28–31).

Jesus calls us to faith in the goodness of God, the power of God, the truthfulness of God, and most of all the personal love of God for each one of us in every aspect of our lives and needs. He calls us to the kind of surrender and abandonment possible only when we know who God is. This kind of faith is centered in a personal relationship with God, Father, Son, and Holy Spirit.

Church leaders are recognizing that many Catholics are impoverished in their personal relationship with Jesus. Recently, while talking to a group of American bishops, Pope John Paul II stressed this point: "Sometimes even Catholics have lost or never had the chance to experience Christ personally: not Christ as a mere 'paradigm' or 'value', but as the living Lord, 'the way, and the truth, and the life' (Jn 14:6)."[3]

Catholics have tended to stress faith as propositional belief and moral obedience, and not so much faith as a personal relationship of trust, surrender, and abandonment to God. I believe that tendency has diminished the worship, life, and mission of the Church and has limited the experience and working of the Spirit. In any event, Scripture clearly presents faith as our lifeline to God. Faith is what inaugurates, sustains, and deepens that relationship. It is as vital to our life with God as an oxygen line is to a deep-sea diver.

Saved from Hell

The gospel is presented as a message with eternal consequences. Apart from Christ and faith in him, we are slaves to sin, to our own passions, "hateful ourselves and hating one another", "foolish and disobedient" (Titus 3:3). Life apart from Christ amounts to hell on earth. Unless we are transferred, by grace through faith, from this kingdom of darkness and to the kingdom of the beloved Son of God, this state of hell becomes intensified and permanent.

Jesus had these grave consequences in mind when he commanded his disciples, "Go into the whole world and proclaim the good news to all creation. The man who believes in it and accepts baptism will be saved; the man who refuses to believe in it will be condemned" (Mk 16:15–16).

Vatican II clearly spelled out the Church's position on the necessity of Jesus for salvation in its constitution on the Church *Lumen Gentium* (no. 16). In summary, the Catholic Church believes that salvation is impossible apart from Jesus but that those who "through no fault of their own" have never heard the good news will be judged on the basis of the light God has given them in creation and in conscience (Rom 1, 2).

Despite this possibility, we should not be lax in preaching the gospel, since "very often, deceived by the Evil One, men have

---

[3] John Paul II, "New Catechism Will Promote National Recatechising Effort", *L'Osservatore Romano,* Eng. ed., March 24, 1993, p. 3.

become vain in their reasonings, have exchanged the truth of God for a lie and served the world rather than the Creator" (cf. Rom 1:21–25). Living and dying in this world without God exposes people to ultimate despair. To bring glory to God and the salvation of many, the Church is mindful of the Lord's command to "preach the gospel to every creature" (Mk 16:16) (LG, no. 16).

Jesus himself frequently spoke about the reality of hell (Mt 22:13; Mk 9:43; Mt 13:42, 50; Rev 20:15; Mk 9:48; Jn 5:25, 29; Rev 2:11, 20:14; Mt 25:46; 2 Th 1:7–10). Despite all the debate about what is metaphorical and what is literal, one thing is undeniably clear: hell is real, unspeakably awful, and you really do not want to end up there. Jesus makes clear that hell is not exactly a long shot but is the way we all drift unless we cling to him. "Enter through the narrow gate. The gate that leads to damnation is wide, the road is clear, and many choose to travel it. But how narrow is the gate that leads to life, how rough the road, and how few there are who find it!" (Mt 7:13–14).

We have witnessed a virtual silence on the reality of hell as a consequence of people having rejected the gospel, not believing in it, or disobeying it—even in some notable official documents of the Church, where an exposition on the reality of hell was virtually required by the subject matter.

Certainly we should make an effort to present the Christian message in a positive and attractive way. We are not at liberty, however, to falsify it by silence where it conflicts with our increasingly secular and pagan culture. To do so is to diminish the gospel's power, distort its saving truth, and remove an essential motivation for evangelization.

If everyone ultimately will be saved and there is no real possibility of hell for the "average person", why be concerned? Many Catholics are not. If it does not matter in the end whether someone repents, believes, and is baptized or not, why bother to preach the good news? Many Catholics do not.

Saved for Heaven

God lavishes his love on all those who receive his gift of salvation through faith and baptism. Joined to Jesus, they become adopted as sons and daughters of God. The Holy Spirit makes his home in their hearts so that they begin to know the joy, peace, and love of heaven right away—in an imperfect, limited, but real way.

Scripture frequently speaks of the reality of heaven, which is described in various ways: eternal life (Mt 25:46); glory beyond compare (2 Cor 4:17); a place in which the redeemed participate in the life of God in glorified, immortal, incorruptible bodies (1 Cor 15:35–55); a dwelling in the heavens (2 Cor 5:1); the city of the living God which is filled with angels in festal garb (Heb 12:22).

While we taste a bit of that heaven here on earth, we await a glorious inheritance far beyond our imagining: a new earth, a new heaven, the new Jerusalem, the holy city, where God will personally wipe every tear from our eyes, where there shall be no more death or mourning, crying, or pain (Rev 21:1–4, 10–11; 2 Pet 3:13).

Our faith is nourished by the body of Christ, by the Church and the Eucharist. The gospel message is good news beyond human comprehension: we are saved by love, for love, for all eternity. And yet there is more. God knows that this life of faith must be nurtured, like a tender shoot, lest it wither and die. Evangelization must lead to catechesis, learning what Christ teaches.

An essential part of the good news is that Jesus, through his Cross and Resurrection, is pouring out his Holy Spirit so we can become one body, a holy nation, a royal priesthood, the Church, his very body, and even his bride. He is gathering together his sons and daughters into a new family, the Church. As part of the way of life of the redeemed community, Jesus has asked us to celebrate the Lord's Supper in memory of him.

In the Eucharist we remember and make present the central realities of our redemption—the sacrificial death of Jesus on the Cross and his Resurrection—and we look forward to his return in glory. We proclaim the good news together: Christ has died, Christ has risen, Christ will come again. We are nourished through the sacramental presence of his Body and Blood. We worship the Father in Spirit and in truth.

Heaven is a *corporate* reality. Together, we begin to learn what it means to live for the destiny for which we were created, to "live for the praise of his glory" (Eph 1:12). The Church and the Eucharist are essential elements of the good news. Christian initiation is not complete, and therefore evangelization is not complete, until the new convert becomes part of Christ's body, expressed in a local congregation, and is invited to participate in the eucharistic feast.

Vatican II recognized the liturgy as the summit toward which the activity of the Church is directed, as well as the fount from which all her power flows. "For the goal of apostolic endeavor is that all who are made sons of God by faith and baptism should come together to praise God in the midst of his Church, to take part in the Sacrifice and to eat the Lord's Supper" (SC, nos. 9–10).

Thus evangelization leads to incorporation into his body, the Church, and is consummated and expresses itself in the liturgy, the formal, public worship of the Church. In the Eucharist we remember that we are saved by grace, through faith, and give thanks and praise to the Father for the immeasurably generous gift of his Son, Jesus. John Paul II spoke about this inseparable link between evangelization and the Eucharist in his first encyclical:

> The Church never ceases to relive his death on the cross and his resurrection, which constitute the content of the Church's daily life. Indeed, it is by the command of Christ himself, her Master, that the Church unceasingly celebrates the Eucharist, finding in it the "fountain of life and holiness", the efficacious sign of grace and reconciliation with God, and the pledge of eternal life.
>
> The Church lives his mystery, draws unwearyingly from it, and continually seeks ways of bringing this mystery of her Master and Lord to humanity—to the peoples, the nations, the succeeding generations, and every individual human being—as if she were ever repeating, as the Apostle did: "For I decided to

know nothing among you except Jesus Christ and him crucified."
The Church stays within the sphere of the mystery of the
Redemption, which has become the fundamental principle of
her life and mission (RH, no. 7).

The Eucharist is a *representation* of the gospel in a very special
way. As we gather at the table of the Lord, we remember the
unmerited free gift of redemption through the sacrifice of Christ's
life, death, and Resurrection and draw nourishment from his
presence in the Eucharist according to our faith.

"Eucharist" in Greek means thanksgiving. The liturgy is sup-
posed to be characterized by a spirit of profound gratitude and
praise for the awesome love demonstrated in the sacrifice of
Christ. But how can we be grateful for something we do not
know we have received or for something we think we deserve
because of our own merits? How can we be grateful if we do not
know what we have been saved from and saved for?

> O stupid Galatians! Who has bewitched you, before whose eyes
> Jesus Christ was publicly portrayed as crucified? I want to learn
> only this from you: did you receive the Spirit from works of
> the law, or from faith in what you heard? Are you so stupid?
> After beginning with the Spirit, are you now ending with the
> flesh? Did you experience so many things in vain? — if indeed it
> was in vain. Does, then, the one who supplies the Spirit to you
> and works mighty deeds among you do so from works of the
> law or from faith in what you heard? (Gal 3:1–5).

Faith in the crucified Christ is important not just initially but is
required daily if we are to follow the Lord, if the Spirit is to be
continually poured out as we and the entire Church desperately
need. A "new Pentecost" must accompany the "new evangelization",
and the key to both is the same: the basic gospel message. We are
sinners saved by grace, through faith; saved from hell, for heaven,
by Jesus Christ, our Savior and Lord.

Ralph Martin is President of Renewal Ministries, which promotes renewal and evangelization through television, publications, and conferences. For more information, contact:

Renewal Ministries
P.O. Box 8229
Ann Arbor, MI 48107
313–662–1730

3

WHY SHOULD CATHOLICS EVANGELIZE?

Fr. Tom Forrest, C.Ss.R.

The Holy Spirit gives us three excellent reasons why Catholics should evangelize: his supernatural gifts of faith, hope, and charity. Concerning all God's gifts, Jesus commanded us, "Without cost you have received; without cost you are to give" (Mt 10:8).

In obeying this command, we have to give exactly the way Jesus gave to us. He shared with us the very best he has to give: his Father, his Spirit, his Mother, his name, his life, his glory and inheritance. This means that we in turn have to share the very best we have to give: and that means the faith, hope, and love that enrich our lives and that we have in our hearts because of him.

Our Faith Unlocks the Gates of Heaven

I remember a few years ago touring some of the ancient ruins of Rome with a pleasant priest. He talked with great excitement about his favorite therapeutic technique, the "primal scream". He spoke about it so much that I was tempted to let out a "scream" of my own, thinking how much good this exuberant priest could do if he were speaking with the same enthusiasm about Jesus.

If an angel were to suddenly announce that I had been granted one wish for the good of the Church, my choice would be clear. I would wish for a new and unshakable faith-conviction through-out the entire Church regarding the incomparable value of knowing Jesus Christ. This conviction is the kind of faith for which martyrs give their lives and which missionaries struggle at tremendous risk to implant in others.

"Incomparable" is a superlative, and superlatives, like absolutes, are out of style in this day and age. Even so, Jesus Christ *is* the supreme good. Nothing and no one can match him or even be compared. Jesus is in a class by himself! He is Emmanuel: God himself among us. St. Paul writes, "I reckon that nothing can . . . outweigh the supreme advantage of knowing Jesus Christ my Lord. For him I have accepted the loss of everything, and I look on everything as so much rubbish if only I can have Jesus and be given a place in him. . . . All I want is to know Christ and the power of his resurrection" (Phil 3:8–10).

In the opening scenes of the poignant film *The Mission,* a priest is martyred by Guaraní Indians of Paraguay. Soon afterward, another young priest sets out to bring Christ to these same Indians. When his companions express their concern that he is endangering his life, the future martyr (canonized by Pope John Paul II in 1988) responded with the simple words, "I *must* go." At any cost, he is saying, I *must* bring Jesus to those who do not know him.

This conviction about the absolute importance of knowing Christ leads us to the supreme charity of making him known to others. This faith, however, is being lost in an age of exaggerated egalitarianism that goes beyond the equal rights of individuals and gives equal value to all beliefs. A young woman once asked me about the hopes of Evangelization 2000 regarding good Hindus, Muslims, and Buddhists. When I answered that our desire and prayer is to lead them gently and freely to Jesus, she responded in bewilderment, "But won't that do damage to their culture?"

I tried to explain some crucial distinctions that place this concern in proper perspective. Buddha is only a teacher; Jesus is the living Word of God. Mohammed is a prophet; Jesus is the fulfillment of all prophecy. Hindus at times worship a confusion of gods; Jesus is the one, true God, King of heaven and earth. At Jesus' name—and at his name *only*—every knee must bend in the heavens, on the earth, and under the earth, because "there is no other name in the whole world given to men by which they are to be saved" (Acts 4:12).

We can perform a vast number of good deeds, but one is supreme: proclaiming Jesus Christ as the only Savior of the world. Those who do not know Christ have no guaranteed way of getting to heaven. *Only Jesus* reveals the Father (Mt 11:27). *Only Jesus* empowers us for godlike loving and godlike forgiving (Jn 15:9–12; Lk 15:31–32). *Only Jesus* gives us a totally new beginning by washing away our guilt and even the memory of our sins (Is 53:11–12; Micah 7:18–19; Jer 31:34; Heb 10:17–18). *Only Jesus* gives us his Holy Spirit to make us the "very holiness of God" (2 Cor 5:17–21).

A disciple of Christ enjoys a tremendous advantage in regard to salvation over the adherents of other religions. As one dynamic cardinal at the Vatican stated during a School of Evangelization, "Buddhists, Hindus, and Muslims can be saved if, if, if, and if!"

Christ commissioned St. Paul "to open the eyes of those to whom I am sending you, to turn them from darkness to light, and from the dominion of Satan to God: that through their faith in me they may obtain forgiveness of their sins and a portion among God's people" (Acts 26:16–18). The task of an evangelist is the delightful one of evacuating hell and populating heaven, a task that draws its power from a burning conviction that the very purpose of life and the measure of all human success are summed up in knowing Jesus Christ and being united with him.

Our Hope Gives Light to a World in Darkness

In his great encyclical *Redemptoris Missio,* Pope John Paul II makes this prophetic statement: "Today, as never before, the Church has the opportunity of bringing the Gospel, by witness and word, to all people and nations. I see the dawning of a new missionary age, which will become a radiant day bearing an abundant harvest, if

all Christians . . . respond with generosity . . . to the calls and challenges of our times" (no. 92).

If, indeed. If there were ever a time when sinners needed
conversion, if there were ever a time when captives needed to be
set free and mountains of pain and depression removed, if there
were ever a time when the human race needed sanctification and
salvation, if there were ever a time when the whole world needed
to hear and follow Christ's teaching on love, mercy, and forgiveness,
that time is now!

So too, if there were ever a time when Christ held the only
answer, if there were ever a time when Christian values needed to
be proclaimed, if there were ever a time when our own faith
needed to be renewed and activated, if there were ever a time
when the Church needed to be united in common and decisive
efforts, if there were ever a time in history for dynamic evangelization, that time is now!

The pope is telling us that if there were ever a time when the
world was ready to listen and respond to the Christian message,
our own moment in history is that time. We all know about the
enormous problems in the world today: racial and ethnic hatreds
fueling wars of unthinkable savagery; children who, if their lives
are not ended in the womb, live in danger of abuse and violence
even within their own homes; city streets too dangerous to walk
that have become dormitories for the lost and homeless; self-
doubts and chronic depression leading to "escape routes" of addiction and suicide; a planet threatened by global pollution and an
over-consumption producing more garbage than we can handle.

Reporters and analysts talk endlessly about crime, poverty,
economic recessions, and global pollution, yet few claim to have
any answers. Leaders have lost the confidence of the people,
while scandals in palaces and rectories shake our loyalties and
even our faith. That is why so many people are hungry to hear
about something and someone in whom they can truly trust and
believe.

Jesus is that someone. Someone so good that he is called the
spotless and innocent Lamb of God. Someone so wise that he is
called the Wisdom come down from heaven, the Word of eternal
life. Someone so faithful and merciful that he is called the Way, the

Truth, and the Life. Someone who promises his disciples an unbelievable destiny, and who carries them as God's own children all the way to paradise.

Doctors need medicine before they can heal. Soldiers need arms before they can do battle. Cooks need ingredients before they can prepare a banquet. Farmers need seeds before they can reap a harvest. Cars need gasoline before they can run. Sailors need wind before they can sail. Orchestras need a musical score before they can enchant audiences with their symphonies. And the world needs Jesus, our *anchor of hope,* before we can find an answer to our problems and needs.

We are the "Easter people", God's own people of hope. St. Peter told us to "always be ready to give an explanation to anyone who asks you for a reason for your hope" (1 Pet 3:15). And the reason for our hope is Jesus Christ, the Lamb of God who washes away all our sins, who gives us a new heart, a new mind, and a new and abundant life.

Our Love Brings Healing to the Brokenhearted

Only one word can fully describe the Christian life. That word is *love.* "If I have prophetic powers, and understand all mysteries and all knowledge, and if I have all faith so as to remove mountains, but have not love, I am nothing" (1 Cor 13:2–3).

Two thousand years ago the invisible love that is God became visible by vesting himself with the flesh of a virgin and dying on a cross for the incredible reason that he loves each and every one of us. The fact that Christianity is a religion of love makes every evangelizer the teller of a love story, the singer of a love song. By example as well as by words, evangelizers must be teachers of love, calling others to love God above all else and to love their neighbors as they love themselves.

Too few Catholics realize that evangelization is the only adequate and convincing proof of their Christ-like love for both God and neighbor. How can I say I have learned from Jesus the Master how to love if I show no interest in continuing the mission he gave me after dying on the Cross (Mt 28:19–20)? How can I claim to have found the pearl of great price (Jn 13:46) yet share it with no one?

Learning how to love means helping others to find the path of righteousness, the green pastures that bring refreshment to the soul, the eucharistic Bread that ends all hunger, the water that conquers thirst, the light that provides escape from the terror of the dark, the truth that sets us free. How can I claim to have learned that truth and yet not release a single prisoner from the slavery of spiritual selfishness — perhaps not even myself?

Christians possess the ultimate treasure! Christians know the name! Christians hold the answer! And until Jesus comes again, they have the finest of all opportunities for sharing that treasure, shouting that name, and announcing that answer to all the world.

There is nothing more natural than wanting to share the good news. When a man wins a million-dollar lottery, he almost falls from the window in his excitement to share that news with a neighbor. Jesus himself talks about shouting, not from a window, but from the housetops, shouting the good news about all he has won for us by his Cross (Mt 10:27). On another occasion, he says that if Christians stayed silent with this kind of good news, "the very stones would cry out" (Lk 19:40).

Paul explains that the love of Christ *impels* us (2 Cor 5:14). He expresses that fact in many ways: "Woe to me if I do not preach the gospel. . . . I have made myself a slave to all, that I might win the more. To the Jews I became as a Jew. . . . To the weak I became weak . . . all things to all men, that I might by all means save some" (1 Cor 9:16–24).

The morning of the first Pentecost offers dramatic testimony to the power of love. A few minutes after the Holy Spirit had fallen upon them, all the disciples were down in the street proclaiming, converting, and baptizing three thousand new believers (Acts 2:40–41). Nor did their fervor cool off as the days and months went by. These first Christians continued to work with a sense of urgency. "Every day in the temple and at home they did not cease teaching and preaching Jesus as the Christ" (Acts 5:42).

Jesus never doubted the urgency of his mission. While still a small boy, he showed his own determination: "I must be about my

Father's business" (Lk 2:4). Using a parable, he tells us to "Go out quickly to the streets and lanes of the city, and bring in the poor and maimed and blind and lame.... Go out to the highways and hedges, and compel people to come in, that my house may be filled" (Lk 14:21–23).

An angel spoke with equal urgency to the women standing in astonishment at the sight of the empty tomb: "Go quickly and tell his disciples that he has risen" (Mt 28:8). After the Ascension, another angel indicated the same urgency when he said to the stupefied apostles: "Men of Galilee ... why do you stand here looking up at the skies?" (Acts 1:11). In his own heavenly way, the angel seems to be saying, *"Get going!"*

Our task of love is so urgent that not even the most valid of excuses is acceptable. Jesus says bluntly, "Leave the dead to bury their own dead; but as for you, go and proclaim the kingdom of God" (Lk 9:60).

We respond with urgency when a baby falls down a well or when someone has a heart attack. If a house begins to rock with an earthquake, no one thinks about first taking a nap or paying the bills. When a father sees his home on fire with his children still inside, does he say, "Let's check the insurance to see if we have full coverage"? Does he procrastinate for a half-hour before calling the fire department? Or when he calls, do the fire fighters respond, "We'll drop by right after our coffee break"? After they arrive at the blaze, do they chat with the father about the outside chance that the kids can find a way out on their own?

In urgent situations, late responses are useless, and any postponement means a lost opportunity. Yet the Church today is staying far too cool, seemingly oblivious that the world is blazing all around them and that people are dying for a drink of life-giving water. With participation at Sunday Mass melting away, some bishops still seem to be saying, "Don't disturb me! I have this important correspondence to finish." With few young people in sight, some priests are still busy only with routine services for the already converted.

With empty Catholic churches being torn down and Muslims flooding the world with new mosques, some theologians tell us to keep calm. They blithely explain that people just may find their way even if we fail to announce that Jesus is *the* Way. With the devil roaring around in search of someone to devour (1 Pet 5:8), many Christians are still using shyness as an excuse for not revealing the only name that saves—even to their own children, his most likely prey.

At least in some parts of the Church, it is no exaggeration to say that the Father's house is on fire and that his beloved children are being trapped by flames. We are not living in a time that calls for no more than a quiet chat or just one more conference, dialogue, or study paper. Faith, hope, and love fuel our urgent mission to share the gospel.

Jesus commands us to "go and make disciples of every nation" (Mt 28:19). Evangelization is a mission for all Christians, the highest expression of Christian love. It is a faith-filled response to the fact that the whole value of any human life depends upon hearing and putting into practice the good news. An unresponsive Church risks an awful consequence: "Because you are lukewarm, and neither cold nor hot, I will spew you out of my mouth" (Rev 3:16).

Go now! Go with urgency! We are heralds of glad tidings (Is 41:27), messengers ready to run ourselves even to death in our determination to deliver the good news of salvation as quickly as possible. We have only so much time. Tens of thousands die daily, many without ever hearing of Jesus. With so many in the world still waiting to be evangelized, we have to run hard and run to win, looking forward to the finish line, looking forward to meeting in glory, spending eternity with the Church made perfect by the blood of the Lamb.

❧

With offices in Rome and on all continents, Evangelization 2000 works through retreats, international prayer campaigns, conferences, and LUMEN television to motivate and mobilize Catholics to share Christ and his love. For more information, contact:

Evangelization 2000
3045 4th Street, NE
Washington, D.C. 20017
202–526–2814
202–526–2871 (FAX)

4

HOW MUST CATHOLICS EVANGELIZE? EVANGELIZATION AND THE POWER OF THE HOLY SPIRIT

Bishop Samuel Jacobs

The call to evangelize is not a new call, even though our Holy Father coined the term "new evangelization". What he says is that it must be new in method, new in expression, and new in zeal. John Paul reiterated this call in 1991 in these words: "The new evangelization needs new witnesses . . . people who have experienced an area of change in their lives because of their contact with Jesus Christ, and who are capable of passing on that experience to others."

Jesus himself issued this call. "This is the time of fulfillment. The reign of God is at hand! Reform your lives and believe in the gospel!" (Mk 1:15). Before his Ascension, he commissioned the apostles to continue and extend his work of evangelization: "Go, therefore, and make disciples of all the nations. Baptize them in the name of the Father, and of the Son, and of the Holy Spirit. Teach them to carry out everything I have commanded you. And know that I am with you always, until the end of the world" (Mt 28:19–20).

What our Holy Father has done is to give new emphasis to the call for evangelization and make us more aware of the urgency of our times. With the third millennium just around the corner, John Paul II has exhorted us to a new zeal for unveiling the love of Christ toward all people. He has called us to a new commitment to "sow Christian hope in hearts thirsting for the living God" (April 8, 1987). As Cardinal Thiandoum put it, "Every person has a right to the good news, and we should leave no stone unturned to announce it to them."

The pope stresses the need for a new evangelization of society in a world torn asunder by war, so that "the liberating truth of the gospel will inspire the building of a new world of authentic peace and justice animated by love" (October 28, 1991, Fifth Centenary of the Evangelization of America). If the truth and life of the gospel were lived out more fully and proclaimed more effectively, then our society would reflect the values of the gospel more clearly.

The call is not just to evangelize, but to evangelize *in the power of the Spirit with new boldness.* After commissioning the disciples to proclaim the good news to all the nations, Jesus tells them to *wait* for the coming of the Spirit promised by the Father. "You will receive power when the Holy Spirit comes down on you; then you are to be my witnesses in Jerusalem, throughout Judea and Samaria, yes, even to the ends of the earth" (Acts 1:8).

Being in Harmony with the Plan of God

What does it mean to evangelize in the power of the Spirit? First of all, we must begin by acknowledging that evangelization is the plan of God and not simply a good idea. As such, our efforts to share the good news will be effective to the extent we are in harmony with that divine plan. We can design all the evangelistic programs and outreaches we wish, but if the power of the Spirit is not the soul of our efforts, then we will be exhausted very soon—just like all those batteries left in the dust by the pink Energizer rabbit.

Pope Paul VI sums up the central role of the Holy Spirit in his apostolic exhortation *Evangelii Nuntiandi:*

It must be said that the Holy Spirit is the principal agent of evangelization: it is he who impels each individual to proclaim the gospel, and it is he who in the depths of consciences causes the word of salvation to be accepted and understood. But it can equally be said that he is the goal of evangelization: he alone stirs up the new creation, the new humanity of which evangelization is to be the result, with that unity in variety which evangelization wishes to achieve within the Christian community. Through the Holy Spirit the gospel penetrates to the heart of the world, for it is he who causes people to discern the signs of the times—signs willed by God—which evangelization reveals and puts to use within history (no. 75).

How important is it for us to follow the plan of God? In one of his books, S. D. Gordon pictures the angel Gabriel as asking Christ a question when he reached heaven: What recognition had the world given to his divine suffering for its sake? Christ replies that only a few people in Palestine knew of it. Believing the whole world ought to know, Gabriel asks, "What is your plan, Master, for telling them of it?"

Jesus replies, "I have asked Peter, James, John, Andrew, and a few others to make it the business of their lives to tell others, and those others to tell others, until the last person in the furthest circle has heard the story and has felt the power of it."

"But suppose they do not tell others—what then?" asks the angel.

Jesus answers quietly, "Gabriel, I have not made any other plans. I am counting on them."

To begin to grasp more clearly the plan of God, we need to look at the life of Jesus, the greatest of all evangelists. What we see is an intimate relationship with the Father. Jesus in his humanity was so in love with the Father that he committed his whole life to doing his will and his work. It was not enough for Jesus to know this in his heart; he wanted to make public his relationship and commitment. He wanted his life to be a public witness of his union with the Father, not just a private, vertical relationship. He wanted his deeds to be a witness of the love of the Father for all mankind.

This profound intimacy with the Father and the Spirit did not happen overnight. Jesus spent the first thirty years of his life being formed in the religious environment provided by Mary and Joseph and by his covenant with Yahweh. He heard the Scriptures in the synagogue every Sabbath and was immersed in God's saving deeds through the various religious celebrations. God's laws were not just words for Jesus but his rule of life.

When the time came for his public ministry, Jesus did not devise his own plan for evangelization. He was impelled by the Holy Spirit to go to the Jordan River and be baptized by John, not because of sin but because of this consuming love and desire to do the will of the Father.

We read in Luke's Gospel: "When all the people were baptized, and Jesus was at prayer after likewise being baptized, the skies opened and the Holy Spirit descended on him in visible form like a dove. A voice from heaven was heard to say: 'You are my beloved Son. On you my favor rests' " (Lk 3:21–22).

Observing the life of Jesus shows us that the effective evangelist must be rooted in a growing, personal love relationship with the Father, which is the call to holiness. Our relationship cannot be something that was experienced years ago as a child or as a young adult. It must be one that is alive and developing today, always open to the new gifts of God's personal love in the present moment. It must be nurtured daily in the quiet of prayer and intimacy, in word and sacraments, in the desert of purification and the valley of restoration.

This call to holiness is parallel and prerequisite to the call to evangelize. How can we effectively proclaim God's love if that love is not effectively visible in our lives? How can the Spirit empower us to evangelize if the life of the Spirit is dormant or stagnant within our hearts?

Evangelization and the Gifts of the Holy Spirit

Jesus began his three years of public ministry following the visible Pentecostal experience at his baptism and the hidden temptations in the desert. The initial response was quite positive. Scripture tells us that "Jesus returned in the power of the Spirit to Galilee, and his reputation spread throughout the region. He was teaching in their synagogues, and all were loud in his praise" (Lk 4:14–15).

Jesus knew, acknowledged, and acted in the power of the Spirit. Peter later attested to this fact when he proclaimed, "Men of Israel, listen to me! Jesus the Nazorean was a man whom God sent to you with miracles, wonders, and signs as his credentials" (Acts 2:22).

Peter later evangelized Cornelius by relating the works of Jesus: "I take it you know what has been reported all over Judea about Jesus of Nazareth, beginning in Galilee with the baptism John preached; of the way God anointed him with the Holy Spirit and power. He went about doing good works and healing all who were in the grip of the devil, and God was with him" (Acts 10:37–38).

The Scriptures establish the direct relationship between evangelization and the gifts of the Spirit. Jesus evangelized and confirmed the words he was sharing with signs and wonders. As an example, recall the encounter he had with the Samaritan woman at the well. As he led her from the external fact that he was a male Jew to the internal faith-realization that he was the Messiah, Jesus exercised the gift of word of knowledge, telling the woman that the man she was living with was not her husband. The power of the Spirit was evident in bringing her to the grace of salvation.

At other times Jesus would heal and then evangelize, bringing the person into an acceptance and response to God's gift of his saving love and freedom. His way of ministering to the man blind from birth demonstrated this approach. Jesus first healed him. As the grace of God continued to work, he was able to bring this man from physical blindness to physical sight, from spiritual blindness to spiritual sight.

We see the power of the Spirit manifested in the process of evangelization both when a person experiences a miracle or sign of wonder and when he makes a proclamation of faith in the saving work of Jesus. For it is the Spirit who opens the heart of the unbeliever, or the heart of one who seeks the fullness of truth, or the heart of the sinner and backslider, or the heart of the indifferent and inactive believer.

Whatever the case may be, it is the grace of the Spirit that triggers the response of faith and deeper commitment in the person who freely chooses to say yes to Jesus' call and plan. The evangelist is merely a chosen instrument in the hands of God, though an important one.

What was evidenced in the life of Jesus was taught, learned, experienced, and imitated by the apostles after their own anointing by the Holy Spirit. The fire of Pentecost still glowed in Peter and John as they said to the crippled beggar at the temple gate: "In the name of Jesus Christ, the Nazorean, walk!" (Acts 3:6). As the temple crowd rejoiced over the miracle, Peter proceeded to evangelize them, proclaiming that the healing was done in the name of Jesus.

Later, after receiving in a vision the message to go to the house of Cornelius, Peter addressed him and his household about God's plan of salvation, culminating with the birth, life, death, and Resurrection of Jesus. He concluded: "To him all the prophets testify, saying that everyone who believes in him has forgiveness of sins through his name" (Acts 10:43). No sooner did Peter finish when the Holy Spirit descended on all who were listening and they began to speak "in tongues . . . glorifying God" (Acts 10:46).

We see this same process, which is the plan of God for evangelization, played out over and over in other New Testament accounts. Philip "went down to the town of Samaria and there proclaimed the Messiah" (Acts 8:5). Because of the preaching and the miracles, many people accepted the word of God and were baptized in water and in the Spirit. Led by the Spirit, Philip then caught up with the carriage of the Ethiopian eunuch. Through the gift of interpretation, he proceeded to explain the passage from Isaiah fulfilled in the person of Jesus. The official asked for baptism in response to the grace of faith (Acts 9:26ff.).

Scripture tells us that Paul and Barnabas, "sent forth by the Holy Spirit, spent considerable time [in Iconium] and spoke out fearlessly, in complete reliance on the Lord. He for his part confirmed the message with his grace and caused signs and wonders to be done at their hands" (Acts 14:3).

How Can We Respond to the Pope's Call for a New Evangelization?

I believe we can best respond to the pope's call for a "new evangelization" by understanding and submitting to God's plan as evidenced in the Scriptures. We do not have to reinvent the wheel or develop a new process. Our primary responsibilities are to be rooted in our relationship with God, to be formed in our faith, to accept the empowerment of the Spirit already given to us, and to trust in God.

As we try to be attuned to the lead of the Spirit and respond with obedience, we need to speak out fearlessly but faithfully the word of God and our own faith-tradition, share the gospel message of salvation in simple terms, and exercise the appropriate gifts of the Spirit as he inspires us.

Like Jesus and the apostles, we need to continue to seek the face of the Lord and to enter into greater intimacy with the living God. Like Jesus, we need to be obedient children of the Father of all. Like the apostles, we need to come under the Lordship of Jesus, to live consciously in the presence of the One who is the beginning and the end.

Like Jesus, we need to be a people of prayer so that our witness and evangelization may flow from union with the Father in the power of the Spirit. An example of this is found in the healing of the paralytic. Prior to this miracle, Jesus had gone to the desert to pray; it is out of this context that the miracle occurs. Our witness and evangelization then need to be brought back to the Lord in thanksgiving and praise, as we see after the healing of Simon's mother-in-law as well as the many sick and possessed brought to him that evening.

Like the apostles, we need to pray for the continual infilling of the Holy Spirit, so that we may boldly proclaim the good news of Jesus. They beseeched the Lord in the upper room, "Grant to your servants, even as they speak your words, complete assurance by stretching forth your hand in cures and signs and wonders to be worked in the name of Jesus, your Servant." God responded in a dramatic way: "The place where they were gathered shook as they prayed. They were filled with the Holy

Spirit and continued to speak God's word with confidence" (Acts 4:29–30).

Like Jesus and the apostles, we need to be open to the lead and power of the Spirit if our work of evangelization is to be authentic and fruitful. How many divine appointments have we already missed because of fear, laziness, a sense of inadequacy, an unwillingness to be a disciple of Jesus at the moment, or any number of other excuses? As a result, how many people have not been given a chance to respond to God's invitation to a new life? How many have missed the grace of repentance, conversion, and sanctification because we did not respond to the grace of evangelization?

Like the apostles, in the words of Paul VI, we must share "the name, the teaching, the promises, the kingdom, and the mystery of Jesus of Nazareth, the Son of God". In all of this, ours is a small part of the process, though by God's choice a necessary one. However, what the Spirit does through us and in the person being evangelized remains the heart of the matter, the essential part of the process of conversion.

We must always remember that the response of the person being evangelized is not the measuring stick God will use in judging *our* efforts. Whether someone comes to a saving relationship with Jesus and becomes a member of the community of faith is not our responsibility but that of the person evangelized. Our responsibility is to do the work of evangelization in the power of the Spirit.

To paraphrase a comment by Mother Teresa, God is not asking us to be *successful* but *faithful* to his command. We are not held accountable before the Lord for the number of people we actually evangelize but for how many times we obediently act on his lead and in his power to proclaim the good news to others.

John Paul II sees the new evangelization as a sign of a new springtime coming for the Church. "Despite the voices of the prophets of pessimism, I would like to repeat once again, with emphasis: as we approach the third millennium of the Redemption, God is preparing a great Christian springtime, the beginnings of which can already be glimpsed" (January 1993).

Having been blessed by the Lord and gifted by his holy and awesome presence, we need to hear his word to Isaiah uttered in our own hearts: "Whom shall I send?" The Lord is waiting to hear the fearless and generous response of Isaiah from our own lips: "Here, I am, Lord, send me."

It is not enough for us to have our ears tickled, our minds instructed and illumined, our hearts challenged. God is looking for men and women who are committed to be evangelizers in the power of the Spirit, who will pursue training if necessary, who will no longer be satisfied with being fed but who will seek to feed others the same good news which brings them life.

To repeat Cardinal Thiandoum, "Every person has a right to the good news, and we should leave no stone unturned to announce it to them." Because we have heard and experienced the saving power and love of God in Jesus, we have the duty and responsibility to share it with others. The reward and the consequences are explicit in the Scriptures: "Whoever acknowledges me before others, I will acknowledge before my Father in heaven. Whoever does not acknowledge me before others, I will not acknowledge before my Father in heaven" (Mt 10:32–33).

Consider these questions from the Letter to the Romans a personal challenge: "Everyone who calls on the name of the Lord will be saved. But how shall they call on him in whom they have not believed? And how can they believe unless they have heard of him? And how can they hear unless there is someone to preach? And how can men preach unless they are sent?" (Rom 10:13–15).

If not you, who? If not now, when? If not the truth of the gospel, what? If not in the power of the Spirit, how? If not in your home or school or place of work, where? God needs us to do our part to help others to know his great love.

PART TWO

Perspectives on Evangelization

5

GO AND MAKE DISCIPLES:
THE UNITED STATES BISHOPS' NATIONAL
PLAN FOR CATHOLIC EVANGELIZATION

Fr. Kenneth Boyack, C.S.P.

The bishops of the United States passed *Go and Make Disciples: A National Plan and Strategy for Catholic Evangelization in the United States* at their plenary assembly in Washington, D.C., on November 18, 1992, by an overwhelming vote of 229 to 2. Every Catholic in this country would benefit from reading this national plan, which I believe will define and shape our efforts well into the twenty-first century.

Prior to the publication of *Go and Make Disciples,* Catholics who wanted to develop evangelization in their parishes had to rely on a thorough reading and study of Pope Paul VI's magnificent apostolic exhortation, *Evangelii Nuntiandi.* Written in 1975, this document defined evangelization as the very mission of Christ and outlined the content, the methods, the beneficiaries, the workers, and the spirit of evangelization.

While extremely instructive, this particular exhortation was intended more as a meditation than an action document. It was also written for a worldwide Catholic audience, not for people in any particular continent or nation. *Go and Make Disciples,* on the other hand, was designed as a plan and strategy to lead Catholics in the United States to develop new attitudes and behaviors for bringing the good news of Jesus Christ to every person in our nation.

The Historical Setting: A New Period of Evangelization

Go and Make Disciples is the first major teaching on Catholic evangelization made by the bishops of the United States since Vatican II. Pope John XXIII called the Council in 1959 as a way to let the light of Christ shine more brightly in the modern world. The dogmatic constitution on the Church *Lumen Gentium* sets forth this primary goal of the Council clearly: "Christ is the light of humanity; and it is, accordingly, the heart-felt desire of this sacred Council, being gathered together in the Holy Spirit, that, by proclaiming his Gospel to every creature (cf. Mk 16:15), it may bring to all [people] that light of Christ which shines out visibly from the Church."[1] Vatican II equipped the Church to live and proclaim the gospel more effectively.

Pope Paul VI called for the Third General Assembly of the Synod of Bishops to meet in the fall of 1974 to reflect on the topic of evangelization in light of the Council, which had ended some nine years earlier. After discussing evangelization from a world-wide perspective, the assembly " . . . decided to remit to the Pastor of the universal Church, with great trust and simplicity, the fruits of all their labors, stating that they awaited from him a fresh forward impulse, capable of creating within a Church still more firmly rooted in the underlying power and strength of Pentecost a new period of evangelization."[2] *Evangelii Nuntiandi (On Evangelization in the Modern World)* was published in 1975 and set forth the elements of this new period.

The bishops of the United States, in *Go and Make Disciples,* acknowledged the historical roots of this new period of evangelization by referring to key Church teachings which had laid the necessary foundation, primarily *Evangelii Nuntiandi* and *Redemptoris*

[1] Austin Flannery, O.P., *Vatican Council II* (Northport, N.Y.: Costello Publishing Co., 1975), Dogmatic Constitution on the Church *Lumen Gentium,* no. 1.

[2] *On Evangelization in the Modern World,* Apostolic Exhortation of Paul VI (hereafter EN) (Washington, D.C.: Office for Publishing and Promotion Services, 1975), no. 2.

Missio (Mission of the Redeemer). In the United States this new period has been characterized by such powerful teachings as the *National Pastoral Plan for Hispanic Ministry, Here I am, Send Me: A Conference Response to the Evangelization of African Americans,* and *Heritage and Hope: Evangelization in the United States.*[3]

This new period of evangelization has indeed produced a stunning array of Church teachings which guide Catholics into a new way of thinking and behaving. All these elements of the new evangelization have one aspect in common: they were produced under the guidance of the Holy Spirit working in the Church. As Paul VI writes, "Now if the Spirit of God has a preeminent place in the whole life of the Church, it is in her evangelizing mission that he is most active. It is not by chance that the great inauguration of evangelization took place on the morning of Pentecost, under the inspiration of the Spirit."[4]

And it is under the same inspiration of the Spirit that Pope John Paul II can write in *Redemptoris Missio,* "I sense that the moment has come to commit all the Church's energies to a new evangelization. . . . "[5]

Why We Need a Plan and Strategy Now

We can only speculate about the reasons the bishops passed *Go and Make Disciples* in 1992, as opposed to 1985 or some other date. Yet we know this plan meets a need. Large corporations, political groups, and other institutions routinely develop strategic plans to meet their needs and to chart their way into the future. Similarly, the bishops approved *Go and Make Disciples* to chart the direction of the Catholic Church in the United States.

The original idea for the national plan was presented in June 1989 by Archbishop Michael Sheehan (then Bishop Michael Sheehan

[3] *Go and Make Disciples: A National Plan and Strategy for Catholic Evangelization in the United States* (hereinafter: GMD) (Washington, D.C.: Office for Publishing and Promotion Services, 1993), p. 10.

[4] EN, no. 75.

[5] As found in GMD, p. 10.

of Lubbock, Texas) as the Bishops' Committee on Evangelization met under the leadership of Bishop William R. Houck. Archbishop Sheehan noted that since other churches, such as the Southern Baptists and the Assemblies of God, were developing plans for evangelism in the 1990s, the Catholic Church should also consider this.

The members of the Committee on Evangelization also knew that the Catholic Church has a unique and valuable contribution to make in this area. Moreover, the committee recognized that a stronger and more defined Catholic evangelizing presence is needed as we experience the forces of a secularized culture which threatens Catholic values and identity.

Contemporary sociologists give us insights into the realities behind the bishops' thinking. In his book *Christianity in the Twenty-first Century, Reflection on the Challenges Ahead,*[6] Robert Wuthnow comments that a Christian identity is no longer supported in our culture by the family or by the neighborhood. As an immigrant Church in the 1890s, for example, Catholics experienced a strong ethnic identity as German Catholics or Irish Catholics.

This experience was strengthened by other key elements of Catholic identity, such as not eating meat on Friday, studying from the Baltimore Catechism, and experiencing the same Latin Mass throughout the world. Not so today. Most Catholics today no longer have an immigrant status but are "mainline", comprising about 23 percent of the U.S. population. Catholics today are affected by the same cultural elements of privatism and relativism and in most cases are indistinguishable in behavior from other Americans. These cultural changes make contemporary Catholic evangelization difficult.

Adding to this discussion, sociologist Wade Clark Roof finds some revealing characteristics of Catholic baby boomers in his study *A Generation of Seekers: The Spiritual Journeys of the Baby Boom Generation.* Clark found, for instance, that of all Catholics

---

[6] Robert Wuthnow, *Christianity in the Twenty-first Century, Reflections on the Challenges Ahead* (New York: Oxford University Press, 1993).

born between the years 1946 and 1962, 33 percent remained loyal to the Church and 67 percent dropped out. Of the 67 percent who dropped out, 25 percent have returned to the Church. He found that only 50 percent of baby boomers baptized Catholic are currently active in the Catholic church today, and another 8 percent are active in other churches.[7]

When interviewing these baby-boomer Catholics, Roof discovered that their definition of what constitutes a "good Catholic" diverged widely from Church teaching on some key issues. For example, when asked if one could be a good Catholic without going to church every Sunday, 77 percent of the males and 90 percent of the females responded yes. Similarly, when asked if one could be a good Catholic without obeying the Church's teaching on abortion, 67 percent of the males and 69 percent of the females said yes.[8] These attitudes reveal the strong influence of secular American culture, a culture in which pluralism and personal opinion are prized.

Other research reveals that the number of American adults who are not active in any church is increasing. In the study *The Unchurched American,* the Gallup Organization found in a 1988 survey that 44 percent of American adults are "unchurched", as compared with 41 percent who were unchurched in 1978. Both studies defined an "unchurched adult" as one who was not a member of a church or who had not attended services in the previous six months other than for special religious holidays, weddings, funerals, or the like.[9]

In spite of the large number of individuals without a church family, both the Gallup Organization in 1988 and Wade Clark Roof in 1993 found that many Americans are seeking a spirituality that answers their questions and gives meaning to their lives.

If we were to summarize why we need a national plan for Catholic evangelization now, we could point to three clear reasons.

---

[7] Wade Clark Roof, *A Generation of Seekers: The Spiritual Journeys of the Baby Boom Generation* (San Francisco: Harper Collins Publishers, 1993), p. 176.

[8] Ibid., p. 233.

[9] See the introductory summary, *The Unchurched American* (Washington, D.C.: The Paulist National Catholic Evangelization Association, 1988).

First, we need a plan to enable Catholics to develop a renewed identity as an evangelizing people in an increasingly secular culture. Second, we need a plan to equip Catholics to share the gospel more effectively, especially with the large number of Americans who do not have a church family but who are open to an invitation. Third, we need a plan for Catholics to evangelize our society and culture, looking for ways in which we can transform this culture through the love and power of Jesus Christ.

Go and Make Disciples is a short but powerful document that meets the needs of our age. The best way to capture the spirit of the national plan is to read this ten-thousand-word document oneself. The NCCB Committee on Evangelization made the decision to write this plan for every Catholic, and not specifically for Catholic leadership. Consequently, the language is engaging and easy to read.

Go and Make Disciples is comprised of two parts, with part one entitled "A Vision of Catholic Evangelization", and part two entitled "Goals and Strategies". The vision section, making up over half the text, is intended to present Catholic teachings on the topic and motivate and inspire the reader to action. The goals, objectives, and strategies of part two form the heart of the document: they present a plan for action.

Part One: A Vision of Catholic Evangelization

The framework for part one, the vision of Catholic evangelization, is taken almost exclusively from Paul VI's *Evangelii Nuntiandi* and rightly so, because the bishops were taking the insights on evangelization from the universal Church and applying them specifically to the situation in the United States. Number 18 of this apostolic exhortation provides a definition of evangelization, the foundation for the three goals of *Go and Make Disciples:*

> Evangelizing means bringing the Good News into all the strata of humanity, and through its influence transforming humanity from within and making it new: "Now I am making the whole

of creation new." But there is no new humanity if there are not first of all new persons renewed by Baptism and by lives lived according to the Gospel. The purpose of evangelization is therefore precisely this interior change, and if it had to be expressed in one sentence the best way of stating it would be to say that the Church evangelizes when she seeks to convert, solely through the divine power of the message she proclaims, both the personal and collective consciences of people, the activities in which they engage, and the lives and concrete milieux which are theirs.

What does evangelization mean? The first section of *Go and Make Disciples* sets forth key Catholic teachings on being a disciple and making disciples. The bishops define evangelizing as "bringing the good news of Jesus into every human situation and seeking to convert individuals and society by the divine power of the gospel itself. Its essence is the proclamation of salvation in Jesus Christ and the response of a person in faith, both being the work of the Spirit of God."[10] The language of this definition speaks to the heart of discipleship: proclaiming the gospel, responding in faith, relying on the power of the Holy Spirit, and bringing the kingdom of God both to individuals and to society.

As teachers and shepherds, the bishops point out that Catholic evangelization casts a wide net; indeed, no one should be excluded. They identify five primary groups who would benefit from the gospel: practicing Catholics, who are called to a renewal in faith and ongoing conversion; inactive and alienated Catholics, who are called to reconciliation; children, who are called to be formed as disciples through the efforts of their parents and religious educators; Christians from other traditions, who are called to the fullness of Christ's message; and those who have no faith in Jesus, who are called to know Christ through his Church.

Why do we evangelize? The section entitled "Why We Evangelize" offers many reasons for proclaiming the good news of Jesus Christ.

[10] GMD, p. 2.

Primarily, we want all people to know Jesus and experience the salvation and the new life only he can give. It is our love for Christ that calls us to evangelize, but it is at the same time a duty. Jesus commands us to "go and make disciples of all nations" (Mt 28:19).

How does evangelization happen? Next comes an explanation of how evangelization happens. The bishops note that Catholics have done well as silent witnesses to their faith through living good lives. However, they also point out that in our society and culture more is needed. Catholics need to learn to share their faith by speaking the gospel message clearly and by giving the reasons for their Catholic faith.

Throughout the vision section, the bishops set forth teaching that is extremely Christ-centered. The methods of Catholic evangelization involve inviting, welcoming, showing love for the unbeliever, entering into sincere dialogue with an inquirer, and trying to discern the working of the Spirit in a person's life. These methods of evangelization reflect the methods and approaches that Jesus used as revealed in the New Testament. Through putting on the mind of Jesus, we are taught to be disciples, so that we, in turn, may make disciples of others.

Three goals of evangelization. One of the final sections of part one presents the three goals that form the heart of the bishops' plan and strategy. These goals are as follows:[11]

Goal I: To bring about in all Catholics such an enthusiasm for their faith that, in living their faith in Jesus, they freely share it with others.

Goal II: To invite all people in the United States, whatever their social or cultural background, to hear the message of salvation in Jesus Christ so they may come to join us in the fullness of the Catholic faith.

Goal III: To foster gospel values in our society, promoting the

[11] Ibid., pp. 7–8.

dignity of the human person, the importance of the family, and the common good of our society, so that our nation may continue to be transformed by the saving power of Jesus Christ.

These three goals contain the essential elements of the definition of evangelization set forth by Pope Paul VI in number 18 of *Evangelii Nuntiandi,* thereby intricately connecting the teaching of the universal Church with Christ's evangelizing mission in the United States. The presentation of these goals reveals that *Go and Make Disciples* is truly part of the new period of evangelization which the Third General Assembly of the Synod of Bishops spoke about in Rome in 1974. And, attentive to the working of the Holy Spirit, this new period of evangelization in the Catholic Church can now move forward with even greater intensity in the United States through the insights of this plan and strategy.

Part Two: Goals and Strategies

Before presenting the objectives and strategies for each goal, the bishops first offer suggestions about the ways in which all Catholics can use this plan. The objectives and strategies are not meant as a recipe to be applied by all people in exactly the same way in every situation. Rather, the bishops present a framework which individuals, parish staffs, parish councils, Catholic organizations, and religious orders can apply to their own situations. All who read the plan are encouraged to affirm the ways in which they are already evangelizing, look for new areas to develop, discern the guidance of the Holy Spirit through the Church, and then engage in the process of evangelizing—going and making disciples.

And, lest Catholics lose their perspective through being either too provincial or too zealous, the bishops offer a number of reflections which set the context for the three goals, a context which renders evangelization truly Catholic. The bishops teach that all Catholics are involved by virtue of their baptism. All evangelizing activity must be steeped in prayer. Evangelization is a ministry of the universal Church—when one Catholic evangelizes, the entire Church evangelizes.

The bishops also teach that evangelization is directly connected to the ebb and flow of everyday life. Further, the parish is the most fitting location for living and sharing the gospel since the goal of all evangelization culminates in the Eucharist—involving all people in the paschal mystery of Jesus Christ within a community of faith. Evangelization involves a collaborative effort, a true partnership in Christ among laity, religious, and clergy. Evangelization involves a consistent witness among all Catholics at each level of the Church. And finally, the bishops teach that these goals will be difficult to attain in our secularized and modern culture.

Goal I: To bring about in all Catholics such an enthusiasm for their faith that, in living their faith in Jesus, they freely share it with others. The key elements of this goal include hearing the gospel at new and deeper levels, responding in faith, growing in holiness. Also, because we have experienced the love of God more profoundly, we want to share this love of Christ more freely with others.

The strategy for achieving this goal centers on creating for people new encounters with Christ through the Scriptures and the sacraments of the Church. As a result, Catholics will pray more intently, listen to Christ's call more clearly, and live as a disciple in the family and the workplace. Moreover, the strategy calls for being attentive to the physical, mental, and cultural diversity among Catholics. All of these strategies enable Catholics to fall more deeply in love with God, thereby becoming more holy.

Of course, all of these objectives cannot possibly be realized at one time. The process of implementing this goal in a parish, for example, involves understanding the objectives, doing a pastoral analysis of one's parish, affirming areas in which the objectives and strategies are already being carried out, then selecting and implementing one or two objectives and strategies that seem appropriate for the following year. After review and evaluation, the parish can celebrate what God has accomplished, then begin the planning process for the next year.

Goal II: To invite all people in the United States, whatever their social or cultural background, to hear the message of salvation in Jesus Christ so they may come to join us in the fullness of the Catholic faith. The bishops summarize the meaning of this goal by teaching that Catholics "are to invite effectively every person to come to know the good news of Jesus proclaimed by the Catholic Church".[12] Along with the invitation must come a welcoming spirit that draws others to Christ. Not only individual Catholics will invite and welcome but also parishes, organizations, hospitals, schools, chanceries—all Catholic organizations and institutions.

The strategy for achieving this goal is threefold: create a more welcoming attitude; develop new understanding and skills for sharing our faith, and actually undertake activities in which we can invite people to know Christ and our Catholic faith.

After a pastoral analysis, parishes can affirm the areas in which this goal is already being implemented. Then, through a process of discernment, they can engage in one or two strategies to help the parish become more welcoming, to train parishioners in the skills of sharing their faith, and to plan some events to invite people to come to know Christ and the Catholic faith. As before, parishes are encouraged to celebrate what God is doing in their midst, evaluate the results, and plan for the next year.

Goal III: To foster gospel values in our society, promoting the dignity of the human person, the importance of the family, and the common good of our society, so that our nation may continue to be transformed by the saving power of Jesus Christ. The third goal draws on and incorporates Catholic teaching on social justice and the common good. It proclaims that the kingdom of God may be seen through signs in which the justice and healing presence of Christ transform individuals and all of society. Without these signs of God's kingdom, the first two goals would be weakened and incomplete.

The bishops' strategy for implementation involves being more attentive to showing the presence of Christ in our neighborhoods, fostering the importance of marriage and family, recognizing the

[12] Ibid., p. 16.

tremendous contribution this can make to the United States, and looking for areas in the workplace, the arts, economics, public policy, and media in which we as Catholics can exercise influence for Christ.

After pastoral discernment, parishes can affirm their strengths in this area and then choose at least one objective and strategy for each of the following: involving parishioners in their neighborhoods; fostering the importance of the family; and working to transform all elements of society. After implementation, the process always involves reviewing the results, giving thanks to God, and looking to the next year.

An Indispensable Catholic Framework

These three goals form an integral whole and are not to be viewed separately. One analogy is that of a tripod. Without all three legs rooted solidly on the ground, the tripod will not stand; if one leg is removed, it will fall. Similarly, these three goals form a solid tripod of Catholic evangelization. If we take away any one of them, or allow one to lie dormant, we weaken the plan by not presenting the fullness of Catholic evangelization.

After presenting these three goals, the bishops appeal to all Catholics to implement this national plan as a way of being disciples of Jesus. They state boldly: "We invite you: Make this plan *your* plan."[13] By virtue of baptism into the paschal mystery of Christ, no Catholic is exempt from carrying on Christ's evangelizing mission. This invitation is extended to all Catholics and to all levels of Church structure, including families, parishes, Catholic institutions, and local, diocesan, and national organizations.

This plan and strategy is a distinctive contribution by the bishops of the United States to the new period of Catholic evangelization. *Go and Make Disciples* is rooted solidly in the vision of Vatican II and sets forth specific ways in which Catholics can carry on the evangelizing mission of Christ in the Church in our contemporary secular culture. An individual's participation in

[13] Ibid., p. 21.

this plan and strategy is empowered through one's baptism and confirmation and is sustained through the Eucharist.

Go and Make Disciples affirms a new way of being church, a new way of being disciples so that we can make disciples. As we develop new evangelizing attitudes and behaviors based on discipleship, we will continue to forge a new Catholic identity based on Vatican II—an identity in which we view evangelization as the essential mission of the Church.

Implementing this plan will enable Catholics to respond to the statement of the bishops who gathered for the Third General Assembly of the Synod of Bishops in 1974: "We wish to confirm once more that the task of evangelizing all people constitutes the essential mission of the Church."[14] As we rely on the guidance of the Holy Spirit, which informs individuals as well as the institutional Church, we will see a Catholic identity emerging through which we are able to live and proclaim the gospel more effectively. And through this proclamation, we will come to love Christ and our Catholic faith more deeply.

As the Vicar of Christ, Pope John Paul II has been preaching tirelessly on the new evangelization. His exhortation in *Redemptoris Missio* is appropriate to all Catholics reading *Go and Make Disciples*. He writes,

> I wish to invite the Church to renew her missionary commitment. The [*Mission of the Redeemer*] has as its goal an interior renewal of faith and Christian life. For missionary activity renews the Church, revitalizes faith and Christian identity, and offers fresh enthusiasm and new incentive. Faith is strengthened when it is given to others! It is in commitment to the Church's universal mission that the new evangelization of Christian peoples will find inspiration and support.[15]

We pray that, under the guidance of the Holy Spirit, the implementation of *Go and Make Disciples* will enable Catholics to become more holy, to grow in missionary zeal, and to have an

---

[14] EN, no. 14.

[15] *Mission of the Redeemer (On the Permanent Validity of the Church's Missionary Mandate),* Encyclical Letter of John Paul II (Washington, D.C.: Office for Publishing and Promotion Services, 1993), no. 2.

even greater impact by making all elements of American society new in Christ.

ॐ

Fr. Kenneth Boyack is Director of the Paulist National Evangelization Association, which either publishes or distributes all of the following resources. To obtain more information or to request a free copy of the PNCEA Resource Catalogue, contact:

> Paulist National Evangelization Association
> 3031 Fourth Street, NE
> Washington, D.C. 20017
> 1–800–237–5515

Resources for Implementing Go and Make Disciples:

Go and Make Disciples: A National Plan and Strategy for Catholic Evangelization in the United States (Washington, D.C.: USCC Office for Publishing and Promotion Services, 1993).

Vayan y Hagan Discipulos: Plan y Estrategia Nacional para la Evangelizacion Catolica en los Estados Unidos (Washington, D.C.: USCC Office for Publishing and Promotion Services, 1993).

DeSiano, Frank, C.S.P., and Kenneth Boyack, C.S.P., *Commentary and Planning Guide for Go and Make Disciples: A National Plan and Strategy for Catholic Evangelization in the United States* (Washington, D.C.: Paulist National Catholic Evangelization Association, 1993).

Summary of Go and Make Disciples: A National Plan and Strategy for Catholic Evangelization in the United States (Washington, D.C.: Paulist National Catholic Evangelization Association, 1993*)*.

Wolf, Susan, S.N.D., *Planning Worksheets for Implementing Goals I, II and III of Go and Make Disciples* (Washington, D.C.: Paulist National Catholic Evangelization Association, 1993).

Additional Evangelization Resources

Boyack, Kenneth, C.S.P., ed., *The New Catholic Evangelization* (Mahwah, N.J.: Paulist Press, 1992).

DeSiano, Frank, C.S.P., and Kenneth Boyack, C.S.P., *Creating the Evangelizing Parish* (Mahwah, N.J.: Paulist Press, 1993).

DeSiano, Frank, C.S.P., and Kenneth Boyack, C.S.P., *Discovering My Experience of God: Awareness and Witness* (Mahwah, N.J.: Paulist Press, 1992).

6

EVANGELIZATION AND THE EXPERIENCE OF INITIATION IN THE EARLY CHURCH

Fr. Kilian McDonnell, O.S.B.

What is the source of evangelization? Obviously evangelization is not just an academic process of imparting Christian information. It communicates life and power. Where does the evangelizer and the evangelized draw this life, this power? Where is the well from which the life-giving waters are drawn?

In my view, the source is the rite of Christian initiation, as understood by the early Church. This process, whose length varied, might last as long as two or three years, culminating in the celebration of what we now recognize as baptism, confirmation, and the Eucharist, all celebrated together on one night. What is primary is conversion, both individual and communal. Conversion effected by grace, born out of a personal religious experience, touches the entire community, always turning toward God, with a new way of thinking, a new way of living, embracing the whole of existence. The rite of initiation, as well as the process of faith leading up to it, was highly diverse, with many local variations. No suggestion is made that everywhere the rite was the same.[1] Nevertheless, the theological and pastoral objective remained the same: to lead the catechumen into a living relationship with the Father, through the Son, Jesus Christ, in the Holy Spirit.

---

[1] Paul F. Bradshaw, *The Search for the Origins of Christian Worship* (New York: Oxford University, 1992), pp. 161–84.

The Architecture of Initiation

A knowledge of the architectural setting in the early Church helps one to grasp the theology of initiation. Though the arrangement was different in various parts of the West and in Syria, a widely used floor plan had the church divided into three basic rooms. See diagram below.

In the first room, the baptistery, the pit was filled with water so that if an adult stood up in it, the water might come to about the waist. There were three steps going down into the water and three steps ascending on the other side of the pit. Here the immersion in water (or the pouring of the water) took place. In the second room was a chair for the bishop. In this room took place the imposition of hands and one of the anointings (what we would recognize now as confirmation). The third, much larger room was the eucharistic room, which contained an altar and pulpit, or ambo, for the reading of the Scriptures. Here the Eucharist was celebrated with the local community as part of the rite of initiation.

At the beginning of the liturgy of initiation, the deacon led the men into the baptistry and told them to take off all their clothes. Individually they were then led down three steps into the water where they were immersed three times, in the name of the Father, Son, and Holy Spirit. Going down into the water was a sign that being a Christian meant sharing in Christ's going down into death. After the third immersion, the candidates rose up out of the water and ascended the three steps on the other side, where a white robe was placed on him, a sign of the Resurrection. To be a Christian, one must share in the Resurrection of Christ. The deacon then led the male catechumens into the second room, while the deaconess exited the church, requesting the female catechumens to enter the baptistery. Although the bishop was clearly the one administering the sacrament of baptism, calling on the three names in the baptismal invocation and anointing the head of each candidate, it was the deaconess who led the women catechumens into the water and completed the anointing. When all the men and women candidates had received the imposition of hands and an anointing in the second room, they were led into the

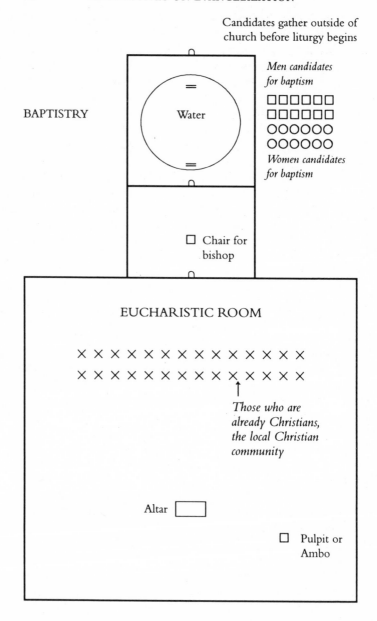

Candidates gather outside of
church before liturgy begins

BAPTISTRY

Water

Men candidates
for baptism

Women candidates
for baptism

☐ Chair for
   bishop

EUCHARISTIC ROOM

✕ ✕ ✕ ✕ ✕ ✕ ✕ ✕ ✕ ✕ ✕ ✕ ✕ ✕ ✕
✕ ✕ ✕ ✕ ✕ ✕ ✕ ✕ ✕ ✕ ✕ ✕ ✕ ✕

Those who are
already Christians,
the local Christian
community

Altar

☐ Pulpit or
   Ambo

eucharistic room, where the local Christian community was waiting, and together they celebrated the Eucharist. To become a Christian, one had to become a member of the church, a worshipping community. No isolated Christians existed, only Christians in community. This whole liturgy, not just the water bath, was called "baptism", or "Christian initiation".

What Is Baptism in the Holy Spirit?

Research indicates that in the early Church the passage of the candidates for baptism through these rites of initiation included what is today called baptism in the Holy Spirit. In fact, Justin Martyr,[2] Origen,[3] Didymus the Blind,[4] and Cyril of Jerusalem,[5] writing from the second to the fourth century, all call the whole rite of Christian initiation baptism in the Holy Spirit. Baptism in the Holy Spirit was not a separate element but was integral to the grace and meaning of initiation. Since the beginning of Pentecostalism around the turn of the century, baptism in the Spirit has referred to a contemporary experience of the power and charisms of the Spirit, which resembles what is described in various texts in Acts in conjunction with 1 Corinthians 12 and 14 and other New Testament texts. Such an understanding is found in various streams of classical Pentecostalism and the charismatic renewal in the historic churches. The same biblical texts cited in classical Pentecostalism for its teaching on the baptism in the Holy Spirit are cited by the authors from the earliest years of the Church's life.

However, in referring to baptism in the Spirit, I am not talking about charismatic renewal. The two are separable. To accept baptism in the Spirit as integral to Christian initiation does not mean that one thereby joins a movement, charismatic or otherwise. One can accept baptism in the Holy Spirit without accepting

[2] *Dialogue with Trypho* 29:1.
[3] *On Jeremiah* 2:3.
[4] *On the Trinity* 2:12.
[5] *Catechetical Lectures* 16:6. Hereafter cited as CL.

charismatic renewal. The issue is not charismatic renewal but baptism in the Holy Spirit.

I will present only enough of the postbiblical texts to demonstrate the broad pattern.[6]

Tertullian

When Tertullian (ca. 160–ca. 225) wrote his small treatise *On Baptism,* probably around 197, he was presenting the view on baptism held by the church of North Africa (not just his personal opinion), against the heretics who rejected baptism. His audience was the catechumens and neophytes, as well as those who believed in baptism without having examined the roots of the baptismal tradition.[7] Tertullian was preoccupied with the apostolic ministry in the Church, the uninterrupted series of bishops who were a sign of apostolicity.[8] To this degree he wanted to retain the traditional doctrine. Tertullian wrote in Latin in a situation where the baptism of adults was the general norm.[9]

At the end of his discourse, when he envisages the catechumens coming up from the water-bath, passing through the rites of anointing, signing, and imposition of hands, and walking into the eucharistic room, he addresses the catechumens (or, more precisely, the neophytes): "You blessed ones, for whom the grace of God is waiting, when you come up from the most sacred bath of the new birth, when you spread out your hands for the first time in your

[6] More extensive biblical and the postbiblical evidence is presented in Kilian McDonnell, George Montague, *Christian Initiation and Baptism in the Holy Spirit: Evidence from the First Eight Centuries* (Collegeville, Minn.: Liturgical Press, 1991). I am not entering into the exegetical material but refer the reader to the first section of the book, pp. 3–80, where the biblical witness is laid out. A popular presentation of the same material is found in *Fanning the Flame: What Does Baptism in the Holy Spirit Have to Do with Christian Initiation,* ed. by Kilian McDonnell and George Montague (Collegeville, Minn.: Liturgical Press, 1991).

[7] *On Baptism* 1:1.

[8] Idem, *The Prescription of Heretics* 32:1; *Against Marcion* 4:5,3; 4:29.

[9] He protests against infant baptism. *On Baptism* 18.

mother's house with your brethren, ask your Father, ask your Lord, for the special gift of his inheritance, the distributed charisms, which form an additional, underlying feature [of baptism]. 'Ask,' he says, 'and you shall receive.' In fact, you have sought, and you have found: you have knocked, and it has been opened to you."[10]

The spreading out of the hands refers to the posture of standing with outstretched arms and palms open, customary when entering the prayer of praise. The expression "your mother's house" refers first to the Christian community and, secondly, to the church building. Tertullian encourages the catechumens to ask God the Father, and their Lord Jesus Christ, for the "special gift of his inheritance", which he names as the charisms which are found in the community. The imparting of the charisms forms "an underlying feature" of baptism.

Tertullian, therefore, sees the imparting of the charisms as an integral part of the process of becoming a Christian, as part of the normal Christian equipment.[11]

Origen

Like Tertullian, Origen presupposes his converts are adults, but he comes out of a Greek culture. At the beginning of a passage on Christian initiation, Origen writes of the great wonders Jesus performed, themselves "symbols of those delivered by the word of God in all ages from every kind of sickness and weakness".[12] These miracles are an appeal to faith. "This [appeal to faith] is true of the water of baptism, symbol of the purification of the soul washed of every stain of sin, and it [baptism] is in itself the principle and source of the divine charisms for anyone who offers one's self to the divinity through the powerful invocation (epiclesis) of the adorable Trinity."[13] So baptism is the "principle" and

[10] Ibid., 20.
[11] Tertullian writes as a Catholic; this treatise contains no hint of his later Montanism.
[12] *On John* 6:33.
[13] Ibid.

"source" of the divine charisms. These two adjectives have almost identical meanings of essential basis, origin, beginning, fountainhead. Placed next to one another, they are an intensive formulation. This concentration of force is itself the object of a further intensive. The immediate context indicates that the charisms are those manifested in the Acts of the Apostles after the Pentecost experience.[14] For Origen, as for Tertullian, baptism is the normal locus for imparting the charisms.

Origen's witness is reinforced by the authority of Basil the Great, an important fourth-century witness and a doctor of the Church, who quotes the passage with approval, the only time in the whole of Basil's writings that he quotes Origen.[15]

Hilary of Poitiers

Hilary of Poitiers (ca. 314–367), apparently an adult convert to Christianity who was named bishop soon after his conversion, writes in Latin in a situation where adults are the usual candidates for baptism. Reflecting on his initiation late in life, he writes: "We who have been reborn through the sacrament of baptism experience intense joy when we feel within us the first stirrings of the Holy Spirit. We begin to have insight into the mysteries of faith, we are able to prophesy and to speak with wisdom. We become steadfast in hope and receive the gifts [plural] of healing."[16]

So Hilary writes of the intense joy when he felt within the first movements of the Spirit during the rite of initiation as an adult. In another context, Hilary returns to the theme of experience: "Among us there is no one who, from time to time, does not feel the gift of

[14] Ibid.

[15] Basil, *On the Holy Spirit* 29:73. After his death, Origen's speculations, which went unchallenged during his lifetime, were dogmatized, which brought down condemnations, now seen as largely unjustified. His doctrine of baptism was never challenged either during his lifetime or after his death. He was one of the most influential theologians in the East during the first thousand years.

[16] Hilary, *Tract on the Psalms* 64:14.

the grace of the Spirit."[17] Care must be taken not to press the text, as though Hilary were saying that only what is felt is real, or that the presence of the Spirit is always perceivable to the senses. Nonetheless, Hilary links the coming of the Spirit to experience.

He, too, specifically mentions the prophetic charisms which were imparted during initiation: word of knowledge, prophecy, word of wisdom, enduring hope, gifts of healing. Elsewhere he insists that the charisms "are profitable gifts".[18] If the charisms are effective, then "let us make use of such generous gifts."[19] Charisms are for the upbuilding of the Church and should not be allowed to remain dormant.

Cyril of Jerusalem

Cyril of Jerusalem has left the text of nineteen instructions for catechumens before the rites of initiation and five for the week after initiation. So we have good knowledge of how the catechumens were instructed. Cyril wrote in Greek for a group of adult catechumens.

Cyril is concerned to make these catechumens aware that the charisms belong to the normal functioning of the life of the community. "Great, omnipotent, and admirable is the Holy Spirit in the charisms."[20] Careful to avoid suggesting that the charisms are the property of the clergy, he maintains that "all the laity" are called to witness the power of the Spirit in the charisms.[21] Twice Cyril appeals to the list of charisms Paul gives in 1 Corinthians 12:7–11.[22] He views the Spirit as the dispenser of the charisms in "the whole Roman Empire", and then "in the whole world".[23]

[17] Idem, *Tract on Psalm 118* 12, 4.
[18] *On the Trinity* 8:30.
[19] Ibid. 2:35.
[20] CL 16:22.
[21] Ibid.
[22] Both occur in CL 16:12.
[23] CL 16:22.

The Spirit is not a reluctant giver of gifts, but pours them out "profusely".[24]

Looking upon the Pentecost experience as a baptismal event, he says that the grace given to the apostles "was not partial, but his [the Spirit's power] in all fullness. For just as one immersed in the waters of baptism is completely encompassed by the water, so they were completely baptized by the Spirit."[25] Two other times he stresses the fullness and completeness of the baptism on Pentecost: "They were baptized without anything wanting, according to the promise";[26] "They [the apostles] were baptized in all fullness."[27]

Toward the end of the baptismal instructions, Cyril, in referring to the gift of prophecy, says: "Only let each one prepare oneself to receive the heavenly gift."[28] And he repeats: "God grant that you may be worthy of the charism of prophecy."[29] "Those who are about to be baptized even now in the Holy Spirit" should bring an expanded expectation.[30] They need only make large their awareness, and "he will grant you charisms of every kind."[31] In the very last instruction before entering into the baptismal rite, he says: "My final words, beloved brethren, in this instruction, will be words of exhortation, urging all of you to prepare your souls for the reception of the heavenly charisms."[32]

Basil of Caesarea and Gregory Nazianzen

Both Basil of Caesarea and Gregory Nazianzen (329–389), writing in Greek, situate the prophetic charisms within Christian initiation, though for historical reasons they are more reserved than Paul is in

[24] CL 16:26.
[25] CL 17:14.
[26] CL 17:15.
[27] CL 17:18.
[28] CL 17:19.
[29] CL 17:35.
[30] CL 16:6.
[31] CL 17:37.
[32] CL 18:32.

1 Corinthians. Basil places the charisms in relation to baptism: "The diversity of the charisms corresponds to the diversity of members, but all are baptized in one sole Spirit."[33] The Spirit is present in "prophecy, or healings, or other wonderful works", all of which are still to be found.[34] He refers specifically to "the distribution of wonderful charisms".[35]

Gregory refers to an inner transformation which can only be accounted for by the divinity of the Spirit: "If the Spirit is not to be adored, how can [the Spirit] divinize me in baptism?"[36] Writing of Paul laying hands on the believers, imparting the Spirit, so that they spoke in tongues and prophesied (Acts 19:1–7), Gregory concludes: "This Spirit does all that God does: dividing into tongues of fire, distributing charisms, coming to expression in apostles, prophets, evangelists, pastors, and doctors."[37]

John Chrysostom

Though John Chrysostom lived in Antioch, the capital of Syria, Greek was spoken in this seaboard city. He finds the matter of the charisms in 1 Corinthians "very obscure".[38] The reason, he says, is "many of the wonders which then [in the time of the apostles] used to take place have now ceased."[39] Many of the charisms listed by Paul are no longer actualities in the life of the Church. But it was not so in the days of the apostles: "Whoever was baptized at once spoke in tongues, and not only in tongues, but many also prophesied; some performed many other wonderful works."[40] "All" who were baptized in the apostolic age received "certain excellent charisms".[41] Specifically with regard to prophecy,

[33] *On the Holy Spirit* 26:61.
[34] Ibid.
[35] Ibid., 9:23.
[36] *Fifth Theological Discourse* 28.
[37] Ibid., 29.
[38] *On 1 Corinthians* 29.
[39] *On Romans* 14.
[40] *On 1 Corinthians* 29.
[41] *On Romans* 14.

Chrysostom says, "this grace was poured out abundantly, and every church had many who prophesied."[42]

Chrysostom regrets the passing of many charisms from the life of the Church. He tells of a beautiful woman who goes to her jewel box, opens it, and finds it empty. "The present Church represents such a woman."[43]

Chrysostom's teaching is significant for three reasons. First, we begin to see the disappearance of some charisms from the broad pattern of the Church's life in one part of the world. Second, Chrysostom is aware of an earlier period in which an experience of the charisms was a normal part of initiation. Third, Chrysostom obviously considered the change a great loss for the Church.

Philoxenus of Mabbug and the Syrians

Tertullian and Hilary wrote in Latin, while Origen, Cyril, Basil, Gregory, and John Chrysostom wrote in Greek, but Philoxenus and those of his tradition wrote in Syriac, a dialect of Aramaic. The previous authors all envisaged a situation in which adults were baptized, while in churches of the Syriac tradition, there was baptism of infants. So his situation was similar to many liturgical churches today.

We would criticize Philoxenus' view of the Christian life as too narrow. Like many of his contemporaries, he belittles the possibility of perfection within the married state. He and other Syrian theologians tie their theology too closely to monastic life. Yet they may preserve an ancient, indeed, apostolic, theology, which only later was narrowed to monastic ideals.

Philoxenus speaks of two baptisms, one received in infancy and the second years later, when one gave oneself completely to the gospel by embracing the monastic ideals. His talk of two baptisms is deceptive, because he actually believes in only one, the first, given at infancy, which is fully actualized years later in adult life

---

[42] On 1 Corinthians 32.
[43] Ibid., 36.

when one surrenders to the gospel. By living the gospel, by emptying oneself, "the sensation" of the divine life given at first baptism, but not then felt, blossoms into "the true experience of the knowledge of the Spirit" in the second baptism.[44] Philoxenus stumbles over himself excitedly when he writes of the second baptism: "You will only know that you experience happiness, but what that joy is you will not be able to express."[45] He does mention the charism of healing, but he implies there are more.[46]

One could mention other Syriac writers who place the charisms in relation to Christian initiation. John of Apamea (first half of the fifth century), like Philoxenus, writes of two baptisms, the second also a later actualization of the first. In the second baptism, one takes possession perfectly "of the power of holy baptism".[47] In relation to the second baptism, he mentions prophecy, healing, and miracles.[48] Theodoret of Cyrrhus (ca. 393–ca. 466) witnesses to the abundant outpouring of charisms at initiation and mentions healing in particular.[49] Severus of Antioch (ca. 465–538), like John Chrysostom, acknowledges that "numerous charisms were bestowed on believers at that [apostolic] time, and those who were baptized by the apostles also received various favors."[50] Finally, Joseph Hazzaya (born ca. 710–713), one of the great Syrian mystics, writes of the "sign through which you will feel that the Spirit received in baptism is working in you", mentioning "a flow of spiritual speech [tongues]", and "a knowledge of both worlds [word of knowledge or wisdom]", in addition to "joy, jubilation, exultation, praise, glorification, songs, hymns, odes. . . . "[51]

Commenting on these Syriac witnesses, Oxford scholar Sebastian

[44] *Discourses* 9:263.

[45] Ibid., 9:289.

[46] Ibid., 2:27. Letter of Sebastian Brock, Oriental Institute Oxford, May 27, 1990, to Kilian McDonnell. Brock also thinks that Joseph Hazzaya (Abdisho) implies the charisms.

[47] *Dialogues and Treatises* 10:117.

[48] *Dialogue on the Soul and the Passions* 9, 10.

[49] *History of the Monks in Syria,* Prologue, 8, 10.

[50] *On Prayer* 25.

[51] See A. Mingana, *Early Christian Mystics* (Cambridge: Heffner, 1934), pp. 165–67.

Brock says the Syriac fathers "are well aware that the pente-costal effects of baptism do not necessarily manifest themselves at baptism itself, but may be delayed until later: the 'pledge of the Spirit'. The potential, however, is already present as a result of baptism."[52] Referring specifically to Philoxenus, Brock continues:

> What Philoxenus is saying here is something of great value. He is looking at the relationship between the personal experience of Pentecost, of the coming of the Holy Spirit upon an individual, and the actual rite of baptism, in a context where, because of the practice of infant baptism, the two events may be separated by many years of time.... The "two baptisms" are thus but two aspects of the one sacrament, the first seen from the point of view of the Giver, the second, from that of the receiver.[53]

Baptism for the Syrians is not a one-time event. Rather, "baptism is seen as just the beginning which opens up all sorts of new possibilities, provided the baptized person responds with openness to the presence of the indwelling Spirit."[54]

Conclusions

These early authors view baptism in the Holy Spirit as being integral to Christian initiation, as belonging to the normal Christian life of the normal Christian community. The experience took place within the rites of initiation for adults, or in a later actualiza-tion of what was received at initiation in the case of someone baptized as an infant. The experience of Christian initiation was one of spiritual joy, issuing in praise and thanksgiving, and of the manifestation, either then or later, of the charisms (tongues, prophecy, knowledge, wisdom, discernment, healing). While classi-

[52] *The Holy Spirit in the Syrian Baptismal Tradition,* Syrian Church Series 9 (Kottayam, Kerala, India, 1979), p. 134.

[53] Ibid., pp. 137–39.

[54] S. Brock, *Spirituality in the Syriac Tradition* (Kerala, India: St. Ephrem Ecumenical Research Institute, 1989), p. 74.

cal Pentecostals and some streams of the charismatic movement see baptism in the Holy Spirit as a second (or third) subsequent work after conversion, the early authors saw it as belonging to the very making of a Christian, that is, initiation.

From this evidence it must be clear that what is called baptism in the Holy Spirit was an integral part of becoming a Christian. There was, and could be, only one baptism, the celebration of which was prepared over a long period of conversion and faith building. Unless conversion took place, the rites were empty gestures. The convert joined a converted community, living a converted life.

The charisms were expected and were imparted during initiation, which is seen in architectural terms in the diagram provided. If baptism in the Holy Spirit is integral to Christian initiation, then it does not belong to private piety but to public liturgy, to the official public worship of the Church. And is normative for all Christians. Baptism in the Holy Spirit clearly does not belong to the charismatic renewal but to the Church.

Further, if the evidence I have placed before you is true, then baptism in the Spirit is not peripheral but central. Justin Martyr, Origen, Didymus the Blind and Cyril of Jerusalem all call Christian initiation baptism in the Holy Spirit. It is a synonym for baptism. The witnesses I have cited come from Latin, Greek, and Syriac cultures, from almost the whole of the Mediterranean seaboard. The witnesses are not minor characters. Five are doctors of the Church (Hilary, Cyril, Basil, Gregory, John Chrysostom), persons especially reliable in identifying the faith and practice of the Church. Origen was the most influential theologian in the East during the first thousand years. Philoxenus was a major figure in Syria.

Classical Pentecostalism has not conceived of baptism in the Holy Spirit in relation to initiation. The research shows that, whatever disagreements there are over the exegesis of certain New Testament texts, the essential insight of classical Pentecostalism about the existence of something called baptism in the Holy Spirit was on target. They were also right in asserting that it was central rather than peripheral. The Christian world is indebted to classical Pentecostalism for its witness to the baptism in the Holy Spirit.

The evidence from the early Church must be significant for evangelization. The intense joy to which Hilary and Joseph Hazzaya refer are a part of an inner transformation to which Basil and Gregory Nazianzen give witness, the dynamism of the charisms. All of this is a source for both evangelization and reevangelization. This is not fluff, not tinsel. Once again, charismatic renewal and baptism in the Holy Spirit can be separated. In embracing the baptism in the Holy Spirit as integral to Christian initiation, one is not joining a movement. The issue is to embrace the fullness of Christian initiation and to utilize the total reality of initiation as the well from which we draw the waters of life and power in the work of evangelization. Leading believers into a living experience of the baptism in the Holy Spirit as an integral part of Christian initiation should be the goal of the evangelizing Church.

7

EVANGELIZATION IN THE CHURCH
OF JOS, NIGERIA

Archbishop Gabriel Gonsum Ganaka

The Lord Jesus tells us that the kingdom of God is like the mustard seed (Lk 13:18–19). This parable can be rightly interpreted as a prophecy about the growth and mission of the Christian Church.

The growth of the Catholic Church in the diocese of Jos, Nigeria, offers dramatic testimony to this parable. From a weak and fragile beginning eighty-seven years ago, the tiny seed of Catholic faith has taken firm root and is growing by leaps and bounds. When human beings cooperate with God's grace, all things are indeed possible.

The first Catholic priests set foot on the shores of Nigeria in 1863. They belonged to the Society of African Missions (S.M.A.), founded in 1856 for the evangelization of the continent of Africa. Because their numbers were few, the missionary fathers could not get to the northern part of Nigeria until 1907, when a team of three priests left France and arrived in the territory of the present Jos diocese. Urged on by a powerful zeal to spread the message of salvation to the people of Africa, many such priests and nuns abandoned the comfort of their homelands and their families. They demonstrated heroic courage in the face of the harsh tropical climate and the strange fever that ended the life of many before they reached the age of thirty. The unfriendly tropical weather combined with the resistance of the inhabitants of the area, who were slow to change from their traditional African religions.

The British colonialists—who for the most part nominally professed Christ and came from traditionally Christian countries—made the task of these first missionaries even more difficult. Out of sheer political expediency, the government forbade them to carry out any work of evangelization in areas officially declared Muslim or in communities over which Muslim emirs exercised political power, even if the majority of the inhabitants did not profess Islam.

For the first few decades, many of the missionaries died on the field without seeing the fruit of their labor. One of the pioneering priests, Fr. Mouren, returned to France almost at the point of death after severe attacks of malaria fever. He noted, "During my stay of two years and eight months in Shendam, I had baptized one child and heard the confession of two passing Christians." Fr. Ernest Berlin died in active service at the young age of twenty-six. Rather then being discouraged, his companions chose these words of Jesus for his funeral Mass: "Except a seed falls to the ground and dies, it remains only a single seed, but if it dies, it bears much fruit" (Jn 12:24).

In the face of so few conversions at the cost of so many lives, the missionaries persevered, believing that their work was not in vain. They hoped and prayed that their humble contribution to the mission of Christ would germinate, grow, and spread its branches to embrace countless numbers of people someday. My own vocation as a priest witnesses to the fact that their hope was not in vain. God is always true to his word. May his name be praised for ever.

Methods of the Early Missionaries

The first priests were seriously handicapped by their small numbers in the midst of a vast geographical area. Unable to speak the various languages of the local inhabitants, they preached the gospel through local interpreters who themselves were not proficient in English or French.

Converts came mainly through the establishment of elementary educational institutions, where reading, writing, and arithmetic were taught. The missionaries gradually found and trained teachers to conduct classes for religious instruction in newly established Vernacular Training Centers (VTC). The graduates of these training centers served as the principal assistants of the missionaries in the work of evangelization by teaching catechism, explaining the Bible, interpreting the message of the priests, and heading the various local community churches as catechists.

These early missionaries also established a few medical clinics and maternity centers run by nuns and lay assistants. These health centers served as important instruments for evangelization as the nuns brought health to the sick and spoke kind words to those in pain. Many of the local people welcomed the message of Christ after having been touched by the love of God in these ways.

Initially the colonial administrators made it extremely difficult for the missionaries to establish schools. As time progressed, however, the local people began to agitate for their rights and forced the government to liberalize and improve the conditions for opening and upgrading schools. The government allowed the classes of religious instruction to run full primary-school programs and also approved the Vernacular Training Centers to run full teacher-training programs. Much later, the missionaries set up a number of secondary schools side by side with those established by the government, thus training Nigerians who would eventually take over from the colonialists as administrators, clerks, and technicians.

These mission-owned schools were used by the missionaries for evangelization. Many of the students were converted while in school, and some went home to convert their parents and relations. Some young people realized their vocation to the priesthood and the religious life while planted in this same fertile soil. I am myself a beneficiary of the early missionary endeavors in northern Nigeria. As one fruit of their tireless labor, I was ordained to the priesthood in 1965 and was appointed bishop of the diocese of Jos in 1974.

With the aid of these schools, the Church grew steadily until about 1965, when the government decided to take over the primary schools from the voluntary agencies in Nigeria—including the Catholic Church. This policy, which was extended to the secondary schools in 1972, had an adverse effect on Catholic evangelism in the whole country. It meant that the Church no longer had total control of the institutions that were the principal instrument of evangelization.

Yet we know that with God all things work together for good, that he can bring the utmost good even out of a policy designed to persecute the Church or stifle her growth. As the Church was rendered helpless without schools, the Spirit who cannot be caged inspired the Church to seek new methods, new avenues, and new instruments for evangelization.

A Period of Enormous Growth, Renewal, and Vitality

In the providence of God, government control of schools coincided with the post-Vatican II era, which encouraged adaptations and innovations in evangelization. The Catholic Church began to use local languages and diverse musical instruments in the liturgy, which proved to be a great boon in Africa. The laity became more actively involved, either as individuals or in various lay organizations within the Church. The era also witnessed a more widespread use of mass media in evangelization.

A few statistics from our diocese alone reflect the enormous growth, renewal, and vitality in the African church in the last two decades: in 1974 there were five indigenous priests, today there are sixty-one; in 1974 there were six nuns, today there are thirty-four; in 1974 there were seventeen parishes, today there are forty-six. Even though the Jos diocese continually opens new parishes, we are nevertheless overwhelmed by the number of new converts to Christianity. Today the Catholic population in our diocese has risen to 515,000.

These figures are consonant with the phenomenal growth of the entire African church, according to those cited at the African Synod held during the entire month of April 1994.

	Catholics	bishops	priests	nuns	seminarians
1927	3,202,903	2 (1939)	127	1,982	336
1993	95,613,000	327	10,903	21,000	121,391

This synod was the first in the history of Catholicism devoted to the church of Africa. About 240 bishops from all over Africa joined representatives from other continents. Together with the pope, we engaged in serious study and reflection on the Church's mission of evangelization in Africa toward the year 2000. The Spirit is indeed moving, may the Lord be praised now and for ever more.

The Fruits of Adaptation and Inculturation

This phenomenal growth of the church in Africa has come about through the grace of God, supported by a number of human factors. Of special significance has been the post-Vatican II program of adaptation and inculturation initiated by the Council, which gave room for the incarnation of the Christian message into different lands and among different peoples, in accordance with the language, culture, music, and social sensibilities of each people.

Until Vatican II, the Mass was said all over the world in Latin. For many Africans, the mode of worship was rather cold and unappealing. This otherwise lively and spirited people, for whom joy and celebration were a way of life, had to sit in church through dull and mournful services, listening to sermons often poorly interpreted.

Africans were also disappointed that this new faith did not provide adequate answers to their most profound questions, fears, and worries about spiritual realities—at least according to their own perceptions. Many therefore fell back on the traditional religions or joined the independent African Christian churches in the southern regions, churches which were more innovative and took the cultural context more seriously in their approach to Christian evangelization.

Christianity for a number of Catholics was no more than the

memorization of abstract theories and concepts that had little bearing on their concrete existence. Thus many of the converts lived ambivalent spiritual lives, with an exterior allegiance to Jesus Christ but with an interior and often more profound allegiance to the gods of their ancestors who appeared to take more interest in the day-to-day problems.

We are now discovering that one cause of this spiritual ambivalence on the part of African converts to Christianity is the lack of adequate inculturation in the traditional mode of Catholic evangelization. When evangelization fails to take into consideration the worldview, thought pattern, or cultural symbols of a people, they may not respond adequately to the Christian message.

The problems that typically arise are highlighted in a letter published in the *Catholic World Report* (March 1992). Sherry Waddle, a reader from Seattle, Washington, was commenting on the active Protestant evangelization in South America. Her letter reads in part:

> Much of the signs and wonders approach associated with evangelical/pentecostal missions stems from the recognition of what, at the Fuller School of World Missions, is called "The Excluded Middle". The theory goes as follows: Western missionaries carried their rationalist and anti-supernaturalist cultural assumptions with them and went to peoples saturated with a spiritual worldview that incorporated minor deities, demons, curses, charms, and spells into daily life.
>
> Western rationalism dismissed these beliefs as mere superstition and converted people to a worldview of a "high" trinitarian God and a "low" strong personal code of behavior. The "middle" realm of demons and spells was never addressed, but it would not go away. These people had lived for many generations with the spiritual realities of the demonic, had seen people die of curses, and knew, whatever the missionary said, that these things were real. To deal with them, they turned once again to their traditional spiritual practices and the result was the various forms of Christo-paganism.
>
> To fill this gap, some evangelical missionaries looked once again to the early Church, and found in the experience of Pentecost and the healings, prophecies, and miracles of the

Book of Acts, a Christian answer for the "excluded middle". This approach has come to be called "power evangelism".

With Vatican II's program of inculturation underway, the Church began to take the worldview of the people seriously. The local church experienced a rapid growth in vocations to the priesthood and religious life. As many young people started becoming priests and nuns, the people were highly encouraged. The liturgy was translated into the various languages, and lay people actively participated in the liturgy.

The spontaneity and creative genius of the African showed themselves in songs, music, and dance at liturgical gatherings. Today in the church of Jos, there is little distinction between the choir and the rest of the people in church. Practically every member of the congregation gets involved in singing and dancing. Most Nigerians are gifted in the art of composing songs, so prayer meetings and liturgical gatherings are further enriched by faith-songs with the accompaniment of modern musical instruments, hand-clapping, and dancing.

The people are particularly excited when they see that the profound spiritual problems that troubled them are being taken seriously by the Church. They can now be delivered of demonic possessions and be assured of the protection of the Lord Jesus from malevolent forces which they know are always seeking to devour them.

The result of inculturation in Catholic worship is that our churches are now overcrowded with joyful worshippers several days a week. Many of those who come to the church with minor complaints of ill health go back home healed after a lively liturgical celebration or prayer meeting. The healing and deliverance Masses are of particular importance for the people and are always crowded with worshippers expecting to be touched in a personal way by the Lord Jesus and his Spirit.

The Charismatic Renewal

The charismatic renewal came into the diocese of Jos in 1974 and has experienced a steady growth. The renewal is now present in thirty-eight of our forty-six parishes. Its Life in the Spirit seminars, combined with such ministries as healing and deliverance, teaching, intercession, and singing, have contributed immensely to the growth of the church in Jos.

An emphasis on the deepening of faith, a profound love for the word of God, and the personal discovery of Jesus Christ as Lord distinguish the charismatic movement. The renewal has also fostered a true devotion to the sacraments, so that many young people now go to sacraments regularly, while a number of those who had lapsed in their faith have been brought back to active participation in the Church's sacramental life.

Besides the Life in the Spirit seminars, Bible studies, and instruction classes organized by the teaching ministry, the renewal organizes crusades and outreach programs aimed at the entire public. Along with their counterparts in the Legion of Mary and the Catholic women's organization (the *Zumnuntamata Katolika*), charismatics try to reach special groups in the community such as students, prison inmates, and prostitutes.

The relationship of the members of the Catholic charismatic renewal with members of different Evangelical groups has fostered the spirit of ecumenism, resulting in mutual enrichment among the Christian churches.

The New Evangelization

During his 1982 visit, Pope John Paul II issued a challenge to the Nigerian church regarding the new evangelization. Since then we have embraced several programs aimed at improving our methods and modifying our strategies toward a more intensive and far-reaching effort to share the gospel. Among these programs are Evangelization 2000, a call to present a birthday gift to Christ by the year 2000 in the form of a world that is more deeply Christian, and Lumen 2000, which emphasizes the creative use of modern audiovisual equipment in the programs of evangelization.

A national seminar on evangelization was held in Ibadan in 1984. Since then, various dioceses have established as many as twenty-six schools of evangelization to equip the clergy and laity with the spiritual gifts and skills required to reach the modern world. They especially stress the need for personal holiness of life and the spirit of community on the part of the evangelizers. The diocese of Jos has already trained two priests, two nuns, three catechists, and one other lay person in these schools of evangelization. We are now poised to start our own school, so that many more people will become trained evangelizers to the people of Jos.

Our diocese held a synod with the theme "Our Call to Holiness" in 1988. As a result, many of our people have experienced a deeper commitment to the message of Christ and devotion to the sacraments, along with the revitalization of the faith of a large number of lapsed Catholics. Today many parishes of our diocese observe an hour-long adoration of the Blessed Sacrament every day before the early morning Mass.

Problems and Challenges

I must however mention that the Catholic Church of Jos is not without her problems. The number of Catholics continues to grow at a very rapid rate, so that our structures, personnel, and resources are often inadequate in the face of this expansion. In spite of the growth in vocations, many congregations cannot hold regular Masses because there are not enough priests to go round. Also, churches are overcrowded in some localities, while Catholics in other localities cannot afford the construction of a church building.

The poverty of our churches shows itself most in the inability of the Catholic Church to purchase air time for evangelization programs on the government-owned radio and television stations. This is a great source of concern to us today, especially since we see many other religious bodies who enjoy financial backing from rich benefactors and then buy up plenty of air time to spread their faith.

Today Islam claims 45 percent of the population of Nigeria. Some Islamic sects are very fundamentalist, militant, and aggressive. In some parts of northern Nigeria, young fanatical Muslims have burned down churches and killed several Christians. Some of these groups wish to claim the whole of northern Nigeria, including Jos, as Islamic territory. And so Christian evangelizers experience ongoing tension with Islamic sects who often become violent at the least provocation.

The Catholic Church has often urged dialogue in dealing with Muslims, but many in the northern part of Nigeria are not willing to dialogue. In the face of violence and arson, the ordinary Christian is often left confused. The church in Jos continues to face up to this challenge, believing that we serve a living God, who on the Cross has conquered Satan and who will not allow the gates of hell to prevail against his Church (Mt 16:18).

Finally, the recently concluded African Synod urged us to pursue intense evangelization in the context of inculturation, justice, and dialogue, making adequate use of the modern means of social communication. This is a great challenge. However, with the help of God, and through the intercession of Mary the Mother of Jesus Christ and the Star of evangelization, we will launch into an evangelization which is "new in its fervor, in its methods, and in its expression".

8

WHICH CHURCHES ARE GROWING AND WHY?

Vinson Synan

Evangelization enlarges the community of faith. Although the term "church growth" represents a specific movement among Protestants, it refers in the broadest sense to what all Christians desire: sharing with the non-Christian world the good news of Jesus Christ as the only Savior.

Simply put, churches that evangelize tend to grow in membership, while those that do not tend to stagnate or even decline. As a rule, churches that are not experiencing growth tend to speak in terms of "quality" rather than quantity. For example, on a recent trip to Malaysia, I met with a group of local bishops and pastors representing most of the churches in that largely Muslim nation. I asked them, "Which churches are growing the fastest in Malaysia and Kuala Lumpur?"

The dozen or so leaders looked sheepishly at each other before replying, "Well, if you are talking about quality and depth, the mainline churches are growing the fastest. But if you are speaking of numbers alone, the Pentecostals and charismatics are growing the fastest."

As the conversation continued, it became clear that indeed the Pentecostals were growing the fastest. But the largest actual increase in membership during the previous months was among the Roman Catholics, who had experienced recent dramatic breakthroughs in certain areas of the nation. The Catholics and the Pentecostals!

How striking that the greatest growth was taking place at opposite ends of the liturgical and sacramental spectrum, from the oldest to the youngest of the world's churches.

We can learn a lot about evangelization from examining which churches in the world are growing and why. Let's review the major researchers who have made it their business to track the growth and size of the churches of the world. Their findings may help us understand the paradox of the Malaysian situation as well as the role of evangelization in expanding the worldwide body of Christ.

The Church-Growth Movement

The increasingly popular church-growth movement was pioneered by Donald McGavran, a venerable missiologist who first became interested in the principles of church growth as a missionary to India in the 1930s. He could not help but notice that some congregations and parishes grew rapidly while others did not.

McGavran's research caused a great stir among missiologists. Due to high demand, he founded in 1961 a new Institute of Church Growth on the campus of Northwest Christian College in Eugene, Oregon. This institute drew so much attention that it soon outgrew its facilities and moved to Fuller Theological Seminary in Pasadena, California, becoming part of the Fuller School of World Missions.

Here McGavran gathered a group of brilliant students and faculty, including C. Peter Wagner, Win Arn, and John Wimber. Almost all of McGavran's previous research had centered on Third World nations. By the mid-sixties, however, church leaders in this country demanded that the same research and principles be applied to the American scene. Thus, a booming church-growth industry emanated from Pasadena, affecting churches in America as well as the rest of the world.

Succeeding McGavran as the leading exponent and popularizer of this influential movement was the prolific researcher, lecturer, and writer Peter Wagner, a man who spread the gospel of church growth to the four corners of the earth. From Wagner, we learned the "pathologies of dying churches" as well as how to do "autopsies" on dead and dying congregations to find out why they died. Here are some of the Fuller findings on why particular congregations die:[1]

Ethnikitis: the ethnic changing of a neighborhood, e.g., from white to Black or Hispanic. This often kills the older church when members flee to the suburbs.

Old age: the "ghost town" disease kills congregations. When small towns die, the churches die with them.

People blindness: the controversial "homogeneous unit principle" states that "people prefer to worship with other people who are like themselves." That would include racial, ethnic, linguistic, social, and economic groupings.

Hyper-cooperativeness: with too much ecumenical cooperation, efforts toward Christian unity can hinder evangelism.

Koinonitis: "spiritual naval gazers", i.e., churches that are too ingrown, that fail to welcome new people who are a little "different" from the in-group.

Sociological strangulation: healthy churches that are choked to death by limited facilities such as small buildings, inadequate parking space, etc.

St. John's syndrome: the "lukewarm church" that is neither cold nor hot, the kind that St. John said would be vomited out of the mouth of God (Rev 3:14–18).

Wagner also describes traits which characterize a growing congregation: a gifted pastor; a well-mobilized laity; churches that are "big enough" to serve the whole family; "celebration plus congregation plus cell equals church"; the homogeneous unit principle, i.e., "mostly one kind of people"; churches that use effective evangelistic tools; and churches that have their priorities straight, i.e., their

[1] C. Peter Wagner, *Your Church Can Grow: Seven Vital Signs of a Health Church* (Ventura, Calif.: Regal Books, 1976), pp. 124–25.

most important function in the community is religious rather than merely social or economic.[2]

Wagner's emphasis on the purely religious factor in church growth was influenced by Dean Kelley, a sociologist related to the liberal-leaning National Council of Churches. He published his ground-breaking book in 1972, *Why Conservative Churches Are Growing,* which simply stated the results of his research: "conservative" churches were growing, while "liberal" churches were declining.

Kelley attributed this situation to the fact that most people are more interested in answers to the "ultimate" question of salvation than in social questions. He said that liberal churches often offer "art or music appreciation, instruction in women's liberation, guidelines to politically correct causes, and dialogues with important local leaders", while most people are generally uninterested in such affairs. Instead, they are "hungry for God" and for the assurance of salvation.

In addition to these insights, church growth researchers discovered the importance of "church planting" as a major evangelistic tool. The movement also developed a method of tracking church growth through a system known as the "decadal growth rate". Through this objective method, churches could estimate their growth or death rates and compare them to the biological growth rates.

Other research introduced us to the "life cycle of churches", which showed that the typical American Protestant church followed a life cycle that looked like the bell curve. New churches tended to grow for ten years, began to plateau at about twenty years, and began a decline after about thirty years. Much of this research appeared in Wagner's best-selling books, *Your Church Can Grow,* published in 1976, and *Leading Your Church to Growth,* published in 1984. In these books, Wagner assured us that "church growth is a science" with theories that can be tested and proven.[3]

Further research by Carl George, head of the Charles E. Fuller

[2] Ibid., pp. 69–155.
[3] Ibid., pp. 38–39.

Institute for Evangelism and Church Growth, also located in Pasadena, centered on the crucial role of pastoral leadership in church growth. From research in the business world, George taught us the differences between the "catalyzers", the "organizers", and the "operators".

Each of these leaders has specific gifts. The CAT (catalyzer) is a charismatic individual who attracts a "pile" of people. This person is disorganized but attractive. The CAT is usually succeeded by the ORG (organizer), who then organizes the "pile" and puts it in logical order. This second person is usually quite critical of the disorganized predecessor. Third, the OP (operator) comes on the scene and operates the church which was created by the CAT and then organized by the ORG. Afterward, the succeeding OPs need only oil the machinery they have inherited from the CAT and ORG. So much for church-growth theory![4]

The main blind spot in the research by McGavran, Wagner, and George, however, was that they never applied their methods to Roman Catholic and Eastern Orthodox churches. They focused solely on the Protestant churches of the world, with a heavy emphasis on mainline denominations in the United States. Surely Catholic churches face the same demographic pressures as urban Protestant churches. Why then were Catholics not studied by the church-growth researchers? Moreover, why did Catholics not study their own situation in America and the world using church-growth methods? Would the results be similar?

Astonishing Survey Results

In 1982, David Barrett and Oxford University Press published his monumental *World Christian Encyclopedia,*[5] the most complete survey of Christianity and other world religions ever attempted. In a

---

[4] Carl George, "Selecting Leaders", *How to Plant a Church,* Fuller Theological Seminary church growth lectures (1983), p. 637.

[5] David B. Barrett, *World Christian Encyclopedia: A Comprehensive Survey of Churches and Religion in the Modern World AD* 1900–2000 (New York: Oxford University Press, 1982).

major review of the book, *Time* magazine said that Barrett had "counted every soul on earth". After the publication of the *Encyclopedia,* Phillip Hogan, world missions director of the Assemblies of God, quipped, "Only God and David Barrett know how many Assemblies of God members there are in the world."

What Barrett revealed astonished people at the time. Based on his research, the Roman Catholic Church was by far the largest religious organization in the world in 1980, with some 809,157,029 members. Next came the Orthodox Christian churches, with 124,419,230 members. To the amazement of many, the largest Protestant family of churches in the world was no longer the Reformation churches, such as the Lutherans, Anglicans, Presbyterians, or Baptists, but the Pentecostals, whose churches had begun only eighty years before.[6] Barrett's figures for 1980 and 1992 were as follows:[7]

	1980	1992
Roman Catholic	809,157,029	999,000,000
Eastern Orthodox	124,419,230	160,737,900
Pentecostals	51,167,200	204,500,000
Anglican	49,706,200	55,000,000
Baptists	47,550,300	55,500,000
Lutherans	43,360,400	52,500,000
Presbyterians	40,209,500	47,400,000
Methodists	29,782,300	31,600,000

The number of Pentecostals by 1992 is truly astounding, since there were no modern Pentecostals before the first day of the twentieth century. When we add the number of charismatics in the mainline denominations—also nonexistent before 1900—the totals are even more incredible. The combined total of denomi-

---

[6] Ibid., p. 14.

[7] David B. Barrett, "The Twentieth Century Pentecostal-Charismatic Renewal in the Holy Spirit, with Its Goal of World Evangelization", in Stanley Burgess, et al., *Dictionary of Pentecostal and Charismatic Movements* (Grand Rapids, Mich.: Zondervan, 1988), pp. 810–30.

national Pentecostals and mainline charismatics for 1992 was 410,626,000.

Unlike most Evangelical Protestant statisticians who tended to count only "born again" believers, or "Bible believers", as true Christians, Barrett also counted all baptized Catholics as Christians. He also counted such groups as Mormons and Jehovah's Witnesses as "marginal Christians". Furthermore, he used demographic techniques that counted entire families as members of churches and movements rather than official church records alone.

The results of Barrett's massive research demonstrated that, in general, Western churches from Europe and North America were declining, while Third World churches were growing. His figures for 1980 were startling. For instance, in that year, 7600 Christians per day dropped out of the Western churches, both Protestant and Catholic, while in an average day, 16,000 Africans became Christians. Indeed, Barrett estimated that somewhere around 1980, the number of nonwhite Christians exceeded the number of white Christians for the first time in history.[8]

Barrett also estimated and projected the numbers and percentages of all churches for the entire twentieth century, beginning in 1900 and ending in the year 2000. The figures were illuminating as far as the growth of the Roman Catholic Church was concerned. His research revealed that in 1900, Roman Catholics totaled 271,990,786, making up 16.8 percent of the world's population. By the year 2000, that number is expected to reach 1,169,462,660 members, accounting for 18.7 percent of the world's population. Barrett's findings indicate a growth of almost one billion souls in one century![9]

John Vaughn's "mega-church" research. If church-growth theory resulted in larger churches, then research was needed to track the largest congregations in the world and to see why they had

---

[8] See Vinson Synan, *In the Latter Days: The Outpouring of the Holy Spirit in the Twentieth Century* (Ann Arbor, Mich.; 1984), pp. 12–19.

[9] Barrett, *World Christian Encyclopedia,* p. 6.

grown. This project was taken on in 1985 by John Vaughn, a professor of church growth and founder of the Church Growth and World Missions Center at Southwest Baptist University in Bolivar, Missouri.

Vaughn first became interested in the fundamentalistic Baptist congregations in America, which were far larger than those in any denominations during the 1950s and 1960s. For years his records showed that the "ten largest churches" in America were indeed Baptist churches, like the ones that sponsored Vaughn's university.

By the middle 1980s, his research took him to the nations of the world, resulting in *The World's Twenty Largest Churches* (1984) and *The Large Church: A Twentieth Century Expression of the First Century Church* (1985). By the time these books appeared, the largest Protestant churches in the world were no longer conservative Baptist congregations but Pentecostal ones, which soon outgrew all others in scope and size.

By 1990, all ten of the largest congregations in the world were either classical Pentecostal or charismatic Protestant. These "megachurches" grew to astonishing proportions. For instance, in the early 1990s in Seoul, Korea, the Yoido Full Gospel Church pastored by Yonggi Cho counted no less than 800,000 members. Other Pentecostal and charismatic churches around the world completed an impressive roster of superchurches.

Biological or Conversion Growth?

A survey of the foregoing research reveals two major ways that churches grow: by biological (demographic) growth or by conversion growth. The two largest families of Christians on earth, the Catholics and Pentecostals, owe their growth to both factors — the former primarily through biological means and the latter primarily by conversion.

Although both methods are certainly desirable, biological growth will never win the world. Muslims and some other religions have much higher birth rates than Christians, many of whom eliminate millions of potential members by abortion. As a matter of fact, if

Western Christians continue to abort millions of babies, even demographic growth will cease.

As a young movement of new churches, the only way Pentecostals could grow was by evangelizing and converting unbelievers and unchurched people throughout the world. Recent estimates indicate that possibly 80 percent of all conversions from paganism come as a result of Pentecostal or charismatic ministries.

Many church leaders are still trying to find the reasons for such rapid growth among Pentecostal and charismatic churches around the world. When asked this question, most Pentecostal leaders would answer simply, "the baptism in the Holy Spirit with the accompanying manifestations of charismatic gifts". Many researchers tend to overlook this answer as being too simplistic, looking rather for more sophisticated sociological or economic causes. At some point, the churches may be forced to face the truth of these Pentecostal claims.[10]

Pentecostals seem to grow in most places because of aggressive evangelism accompanied by such "signs and wonders" as healing, speaking in tongues, casting out of demons, and prophesying. In his book *Power Evangelism,* John Wimber points to "power encounters" as the most significant points of dramatic breakthrough into non-Christian cultures.[11]

Many other factors could be cited for the growth of Pentecostalism in this century: the renewal of expressive worship and spontaneous public prayer; a love of Scripture; the use of cell groups; massive church planting; and cultural adaptability. Yet, it seems that the Pentecostal's dynamic and expressive worship coupled with an expectant faith that miracles could happen at any time go far to explain their explosive growth.[12]

---

[10] For the relationship between the church-growth movement and the Pentecostals, see Grant McClung, *Azusa Street and Beyond* (South Plainfield, N.J.: Bridge Publishing, 1986), pp. 109–32.

[11] John Wimber, *Power Evangelism* (San Francisco, Calif.: Harper & Row, 1986), pp. 15–31.

[12] For a discussion of reasons for Pentecostal growth, see Vinson Synan's "Pentecostalism: Varieties and Contributions", in *Pneuma: The Journal of the Society for Pentecostal Studies* 9, no. 1 (Spring 1987): 31–39.

Of Pentecostals, Catholics, and Liberal Protestants

Not surprisingly, Pentecostal churches are growing in Africa. The cultural freedom of Pentecostals to dance, shout, sing, and exercise the gifts of the Spirit constitutes an undeniable attraction to Africans as well as other Third World peoples, most of whom remain unmoved by the more conventional church life represented by most Western Protestant churches.

On the other hand, the Roman Catholic Church is also growing explosively in Africa, faster than it is growing anywhere else in the world. Some of my African friends explained that Africans are not only attracted to the spiritual freedom of worship that is found in Pentecostal worship but are equally attracted by the liturgical pageantry of Roman Catholicism. Imagine the growth potential in Africa of a church life that combined these qualities in a Pentecostal Catholicism!

A factor balancing Roman Catholic growth in Africa, however, is the problem of massive defections in the West for various reasons. In Europe and North America, millions of Catholics have left the Church for the same reasons that Protestants have dropped out. It has been commonly stated that in America, lapsed Catholics, which number some sixteen million persons, would make the second largest denomination in the nation if they were organized into one body. Millions of other Catholics have left to join Evangelical and charismatic churches.

While Roman Catholics have increased their percentage of world population since 1900, the figures for mainline Protestants show an overall decline. In 1900, all Reformation Protestants numbered 103,056,655 persons, making up 6.4 percent of the world population. By the turn of the century, that number will swell to 345,709,110, but this figure will account for only 5.5 percent of the world population.

These trends mean that, for reasons already explained by Dean Kelley, mainline liberal Protestant churches will not play as significant a role in the next century as they did in the past. This marked decline among mainline Protestants stands in stark contrast to the burgeoning growth of the Pentecostal and independent charismatic churches during the century.[13]

The growth among Evangelical churches not associated with the Pentecostal/charismatic movement proves to be an exception to the losses among the mainline Protestant churches. The best example is the Southern Baptist church, which is now the largest Protestant denomination in the United States, with 15,500,000 members. Added to these numbers are the Afro-American Baptist churches, e.g., the National Baptist Convention, with over seven million members. These evangelistic churches send thousands of missionaries around the world.

To summarize the most recent findings about which churches are growing and why, I offer the following scheme (suggested by Michael Jaffarian, assistant researcher to David Barrett). Looking at it *denominationally,* Pentecostals, charismatics, Evangelical Protestants, and Roman Catholics are growing. Looking at it *regionally,* Third World churches are growing (especially in Africa and Korea); Eastern European churches are growing (due to the vacuum left by the fall of communism); Chinese house churches are growing (85 percent are charismatic); the greatest growth in the world is in the southern hemisphere. Looking at it *ethnically,* nonwhite churches are growing.

Looking at it according to *internal church life,* churches are growing that have gifted leadership; a genuine spirituality (such as the baptism in the Holy Spirit); an emphasis on missions and church planting; an emphasis on Bible study and teaching; an emphasis on worship and community life; an emphasis on signs and wonders; an emphasis on evangelization by *doing it, not just saying it!*

In the end, Peter Wagner makes the important point that despite all the research and techniques of church growth, the ultimate reason churches grow is "God at work through the Holy Spirit".[14]

---

[13] Barrett, *World Christian Encyclopedia,* p. 6.

[14] Wagner, p. 28.

PART THREE

How *You* Can Evangelize!

9

SIX STEPS TO EFFECTIVE EVANGELIZATION

Susan Blum

The thought of doing evangelization intimidates most of us, yet it simply means loving people into the kingdom. This responsibility is not an optional contribution on the part of Catholics, not something we have decided to do in the last fifteen years because we had nothing else to do, or because we thought it might be fun, or because we thought the Protestants were doing it better. Bringing people into the kingdom is the very reason for the Church's existence.

My favorite definition of evangelization is this: one blind beggar showing another blind beggar where the bread of life is, and both being healed in the process. I am not saying that evangelization is the blind leading the blind. What I am saying is that we are all broken, we are all wounded, we are all scarred. We have sorrows, disappointments, and disillusionments. We also have joys, successes, and dreams for the future. But the crucial point is that we are all in this together.

Likening ourselves to beggars reaching out to help other beggars implies a spirit of mutuality and respect between us and those whom we are evangelizing. Effective messengers of the good news do not operate out of a position of power or superiority, feeling that they have all the answers and are going to set others straight whether they want it or not. If we truly desire to bring people into the kingdom, we need to start looking at evangelization inside out and upside down — not the way we always have in the past.

Called to Evangelize Whom?

We are called to evangelize five major groups: the active Catholics, the inactive Catholics, the unchurched, the Protestants, and the non-Christians. Recent statistics indicate that we have somewhere between fifty-five and fifty-nine million active Catholics in the United States, plus sixteen million inactive Catholics. We have an enormous population of eighty million unchurched people, those who say they have no church affiliation. We have seventy-five million Protestant believers. And finally we have twelve million people who practice non-Christian religions. In the past, Jews constituted the largest block of those practicing non-Christian religions in America, but this year Muslims overtook them.

We certainly want to evangelize this last group, but they usually account for only a small number of the people we actually encounter during the course of our daily lives. And while we want to share our faith with practicing Protestants, Catholics are not into "pew-snatching". We should praise them and respect them for their beliefs and not attempt actively to proselytize Christians committed to Protestant denominations.

So I suggest that we look at three major populations as primary targets for Catholic evangelization: the active Catholics, the inactive Catholics, and the unchurched. It is fairly obvious why we want to evangelize those who say they have no church affiliation, who may account for up to 40 percent of any given community. Inactive Catholics are also obvious targets for evangelization. Current estimates indicate that one out of every four baptized Catholics becomes inactive at some time during his life. That is 25 percent! So, of course, as Catholic evangelizers, we want to invite anyone in this group to return to the Church.

I have seen many instances in which the inactive Catholic is looked down upon. The very term "fallen-away Catholic" automatically implies some degree of inferiority, that something is wrong with such a person. I would invite all of us to change this viewpoint by acknowledging that inactive Catholics have made their decision to leave the institutional Church for a reason, whatever it may be. We need to respect and esteem such people by assuming that they have been hurt or had some sort of experience that has led them away from the Church. They must have a good reason. We may not know what it is, but we would like to hear it. While some may leave the Church out of sheer laziness or lethargy, most have left after a great deal of pain and soul-searching.

I was an inactive Catholic for four years, and believe me, I spent more time on my knees during that part of my spiritual journey than when I was attending Mass regularly. I also read more Scripture because I was searching for the truth. After seeking long and hard, I found a loving community that did not put me down but instead welcomed me back as a worthwhile person whose spirituality and morality had not gone out the window. They even told me they needed me and invited me to use my teaching skills in a first-grade CCD class.

The need to evangelize the unchurched and those who have left the Church may seem obvious, but why are we called to evangelize active Catholics? One day in my own parish, I was sitting over on one side of the church where I could see the faces of all the people in the center section and on the opposite side. We were at the point of singing the responsorial psalm, one that says, "This is the day that the Lord has made. Let us rejoice and be glad in it." I happened to look around, and I have never seen such sad-looking Christians in my life! It was just shattering to me. I thought, *My dear brothers and sisters in Christ, if you really believe that "this is the day that the Lord has made, let us rejoice and be glad", would you please inform your faces?*

So I am convinced that we need to zero in on the active Catholics. All five of these groups need evangelization, but if we could *reevangelize* the active Catholics among us, the rest would be a piece of cake. Our parishes would be so dynamic, so exciting, so magnetic that we might need to schedule ten Masses every Sunday. We might have waiting lines outside of church and have to build five-story parking lots! So I say, "Let's focus on the active Catholics!"

George Gallup published a study in 1984 called *Religion in America,* in which he looked at two populations across all Christian denominations, namely, the "churched" and the "unchurched". The "churched" were those who attended Mass or church services at least two times a year other than Christmas or Easter, weddings, or funerals. The "unchurched" were those who attended church even less often or not at all. Gallup made a further distinction within the category of the "churched" Christians. Based on responses to various questions regarding spiritual commitment (such as believing in the divinity of Jesus, seeking God's will in prayer, trying hard to put one's faith into practice, etc.), Gallup identified 12 percent of the "churched" as "highly spiritual" Christians and 88 percent as "nominal" Christians.

After quizzing the "churched" and the "unchurched" on all kinds of ethical and spiritual issues, Gallup then compared the responses of the 88 percent of the "churched" with the responses of the "unchurched". The only statistically significant difference between these two groups was that one went to church and the other did not! He found absolutely no significant difference between most "churched" Christians and the "unchurched" in terms of cheating on income tax, infidelity in marriage, lying, pilfering in business, all kinds of things.

However, Gallup's survey revealed enormous differences between the 12 percent he called "highly spiritual" Christians and both the 88 percent of "nominal" Christians and the "unchurched". To mention only a few, he concluded that this committed group was more satisfied with their lot in life and far happier, placed a greater importance on family life, were more tolerant of other races and religions, and were vitally concerned about the betterment of society.

I believe this 12 percent figure holds true for the approximately fifty-nine million active Catholics as well. In your parish, do you not find a handful of people who do the bulk of the work? They regularly attend Mass, they are committed in time and money, they are members of the prayer group or the CCD program or some other volunteer service. If anywhere close to 88 percent of active Catholics are still sitting on the sidelines, so to speak, then we have plenty of need to evangelize Catholics in today's society.

One of our first tasks as evangelizers reflects the first goal stated in the American bishops' document *Go and Make Disciples:* creating a new enthusiasm in active Catholics so that they will go out and share their faith. Our faith is a free gift that is far more valuable than any material possession in our lives and one that will outlast any human relationship.

If we are excited about that good news, should we not be sharing it with our relatives, our neighbors, even total strangers? We should be shouting it from the rooftops. Given the enormous hunger for the bread of life, how can we become more effective evangelizers?

First Step: Becoming Disciples

Discipleship is both the beginning and the end of evangelization. In order for us to be effective messengers of the good news, we first have to be sure of what we believe. We have to be steeped in prayer, we have to be rooted in Scripture, we need to belong to a worshipping community, and we need to be active in serving others.

Those four basic marks of the Church, which are related in the early chapters of Acts, are extremely critical to this whole sense of discipleship. You cannot *make* a disciple unless you *are* a disciple. Have you ever thought about that? Who makes sheep? Do cows make sheep? Sheep make sheep. In the same way, disciples make disciples. You cannot share something unless you possess it yourself. Most people quickly see through a facade, just mouthing the words, "talking the talk but not walking the walk". Your faith must be genuine.

Step Two: Befriending People

I use another definition of evangelization that I borrowed from Dr. Scott Peck, the psychiatrist and author. In *The Road Less*

Traveled, he gives a wonderful definition of love which serves equally well in terms of evangelization: "extending yourself in order to nurture the spiritual well-being of another person".

I especially like the word "extending". Evangelization is a very active ministry rather than a passive one. You cannot pray all day long and evangelize. It just does not happen that way. Prayer is an absolutely necessary *foundation* for effective evangelization, but eventually you have got to get out of your prayer chair and move! "GO and make disciples." After becoming disciples ourselves, we begin to practice this second step of evangelization by reaching out and befriending people.

My own spiritual journey includes being raised in the Presbyterian Church, where I experienced an enormous amount of hospitality. This was partly the natural result of belonging to a smaller community. The average Protestant church has two hundred members, while the average Catholic parish has two thousand members. It is difficult to establish a sense of community when you are one of thousands. But extending hospitality and being a welcoming community is absolutely essential to loving people into the kingdom.

I attended a national conference several years ago put on by a well-known Catholic organization. Their official welcome of myself and the eleven other newcomers impressed me a great deal. We were given "newcomer" ribbons and wore pink badges when everybody else had blue. The program listed a special luncheon where they were going to introduce each newcomer, so that the other folks would know who we were and be able to welcome us, plus a special cocktail reception for us one evening. I thought, *Wow, this is real hospitality. I don't think I've ever seen the welcome mat extended like this.*

All of this looked good on paper, but what actually happened was quite different. This conference turned out to be what Southerners call "a good old boys' club", where the veterans did not want to meet or talk to newcomers. The twelve of us got together and made some new friends among ourselves, but everyone else at the reception had their own little groups. At the luncheon, they had their own tables. I am a fairly gregarious person, and I like to meet new people, so I tried. And I was given a cold shoulder. I left that conference early the next morning because of it.

Visitors or newcomers can experience this sort of "negative hospitality" when they visit a parish for the first time. You may have a welcoming committee that greets people at the door and serves coffee and doughnuts afterward, but any such efforts will fail miserably if the people in the pews do not want to extend hospitality to visitors.

I am talking about *sincerely* befriending people, not approaching someone with the thought, *Aha! There's a prospect. She'd make a good Catholic!* Evangelizing does not mean looking at people as prospects from a sales point of view but putting into practice the Scripture passage that tells us always to put the needs of others before our own. Become genuinely concerned about the people who visit your parish, the people you visit in their homes, or those you encounter in your daily life.

Reflecting again on the image of two blind beggars: always approach others out of mutual respect, never with an attitude of "one-ups-manship" or feeling "holier-than-thou". We always want to extend a warm welcome to people, whether we are inviting them into the whole community or into our homes for a cup of coffee.

A wonderful experience of getting to know people in church happened in a parish in Albany. A small group of us were a marriage-encounter community of ten to fifteen couples. We decided on our own that whatever Sunday Mass we went to, we would find somebody we did not know—maybe a family with children the ages of ours—and invite them home for breakfast. And we just did it.

The first thing that happened was that people nearly passed out cold when we invited them, and we would have to explain what we were doing. "No, we're just having coffee and dough-nuts and juice for the kids. Come on, we'd love to get to know you." And then before they would leave our homes that morning, we would encourage them to do the same thing the following Sunday. Pretty soon, that whole parish really got to know each other.

Step Three: Sharing Your Faith

After focusing on the first step of becoming disciples and then extending ourselves in order to nurture the spiritual well-being of others, we come to the third step of sharing our faith. Most Catholics are pretty good at what Pope Paul VI calls "the silent witness of our lives". We go to Mass on Sundays. We may send our children to Catholic schools. We may show up at work with the sign of the cross smudged on our foreheads on Ash Wednesday. Or visitors may see sacred pictures or religious artwork in our homes.

I grew up in a very anti-Catholic family and was not allowed to have any Catholic friends. I did manage to sneak one in, however, an Irish Catholic named Maggie. When I would go over to her house, I was absolutely fascinated by the twenty-seven different statues her mother kept on top of their upright piano. To me they looked like little dolls, especially the Infant of Prague. This simple witness of faith was my introduction to the Catholic faith. One day I went into Maggie's parlor and said, "What's wrong? All the statues are turned around and facing the wall!" And Maggie's mother vehemently told me, "Until my prayers are answered, they're all going to face the corner!"

I always wear a crucifix, one of the silent witnesses in my life that often attracts people when I am on an airplane. Complete strangers will look at me and say, "Oh, you're Catholic." And then they will say, "I was Catholic, too." We do many such things that reveal our faith without saying a word.

However, we are not nearly as comfortable in terms of verbal witnessing. We all have many faith stories to share that offer evidence of ongoing conversion in our lives. You may have entered into this continual process by being baptized as an infant, being confirmed as a child, being raised in a Catholic family, or entering into holy matrimony. In your middle years, you may have attended a powerful retreat and come alive in the Spirit. The fact that your whole life changed at this moment in no way negates everything that went before.

We always should be growing spiritually, constantly coming

closer to Jesus. If Mother Teresa or Pope John Paul II were sitting here right now, I would be the first to tell them that God wants them to draw even closer. Jesus himself might say, "Mother, there are a few things you still need to do. I have some other things in store for you. Have you ever thought about . . . ?" And I believe that Mother Teresa would agree, "Yes. I want to come even closer. Even closer."

This is what evangelization is all about: ongoing conversion. Sometimes we experience a more profound moment of conversion, like St. Paul falling to the ground or, in less dramatic circumstances, like Elijah hearing God, not in the earthquake, not in the storm, but in the gentle whisper of the wind. When Jesus touched me, the Holy Spirit came into my life in such a gentle way, healing, perfecting, forming, molding, melting. We all have these whisper-in-the-wind stories. And we need to tell one another how God has touched our lives in a powerful way.

Step Four: Proclaiming the Gospel

If we have trouble telling faith stories, proclaiming the good news of Jesus Christ is usually even more challenging. Many of us do not know what we believe, or if we do know, we cannot articulate it. Two reasons may account for this inability. One, we have never been expected to verbalize our beliefs; and two, we have never been trained to do so.

Growing up in the Presbyterian Church, I was taught how to proclaim the four central truths of the gospel. Most Protestant children learn how to do this by eight or nine years of age — certainly not in its entirety, but a brief and simple statement of faith that would make sense to someone else. I do not know many Catholic children who could do that. In fact, I do not know a whole lot of Catholic adults who could do that!

You need to be able to proclaim what you believe. You do not have to be a theologian. You do not have to be a professional evangelizer. You do not have to be an ordained member of the clergy. You do not have to have a master's degree in religious studies, but you do have to know what you believe. Remember that the best gift you have to offer may not be your theological knowledge but yourself. *You* are your best ammunition in terms of proclaiming the gospel. People can argue with your theology; they cannot argue with your personal experience.

Step Five: Inviting Others to Conversion

Let's say we have befriended people, shared a faith story (and invited them to tell their own faith stories in a mutual sharing), and explained what we call the Christ-story—the proclamation step. It would be absolutely horrible if after all of that we just dropped them like a hot potato and said, "Well, I've told you all this good news. Hope it helps. Bye!"

The next step in leading people into the kingdom is extending an invitation to conversion. What does this mean? Again, the goal of evangelization is ongoing conversion. We ourselves, of course, cannot convert anyone—even ourselves. Only the Holy Spirit can change the hearts and minds of people. So I define the role of evangelizers as facilitators of conversion.

We can help conversion along by creating a setting or an atmosphere conducive to drawing closer to God. We can organize an evangelistic event or bring someone to a prayer meeting, a Sunday Mass, or a healing service. Facilitating conversion is sometimes only a matter of listening to people—really listening with your heart, and then inviting them to take that step of coming closer to Jesus, committing their lives to Jesus, or recommitting their lives, as the case may be.

The invitation to conversion might mean asking a simple question. I might say, "Would you like us to pray with you, or for you and your family?" Always ask for permission. Only one or two people have said no to such an invitation in the course of all the home visits I have made over the years. Remember that this might be the first time they have ever prayed together in a small group or prayed out loud, so make it as nonthreatening as possible.

If they answer yes, then I always tell them exactly what we are going to do. I might say, "What I'm going to do is just say a short prayer, just to quiet us down a little bit. Do you mind if we hold hands in a circle? And then I'm going to lead a prayer for your family. Is there anybody special you'd like to pray for? . . . Oh, your son? OK. We'll make sure that we pray for him. . . . And if you're comfortable with this, maybe at the end, if you'd like to offer a prayer, fine. Or we can close by saying the Our Father together."

Then they know what to expect. They're not sitting on pins and needles, worrying about what's coming next. They can relax and really enjoy the prayer as communication with God, inviting God more fully into their lives and into their families. This invitation to conversion brings us back to discipleship, which makes us all brothers and sisters and also means inviting them into our own lives, into our families, and into the community of faith.

Step Six: Integrating Converts into Community

Integration into community is the phase where catechesis or sacramentalization takes place, depending on the person's situation. Inactive Catholics may need to sign up for an RCIA program and be updated in the Vatican II Church. Non-Catholics may need something else. Our aim is to involve newcomers on an individual level in the faith community.

This final step in the evangelization process might include formation of ministers within the parish, pastoring or discipling people, setting up Bible studies or support groups. It would involve the whole communal life or family spirituality in a particular parish. Our hope is that these new converts will become disciples, who will go out and start the whole cycle over again: befriending people, witnessing to their faith, proclaiming the gospel, inviting others into conversion, integrating newcomers into the community, making them disciples, who then will go out. . . .

This ongoing, cyclical process reflects the order that Pope Paul VI suggests in his document *Evangelii Nuntiandi.* And I think it makes all the sense in the world. But in reality, I think we miss the mark here somewhere. It seems to me that we often put the cart before the horse. Many of us tend to jump right into step number six, integration into the community, long before we have laid the necessary foundation.

These six steps can be applied to both *relational* evangelization and *institutional* evangelization. All of the formal programs or ministries in your parish—the RCIA, prayer groups, "Re-membering Church", "Come Home for Christmas"—are forms of institutional evangelization. Relational evangelization refers to the level of interpersonal relationships. How do you share your faith with your daughter-in-law over a cup of coffee at the kitchen table? I call it the "hedgerow ministry", because it is through our one-on-one efforts that we invite folks to come to the larger, formal programs that are being offered in the parish.

No matter how well trained we are in theology and evangelization, we must always remember that only the Holy Spirit can convert others to Christ. And we often run into the most stubborn roadblocks with members of our own families. I tried every way I could think of to bring my atheist mother to Jesus. To my knowledge, she never set foot into a church except on two occasions: my wedding and my brother's wedding. And my being converted to the Catholic faith and then becoming so strongly involved in Catholic evangelization made matters much worse.

Mom eventually had to go into a nursing home because of Alzheimer's disease. Many times when I would be visiting, she would not recognize me. But one day I went in and my mother greeted me by name. And then she asked me about my four children by name—for the first time in three or four years. She knew what day it was, what year it was. We had a wonderful visit. When I got up to leave, Mom said, "No, I have to tell you something first. Last night, my mother and my father and that other person came and stood at the foot of my bed."

My mother was eighty-six years old, and I know that it is not unusual for elderly people to see long-departed loved ones. Maybe she had dreamed about them, but I could not figure out who she meant by "that other person". I asked her if it was one of her two brothers. She said, "No, Susan, it was that *other* person." I said, "Mom, I just don't know who you're talking about."

Mom was so exasperated with me. She said, "Susan, you've just got to help me. You know, it's that 'separate person'." I still could not figure out who she was talking about. She kept struggling to explain it. "That *separate* person. That *savior* person." And I said, "Mom, do you mean Jesus?" And she said, "Yes, *that's* who it was! My mother and father and Jesus came and stood at the foot of my bed last night. And they told me I could come home now."

I almost fell off the chair. My mother told me that this experience was so strong and so real that she felt that she was now ready to go home. And for the first time in my life I was able to pray with her. We sat and we held hands, she in her wheelchair and I in a little folding chair, and we invited Jesus to come into her life and thanked him for coming in the way that he chose.

I have often wondered why Jesus did not come sooner. It could have been so much easier, but I will let God be God for this one. The most wonderful gift was that we were able to pray together, and I was able to leave my mother that day filled with joy. As it turned out, it was the last time I would ever see her. Shortly after I returned to Florida, my mother died peacefully in her sleep.

St. Paul tells us that "nothing will separate us from the love of God in Christ Jesus. Neither principalities, nor powers, nor the future, nor the past, nor the present." I can add a few more things to that list: not alcoholism, not old age, not Alzheimer's, not agnosticism, and not even atheism. Our God is a faithful God. As Mother Teresa says, "We're not called to be successful. We're called to be faithful." And that, I believe, is the essence of Catholic evangelization.

ɵ

Dr. Susan Blum is the Executive Director of Isaiah Ministries, which promotes renewal and evangelization through parish missions. Her publications include *The Ministry of Evangelization* and *Text, Study Guide, and Implementation Process for Go and Make Disciples.* For more information, contact:

Isaiah Ministries
74 Piper's Pond
Bluffton, SC 29910
803–757–7799

10

EMPLOYING CHARISMS
IN EVANGELIZATION

Peter Herbeck

"The eleven went forth and preached everywhere. The Lord continued to work with them and confirmed his word by the signs that accompanied it" (Mk 16:20). As the disciples go forth to preach the gospel after Jesus' Resurrection and Ascension, the Lord *"works with them"* by demonstrating his presence through confirming signs.

These signs are "manifestations of the Spirit" (1 Cor 12:7), works of power through which God communicates his life and truth to men and women. Throughout the New Testament we see evidence of the important role these signs or works of power play in bringing people to Christ. In Acts 9:41–42, Peter raises Tabitha from the dead. "This became known all over Joppa, and many people believed in the Lord." On another occasion, Peter heals Aeneas, a paralytic, and "all those who lived in Lydda and Sharon saw him and turned to the Lord" (Acts 9:35).

Jesus' mission was to reveal and establish his Father's kingdom (Lk 4:43). When the disciples performed signs and wonders, they experienced Jesus carrying on his ministry through them. He had told his disciples that visible signs would accompany their preaching (Mk 16:7). These extraordinary works of power, such as healing the sick and driving out demons (Mt 12:28), were an indication to many that God's kingdom was present.

Works play an essential role in establishing God's kingdom in the world. If a new evangelization is to succeed in our day, we must rediscover the indispensable role these signs play in evangelization and conversion. It is important to see clearly that the disciples were able effectively to communicate the life of the kingdom because Jesus had given them the power to do so. He gave them charisms—spiritual gifts which enabled them to do his work (1 Cor 12), something they could not do on their own power.

That is why a resurgence of the sign-gifts in our day is so important for the work of evangelism. We cannot reveal the kingdom of God by our own strength or eloquent words. Like the disciples, our proclamation of the gospel needs to be accompanied by the confirming signs, making clear to all who will hear and see that God himself stands behind the message.

The Forgotten Gifts

The charisms the Spirit bestows upon the Church are many and varied. All of them contribute to the building up of the body, and many are exercised in the Church today. Paul enumerates many spiritual gifts but reminds us that "the greatest of these is love" (1 Cor 13:13). Our particular focus here is on what is often referred to in the Scriptures as "signs and wonders", the many miracles of healing and deliverance performed by Jesus and his disciples.

Unfortunately, many Catholics forget or ignore the sign-gifts when discussing and practicing evangelism. For some, the use of these gifts is not an acceptable part of Catholic culture. Their operation is viewed from a distance, outside the Church, and often associated with Protestant faith healers such as Oral Roberts or Katherine Kuhlman. For others, these gifts are viewed as part of Catholic experience yet limited to the miraculous deeds performed by the saints, those who were exceptionally holy and favored by God.

Secular society often ridicules and disparages outward signs of God's power. As a result, some Catholics shy away from anything that may cast them in a negative light. Most of contemporary culture is steeped in scepticism, uncomfortable with the supernatural. Simple unbelief or lack of faith is a significant reason many Catholics no longer employ these charisms.

In addition to all these considerations, perhaps the one that most stifles the use of these gifts is a prevalent understanding of personal faith. Many Catholics view Christianity as a higher morality whose duties are fulfilled through strength of will and personal discipline. Catholics do not typically regard their faith as a new life empowered by the Holy Spirit. Few are conscious of possessing spiritual power, therefore, the particular gifts bestowed on them through baptism lie dormant.

The New Testament is characterized not only by signs and wonders but also by the disciples' *awareness* of the spiritual powers they possess. The third chapter of Acts recounts the story of Peter healing the crippled man at the gate Beautiful. Strongly conscious of possessing spiritual power, Peter spontaneously responds to the man's appeal by saying, "... what I have I give to you. In the name of Jesus Christ of Nazareth, walk" (Acts 3:6).

We are witnessing a fresh awakening to the importance of these spiritual gifts and the role they must play in the revitalization of the Church. Paul VI prayed, "God grant that the Lord would increase the rain of charisms to make the Church fruitful, beautiful, marvelous, and capable of inspiring respect, even the attention and amazement of the profane world, the secular world...."[1] These charisms capture the imagination by communicating the transcendent dimension of the Church.

John Paul II also acknowledges the role of different charisms: "At the beginning of the Christian era extraordinary things were accomplished under the influence of charisms.... This has always been the case in the Church and is so in our own era as well."[2] Archbishop Gabriel Ganaka of Nigeria attests to the working of signs and wonders as one of the primary reasons for the phenome-

---

[1] *Open the Windows: The Popes and the Charismatic Renewal,* ed. by Kilian McDonnell (South Bend, Ind.: Greenlawn Press, 1989).

[2] *L'Osservatore Romano,* March 16, 1994.

nal growth of the Church in Nigeria and the evangelization of the Muslims.[3]

We Need to Do It God's Way

Jesus promised his disciples that "these signs would accompany those who believe" (Mk 16:17). Even though they had witnessed Jesus as he performed many miracles, they were nonetheless often surprised that the power of God was working through them. When Jesus sent out the seventy-two to minister, they returned to him joyful yet incredulous: "Lord, even the demons submit to us in your name" (Lk 10:17).

We are similar to the disciples in this way. Even though Jesus told us it would happen, we rarely *expect* signs to follow the preaching of the gospel. This lack of expectation and faith often hinders the release of these gifts. We can define and limit God's action through a human and rational understanding of how we "think" he should work. Yet throughout creation and salvation history, God has often expressed his presence through both words and deeds. "It pleased God, in his goodness and wisdom, to reveal himself and to make known the mystery of his will.... This economy of revelation is realized by words and deeds, which are intrinsically bound up with each other."[4]

At the summit of revelation, God spoke his word to the world in Christ Jesus, the Word of God who became incarnate. This taking on of human flesh was a specific act, a deed, a sign, a wonder. The Council Fathers point out that God reveals himself through both the words and works of Jesus. He speaks to human beings in the language of words and deeds.

We must realize that God's message to us is incomplete without the deeds—not only those of love and kindness but the deeds of power. When the word is communicated in its fullest measure (in

[3] See Chapter 7, "Evangelization in the Church of Jos, Nigeria", by Archbishop Gabriel Gonsum Ganaka.

[4] *Dei Verbum,* in *The Vatican II Documents,* ed. by Flannery, new rev. ed. (Eerdmans, 1992), pp. 750–51.

both speech and deeds), then people will know God and understand that a transcendent kingdom has come into the world.

The Kingdom of God Is at Hand

John Paul II reminds us in *Redemptoris Missio* that the proclamation and establishment of God's kingdom are the purpose of Jesus' mission.[5] In his coming, Jesus brings the kingdom of God. John says, "Repent, the reign of God is at hand" (Mk 1:14–15). The kingdom of God is the dynamic rule and reign of God. It is "the manifestation and the realization of God's plan of salvation in all its fullness".[6]

This heavenly kingdom is characteristically revealed through Jesus' words, his actions, and his own person. It includes healing, miracles, and deliverance. "If I drive out demons by the Spirit of God, then the kingdom of God has come upon you" (Mt 12:28). Jesus instructs his disciples and interprets for them the meaning of his actions.

Signs are important because these extraordinary works of power point to and confirm the reality of God's kingdom. Deeds "show forth and bear out the doctrine and realities signified by the words".[7] The greatness of God and the wonder and nature of his kingdom are made manifest through powerful signs. Evangelization is essentially a continuation of this work of revealing the kingdom of God.

We *need* charisms to carry on Jesus' work. "To each has been given the manifestation of the Spirit for the common good" (1 Cor 12:7). Jesus gives us his power to do his work: the task of revealing his Father's kingdom. Therefore the Apostle Paul emphasizes that, "the kingdom of God is not a matter of talk, but of power" (1 Cor 4:20).

The contemporary world awaits a fuller revelation of the

[5] Cf. *Redemptoris Missio*, no. 30.
[6] Ibid., no. 15.
[7] *Dei Verbum*, p. 750.

kingdom of God. For too many, the kingdom consists only in words. Yet words alone will not capture the heart and imagination of millions of Chinese yet to hear the gospel. Neither will they penetrate the ever-growing world of Islamic fundamentalism. It is time for the world to see God's power and glory manifest in the life of his people.

How can we minister in these gifts? We must begin by praying for a greater understanding of the power of God already within us. Paul earnestly prays for the Ephesians that the "eyes of your heart may be enlightened in order that you may know his incomparably great power for us who believe" (Eph 1:18–19). We must keep asking God, like the persistent widow, to open up these treasures and to help us overcome our fear in using them.

Secondly, Scripture instructs us to "eagerly desire the spiritual gifts" (1 Cor 14:1). We cannot pick and choose, but we need to accept the gifts *God* wants to give us, even if what he gives us shakes us out of our comfort zones.

Finally, "just do it!" Like Peter in the boat, we need to step out with expectant faith and act on God's promise to us, believing that "greater signs than these will accompany those who believe" (Mt 16:17). The Catholic Church boasts a wonderful collection of documents that speak of the value and necessity of gifts and charisms, yet few people actually exercise them. We must move from theory to practice.

We Learn Best by Personal Experience

Because most of us feel awkward when trying to pray with someone, it can be helpful first to find others in your parish or town who have had some experience in exercising these gifts. We have learned a great deal of practical wisdom from listening to and praying alongside of others who are more experienced.

A few years ago I attended a conference on exercising spiritual gifts. Up to that point I had read a quite a bit about this topic, and

I had gained some experience in praying with people for the baptism in the Holy Spirit, yet I usually felt a bit intimidated when praying for healing or deliverance. Most of my anxiety was due to a lack of experience and fear of failure.

In order to gain some firsthand experience, I asked a conference leader if I could pray alongside one of the team members. He obliged. I spent the next three days praying with a team of people who had years of experience in praying with others. I watched how they did it, asked them questions, and by the end of the three days I was leading some of the prayer under their guidance. My confidence level grew tremendously as I saw the Lord working through our prayers.

Receiving this kind of training can be helpful in terms of getting beyond initial fears and awkwardness, but it can also provide additional discernment and a deeper understanding of the kind of gifts God has given to you personally. As I prayed with the small team at the conference, I could see there were different kinds of gifts present as well as different levels of gifting.

That conference experience also enabled me to see that praying with people is often a relatively simple thing. You do not have to be a theologian or a ministry expert to ask the Lord to touch a person's life in a particular way. It is easy to think this kind of prayer is complicated or needs to follow a certain preset form. It does not. Look closely at the ministry of Jesus or the disciples, and you will not find set formulas. What you will find is an expectant faith that enabled them to follow the leading of the Holy Spirit in a given situation.

Jesus claimed a direct connection between his deeds and the Father's. He said, "My Father is always at his work to this very day. . . . The Son can do nothing by himself; he can do only what he sees his Father doing" (Jn 5:17–19). God is still at work today, healing the sick, setting captives free, and drawing men and women to himself. Like Jesus, we simply need to do what we see the Father doing.

How can we know what the Father is doing in a given situation? Ask him. Expect a response. Is that presumptuous? I do not think so. It is simply a matter of obedience. Jesus commands all the baptized to carry on his work. His work was to do what he saw the Father doing. Our charge is to do the same.

God has given us his own Spirit, who "will speak only what he hears, and will announce to you the things to come" (Jn 16:13). The Holy Spirit is our helper, our counselor. He will enable us to carry on this work. Jesus' word is clear to us: "The Holy Spirit, whom the Father will send in my name, will instruct you in everything, and remind you of all that I told you" (Jn 14:26).

When an opportunity arises to pray with someone, we can begin by simply asking the Holy Spirit to show us how to pray. A friend recently told me about a number of experiences he had had praying with people he was evangelizing. This man is a professor at a midwestern university. On one occasion a Chinese graduate student came to his office to discuss a research project he had been working on. During their discussion, my friend noticed the student was experiencing back pain. He then asked the Holy Spirit if he ought to do anything or say anything to the student. He felt the Spirit prompting him to pray for him.

When my friend asked about the back pain, the student told him he suffered from chronic back trouble which caused him a great deal of pain and discomfort. My friend then asked if the student would like him to pray that Jesus would heal his back. The student agreed. My friend simply reached out and touched the point where the pain was the sharpest and prayed a simple prayer, "Lord Jesus, I ask you to heal this man's back problem."

After a few minutes, the young Chinese man began to experience complete relief from the pain. He was overjoyed and amazed. Not long after their meeting, this man gave his life to Christ. Now, one year later, he is leading a Bible study with other students.

My friend's prayer was simple and powerful. He did not use any preset formula. He simply responded with compassion and expectant faith to what he believed God was doing in that situation. Like Jesus, he knew his Father is always at work. Living in a posture of active faith equipped him with this readiness to recognize the needs of others and respond. As a result, this student has an experiential knowledge of God's love for him that "rests not on men's wisdom, but on God's power" (2 Cor 2:5).

Expect the Unexpected

I would like to relate some of my own experiences of learning how to minister to others with gifts of power. Last September I spoke at a large evangelization rally in a new diocese in Ghana, Africa. At one point I sensed the Lord showing me that we should pray for those in the audience who had gone to the voodoo masters and witch doctors to receive power over some difficulty in their lives.

When I stood up and addressed anyone who fit this description, about sixty people came forward. I spoke quietly and calmly about Jesus' presence and the need for repentance. We prayed, "Come Holy Spirit", and asked Jesus to free those who had responded from the domination of various demons.

Almost immediately there were signs and manifestations of the working of the Holy Spirit. One woman's head jerked back, her eyelids flipped open exposing only the whites of her eyes, and she fell backward like a board. To my amazement, her body then began to flip back and forth, like a fish on a dock, at an incredible and humanly impossible speed. There was a clear resistance raging within her, an encounter between two opposing powers.

Watching from the stage, I was stunned. Although I had prayed for her, I honestly had not expected anything that dramatic to occur! A priest bent down over her and prayed a simple prayer of deliverance. Immediately, the woman's body went limp and she lay there peacefully. When someone helped her up fifteen minutes later, she was totally free.

Last May we were preaching at an evangelistic conference in Lithuania. During a time of ministry I began to experience an intense pain in my right ear. I tried to ignore it, thinking I must have caught a cold the night before. As the pain persisted, I sensed that the Lord wanted us to pray for people with right inner ear problems. A number of people came forward to be healed.

One of our team members, an architect who believes that God commands us to pray for the sick, prayed over a twenty-three-year-old man. This young Lithuanian had lost his hearing three years earlier during the struggle for independence in Vilnius, when a tank cannon went off nearby and blew out his right ear drum. As they prayed he was able to hear, first faintly and then more clearly. The young man was ecstatic, as were many around him. People were stunned and awed by the power and grace of God at work.

Because we are human, we all experience a risk factor when we step out in faith to exercise these gifts. We are afraid of being wrong: "Is God really speaking to me?" Or of embarrassment and losing our reputation: "What if I look strange or it doesn't work?" We are called to be obedient and not necessarily successful. God has freed us to follow and obey him. "Where the Spirit of the Lord is, there is freedom" (2 Cor 3:17).

In this new era of evangelization, God wants to reveal his presence and the glory of his kingdom in a renewed way through the manifestation of signs and wonders. The Lord is sending forth his word through us, his Church, not only as we preach the gospel but also as we do the works that Jesus did.

As Catholics, we must respond to the challenge of these times by freely employing the gifts and charisms God has given us. We must also learn how to train and help others to use their gifts so that evangelization will move ahead with greater power and effectiveness. Let us be like the apostles Paul and Barnabas, who "spent considerable time there [in Iconium] and spoke out fearlessly, in complete reliance on the Lord. He for his part confirmed the message with his grace and caused signs and wonders to be done at their hands" (Acts 14:3).

❧

Peter Herbeck is Mission Director of Renewal Ministries, which promotes renewal and evangelization through television, publications, and conferences. For more information, contact:

> Renewal Ministries
> P.O. Box 8229
> Ann Arbor, MI 48107
> 313–662–1730

II

CATHOLIC STREET EVANGELISM IN PRACTICE TODAY

Leonard Sullivan

Almost thirty years ago, a small group of Catholics enthusiasti-cally told their parish priest about a meeting in a nearby city. They had witnessed healing and heard prophecy, seen people raising their arms and heard them praising God in words and in song, in their own and unknown languages.

The priest listened patiently and asked a few questions about the last detail. Then he observed, "I see. You call it 'praying in tongues'. So *that's* what I've been doing for the last thirty years! I often wondered what it was."

I had the same experience when I read the extracts of the sermon Pope John Paul II delivered at Denver on August 15, 1993. When he challenged Catholics to go out and proclaim the good news on the streets and in public places, I thought, *That's what I've been doing for the last forty-three years!* I belong to the Westminster Catholic Evidence Guild, which has been doing street evangelization in London for seventy-five years. So the new evangelization is not quite so new to me.

If evangelization is new to you, you may be wondering where to start and how to go about it. I would like to share some of the knowledge and experience I have gained through the Catholic Evidence Guild. My hope is that it might pave the way for you to participate more actively in sharing the good news with the people around you.

The Nuts and Bolts of Evangelization

The word "evangelization" means different things to different people, and this has caused a lot of confusion. Here is the best definition I have found: *Evangelization is the Lord Jesus Christ proclaiming his good news, through the members of his body, which is the Church, to those who are not so fortunate as to hold the one true faith.*

Some people have questioned me about the last part. It simply means the "haves" sharing with the "have-nots". This definition excludes the idea of Catholics being evangelized. Catholics can be instructed, retreaded, recycled, rejuvenated, rehabilitated, resuscitated, revitalized, renewed, enriched, and many other things. But once people direct the spotlight of evangelization toward Catholics, they can easily lose sight of the call to reach out to those who do not know Jesus Christ.

We can spread the good news in many ways. Priests can preach sermons expressly aimed at non-Catholics. Trained evangelizers can participate in an organized door-to-door campaign. Radio and television offer other avenues. In brief, we street talkers are not the only workers trying to gather in the harvest as Jesus builds his kingdom.

While the street evangelist may reach only a few people, this personal contact can build a mutual rapport often missing when a speaker is talking *at* people in an auditorium or on the radio. Street evangelization can also be conducted in different ways, perhaps by pushing a wheelbarrow full of literature, free or for sale, with people available to talk about the Church.

Not all of us are commissioned *evangelists* called to take the initiative in seeking out lost sheep. But by the privilege of our baptism, we all have the responsibility to do *evangelization* when the opportunity arises. Scripture says, "Honor Christ the Lord in your hearts, and always have your answer ready for people who ask you the reason for the hope which you all have. But give it with courtesy and respect, and with a clear conscience" (1 Pet 3:15).

This verse should raise a few questions in your mind. *What in my life radiates the hope I have? What will lead people to ask what it is that makes me tick? What answers can I give for the questions that come my way? My answer may fit the question, but will it fit the questioner? How could my answer be improved or varied?*

Consider a simple example. A man might comment, "I read the newspaper every day from cover to cover. The world is a mess." A Christian might reply with a question: "Have you tried reading the *good* news?" This response would leave the field open for the man to ask about the good news.

From my experience in England, I suggest that any Catholics wanting to work in evangelization need to consider the following three points. First, do you know Catholic teaching accurately? In practice I have met a lot of Catholics who thought they did but in fact held ideas that were not true to Catholic teaching, like someone who recently said to me that it did not matter to which denomination you belong.

Second, can you explain the teaching in a clear way, one which the listener can understand? Thinking over the ways in which I have heard some Catholic teachers of children and adults trying to do this, I have seen some dismal results.

Third, have you considered the questions a listener might ask, and will your answers be clear—especially if a listener belongs to a different religion and knows something about that religion? In brief, we may do our best to evangelize; but, without some thought or further instruction, we may not get very far. But in these instances, keep in mind that we are sharing our faith as individuals and not as commissioned teachers proclaiming the good news in the name of the Church.

If I Can Do It, So Can You!

I see my task as an evangelistic speaker as quite simple: somehow or other, the Lord Jesus Christ is trying to introduce himself, even through me, to those who do not know him. This is a variation of Jesus' statement in Luke 10:16: "Anyone who listens to you, listens to me; anyone who rejects you, rejects me; and those who reject me, reject the one who sent me."

If you read the *beginning* of Luke 10, you should get a shock: Jesus was not speaking to the twelve apostles but to the seventy-two others who suddenly pop up from nowhere. They had not had Catholic parents, they had not been to Catholic schools, and they were probably not trained as teachers—yet these seventy-two were called to be evangelists.

If they could do it, so can I. And if I can do it, so can you! Before you start thinking of excuses, I will give you three of them: (1) *I don't know my faith* (in London, this is usually put to me by people who *have* been to Catholic schools); (2) *I don't know anything about public speaking;* and (3) *I might do more harm than good.* If these were valid reasons, then how did somebody like me ever become an evangelistic speaker? I had the good fortune of stumbling over the Catholic Evidence Guild.

Let me provide a little bit of history. In 1917, during World War I, a New Zealander traveling through London noticed the Speakers' Corner at Marble Arch and thought that the Church ought to be there having her say as well. After a discussion with the Cardinal Archbishop of Westminster, a meeting of those interested was held in January 1918. In April, the Catholic Evidence Guild was formed. After some training by the clergy, these few brave souls started speaking in public on August 4, 1918.

The system of qualification that had evolved by 1921 is still in use today. When men and women decide to be trained as Guild speakers, they choose one subject from the many listed as "junior subjects" in the Catholic Evidence Training Outlines recently published in Ann Arbor. Those who are wise select an easy subject and then study it, ignoring all the rest of theology. After preparing a fifteen-minute talk on this topic, they then deliver it at an indoor practice class, and the rest ask awkward questions. The instructor sums up the effort with constructive criticism.

This practice is repeated until candidates have satisfied the instructor that their presentation and technique are adequate and that they know enough theology *on this one subject* to be tested. The test is private before two persons: one is a priest appointed as "examining chaplain" by the bishop; the other is an experienced speaker of the Guild. The test follows the same pattern as the practice class.

If both examiners are satisfied, the beginner is licensed to speak for the Catholic Evidence Guild on that *one subject,* and to answer questions *only* on that subject and *only* in the presence of a chairman speaker. With those safety catches in place, the beginner is let loose on the public. The point to note here is that within a couple of months or less, a would-be speaker can be doing street evangelism.

Speakers then extend their repertoire by studying and passing tests on other subjects. A major step is the test on the divinity of Christ. Later on, speakers may be encouraged to go before a priest and senior Guild members to take the chairman's test, a question-and-answer exam on the general knowledge of dogmatic theology. Those who pass this exam can lecture on specific subjects according to their ordinary license but may also field other questions and run outdoor meetings, which includes supervising and training less experienced speakers.

Targeting Those to Be Evangelized

A few public places in London are recognized as speakers' areas, where, subject to a few rules, people can stand and say whatever they like. The best known is the Speakers' Corner at Marble Arch in Hyde Park. If you have such a designated area in your locality, you may not have to look farther. If you have to find somewhere to speak, what you want is a place suitable for a public meeting where many people pass by who might have time to stop and listen.

Four considerations need to be kept in mind in determining a location: avoid noisy traffic; make sure that the meeting will not obstruct other people; find out whether you need permission to hold a meeting from the owners of the property, the local civil authority, or the police; and find out how the local Catholic clergy view your intentions (they may have to pick up the pieces).

Identifying potential listeners can be even more difficult. As a rough guide, you will likely encounter three varieties of people:

those who come deliberately to listen to a speaker on a matter of religion; those who come hoping for a bit of free entertainment; and those who are passing by and stop to listen, even for a minute or two.

What may potential listeners be thinking, especially on matters of religion? This question is vitally important, because we need to know something on which to build our proclamation. Our Lord's listeners were almost exclusively Jews, which made life simple. When St. Paul evangelized the Jews in synagogues, he used the truths of Judaism on which to build the Christian message. He used an entirely different approach with the pagans in Athens.

In practice, listeners usually turn up with no indication as to what makes them tick, so the speaker may have to try various approaches before noticing a change in facial expression to indicate that some remark is on target. A few months ago at Tower Hill in London, I had two listeners with whom *nothing* seemed to register. I finally learned they were tourists who did not understand English! Remember that when one attempts the study of mankind, nine-tenths of the training is done in the hard school of practical experience.

Our Lord often started his teaching with some common item that was under the noses of his listeners, like a shepherd who had lost a sheep, or a story of a rich man and a poor man. You would also be wise to start with something that is already in the minds of your listeners. You must try tuning in on their wave length on a subject that may hold their interest and from there lead into the proclamation of the gospel.

Keep in mind that the listeners at an outdoor platform usually have to stand and are free to come and go as they please. Some will actively listen, indicating by their facial expressions that they understand the message even if they do not ask questions or comment. Some will passively listen, just standing and staring blankly. You should also watch for listeners who know practically nothing about the Catholic faith. Especially watch for those who *do* know something about the Catholic Church and don't like the look of it.

My experience suggests that listeners tend to belong to one of two general groups: the minority, who accept and read the Bible as the words of God; and the majority, who have not read and do not read the Bible, which they regard as a collection of myths now disproved by science. An evangelistic speaker can often use biblical ideas with effect, without saying where they come from.

Many people believe in some parts of the Catholic faith, and they are willing to accept Scripture as evidence for an extended understanding of the truths revealed by Jesus Christ. You can often discern the attitude of listeners by their reply to a touchstone question, "Do you believe and accept as true that Jesus Christ rose from the dead?"

How to Conduct an Outdoor Meeting

In theory, the first step is to grab the listeners' attention with a story related to your subject, in which you should state clearly and briefly what the Church teaches. You then provide evidence to support this teaching, show the richness of the doctrine as it stands, and then perhaps show its relationship to allied teachings. Finally, you may say something about why this teaching is valuable to you personally. (You usually have to improvise and try variations of this approach, especially when the listeners decide that they do not want to hear that particular subject and begin to drift away from the meeting.)

The result is that listeners receive a fragmented presentation of the Catholic faith. It is perfectly possible to start a talk with one set of listeners and to finish it with a different set. This is a typical scenario: a man (or woman) with no thought of religion pays a casual visit to Marble Arch. Pausing near the speaker's platform in hope of a bit of free entertainment, he may hear something that starts him thinking. He then returns, perhaps weeks later, and is further stimulated, so he starts to come regularly.

This man is learning about the Catholic faith in bits and pieces, but he is beginning to see how they interconnect. Eventually he sees an overall picture, albeit with significant gaps. He may approach a speaker who has climbed down from the platform and ask questions about becoming a Catholic, or he may remember a distant relative whom he knows to be a Catholic. Either way, this man finally decides to take instruction and is received into the Church. In many such cases, the Guild speaker knows nothing about this conversion. He has tilled the soil, and God has planted the seed of faith. That is what matters, not vanity for the speaker.

Our meetings in England are usually quite lively since many listeners respond with comments and questions. Guild speakers work at producing a *constructive* dialogue rather than getting into an abusive, verbal slinging match. If the audience happens to be too polite and reserved on matters of religion, I would suggest challenging them along these lines:

> This is the proclamation of Jesus Christ. The stakes are high: either life in the friendship of God or death in sin. You have heard something of the truth which God wants you to have. You may need to know more before you are in a position to accept or to reject what he wants you to have. Deliberate ignorance is the same as rejection. Each one of you must make your own decision, and this can decide where you will spend your life after you die.

If this sounds too strong for your taste, I suggest you read Mark 16:15–18. Further study of the Gospels and the Acts of the Apostles shows a pattern of demonstration, proclamation, and demonstration. Thus far the Westminster Catholic Evidence Guild has concentrated on the proclamation of the truth and has hardly touched on the possibility of employing signs and wonders in this effort. I consider this an important subject for the present time and for the future.

I believe signs and wonders are Jesus Christ at work through the members of his body, to attract attention and to confirm the truth of the good news. Street-corner evangelists or everyday evangelizers need to resolve two basic questions in their own minds. First, how much does the Lord Jesus Christ want to use signs and wonders now and in the future in his work of building the kingdom? In other words, are signs and wonders intended to be used on a wide scale or only on rare occasions? Second, how far are the evangelists or evangelizers themselves willing to be used by the Lord in his working of signs and wonders?

You will need to pray with a listening heart to learn how God wants you to participate in the new evangelization. He will provide the necessary gifts, but he can use only those who are willing to be used. So whatever he tells you to do, do it. I would suggest that you prayerfully consider joining any evangelistic efforts being made in your area. On the other hand, the Lord may have other ideas as to how he wants you to participate in building his kingdom. Pray.

If you are interested in starting a local Catholic Evidence Guild, I suggest you gather a group of lay enthusiasts and find a friendly priest. Then discuss the idea and determine how to get started in a way that fits in with the Church's work on evangelization. You also need to consult with your diocesan bishop about the use of the word "Catholic" in proclaiming the good news.

If the bishop agrees, formally set up a local Guild with a constitution and leaders. Under the guidance of the bishop, organize the training and qualification of lay speakers. You should also link up with other Guilds to share information and mutual support. Then go out and proclaim the good news, ready to take those who seek the Lord farther into the kingdom.

Even though Jesus commands us to go out and proclaim the good news (Mk 16:15–18), at times we may face "no-go" areas like Paul did in his attempt to enter Asia and Bithynia (Acts 16:6–7). We do not know the Lord's detailed plan for the building up of his kingdom in the world of today. All we can do is to ask him, with listening hearts, to guide us step by step in his work, doing whatever he tells us to do.

What Role Can the Laity Play in Evangelization?

The prevailing view during the early days of the Guild in England was that priests could teach and preach but that the laity should refrain from "preaching" on the outdoor platform. In hindsight, I believe this attitude resulted in weakening the effectiveness of lay speakers. They had contact with the *minds* but not the *hearts* of listeners, which left the listeners to ask, "You have explained this teaching—so what?"

Explaining the value of a truth is still a long way from inviting the listeners to pray for the special gift of acceptance and to offer a prayer to this effect from the platform. Our goal today in the new evangelization is to proclaim the good news—with teaching and preaching—and to make potential disciples whom God can enrich by whatever means he chooses.

Recent papal teaching has also stressed the importance of personal example and witness in evangelization. Some reduce this concept to "Just be a good example to your neighbor", which could apply equally well to paganism. As a well-known Guild speaker pointed out some years ago, "You will not proclaim that adultery is wrong just by not practicing it in public."

Speakers can witness to Christ by being courteous to their listeners, especially the awkward ones, and by telling from their own experience the value of the particular teaching they are giving and the riches they have in being a Catholic. Telling your personal story first tends to put the emphasis on the speaker rather than on Jesus Christ. I have heard speakers from other Christian groups begin by saying in effect, "I was once a sinner and now I am saved." Their listeners could offer a reasonable rebuttal: "Your Christianity may suit you, but I don't think it will fit me."

Even though personal witness can be quite convincing, without the teaching of Jesus Christ, there is nothing much about which to be convinced. A teacher passes on the definitive truths of Jesus Christ and the Church. Teaching does not require us to be theologians, whose role is to clarify statements of truth, develop a fuller understanding of these truths, and extend the present limits of the truths so far defined. Theology can enrich those who already accept the truth but is usually too deep for those who do not. In fact, apart from the clarifiers, I try to keep theologians *off* the outdoor platform, since they can distract listeners from the basic truths I am trying to communicate to the have-nots.

Those who already profess faith in the gospel are known corporately as the body of Christ, which has two basic dimensions.

First, the Church is the continued life on earth of the Lord Jesus Christ. We are members of his body and he is the head. Most people outside the Church know nothing about this "insider" dimension, and so we need to enrich them with this truth and its implications.

Second, the Church is an institution of human beings, which is how "outsiders" see her. Their questions and comments focus on the *people* in the Church, especially the well-known sinners. These two dimensions are connected by the fact that Jesus Christ came to save sinners, not those who thought they were good. The Church is Jesus Christ trying to turn sinners into saints fit for heaven as individuals, while the Lord is simultaneously trying to build up his body as a whole.

Temptations for the "Decade of Evangelization"

The so-called "decade of evangelization" started in January 1991, nearly three and a half years ago. We have got to recognize that Satan does not like evangelization and will target evangelists and would-be evangelists for special attention. With apologies to C. S. Lewis, I will conclude this chapter with a recently intercepted memo from Satan to his demons:

1. The half-truth or innuendo can usually do more damage than a lie.
2. Tempt people to do good—in the wrong place at the wrong time. For example, someone with an unused talent for outreach in a parish should be encouraged to take on the flower arrangements around the altar. Those already using their talents in outreach should be guided to take on another good work so as to make them almost useless in both.
3. Tempt people to admire the view of the Christian horizon, especially of the past (tinted glasses can be provided), so that they will be mesmerized, stay put, and do nothing.
4. As it is often worse than useless to tempt active Christians

to sin seriously, suggest minor sins. When they descend to the level where they say, "Venial sins don't matter", then leave them to their own inertia. They will drift so far from Jesus Christ that they won't want him even at the hour of death, as they will have forgotten him.

5. Encourage people to promote peace in a pompous, self-opinionated way. Use the fact (but don't remind them of it) that in spite of the crucifixion and in spite of being baptized, people are still prone to sin. This tactic can result in quite a lot of infighting for the cause of peace.

6. Get people to talk, write, discuss, and argue about evangelization—a clear way to make sure that little or nothing is done.

7. Remind them that an actively evangelistic church may cause offense to other Christian churches. Better to do nothing, or offer a watered-down, lowest-common-denominator Christianity—the kind that wouldn't make a self-respecting cat open one eye.

8. Get bishops and clergy to preach "Just be a decent sort of person and set a good example." On the assumption they're already doing that, the congregation will turn off mentally and ignore anything else that may be said. The result will be to leave Jesus Christ out of their Christianity.

9. Encourage new religious societies and groups so as to duplicate what is already being done. This will make active Christians think they're busy and in fact steer them away from what Jesus Christ actually wants them to be doing.

10. Pay special attention to the Catholic Evidence Guild platform. When a speaker is answering a question, get listeners to interrupt with another, so that the full answer to the first question is never given.

11. Get some Guild members to complain and moan about their miseries. This can be very infectious and weaken the entire organization.

12. Distract their leaders with irrelevant issues so as to waste their efforts.

13. Encourage humility (false, of course) so that Christians will underrate their value to Jesus Christ in the building up of his kingdom. Make them feel so useless that they will want to do nothing.

God spoke the words to the prophet Jeremiah: "Before I formed you in the womb, I knew you. Before you came to birth I consecrated you. I have appointed you as a prophet to the people." Jeremiah immediately made excuses: "But, Lord Yahweh, look: I do not know how to speak. I am a child."

The Lord replied, "Do not say 'I am a child.' Go now to those to whom I send you, and say whatever I command you. Do not be afraid of them as I am with you, and I will protect you. It is Yahweh who speaks."

Jeremiah heard and obeyed. And so should we.

Leonard Sullivan is the current Master of the Westminster Catholic Evidence Guild in London, England. This international organization promotes training for street evangelism in the Catholic Church. For more information, contact:

> The Catholic Evidence Guild
> 25 Banstead Rd.
> Purley Surrey CR83EB
> United Kingdom

12

PREACHING EVANGELISTIC HOMILIES

Fr. Bruce Nieli, C.S.P.

Evangelistic preaching, as the name implies, is a proclamation of
Jesus Christ designed to convert people to the life of the gospel. It
is, in the words of Pope Paul VI, a "living preaching" that "invites
to belief" (EN, no. 42).

Scripture tells us that "faith comes from what is heard, and what
is heard comes through the word of Christ" (Rom 10:17). Thus the
aim of evangelistic preaching is to inspire people to fall in love with
Jesus, to embrace him, and to imitate him in his body, the Church.

Since it is a form of preaching specifically directed to touching
the heart, it can be a highly emotional experience, yet not necessarily nor exclusively. Evangelistic preachers like Jonathan Edwards
and Phoebe Palmer were learned theologians who appealed to the
mind as well as to the heart.

Moreover, periods of great evangelistic preaching and related
activities produced much-needed social change and reform in the
history of the United States. During the eighteenth-century era
known as the Great Awakening, the labors of people such as
Jonathan Edwards and George Whitefield not only helped convert individual hearts but also helped form the heart of a nation.
Evangelistic preaching helped inspire the unification of the thirteen colonies just prior to the American Revolution as well as the
birth of some of our country's earliest universities. In fact, Jonathan
Edwards served as the first president of one such institution named
Princeton.

The nineteenth century began with a period of intense evangelistic preaching known as the Second Great Awakening. Charles Finney and others helped mobilize social and political reform as diverse as abolition, higher education, and women's rights. Ohio's Oberlin College, the first institution of higher learning in the United States to admit women and African Americans, was launched by a team of well-known and respected evangelists.

Like-minded women also made significant contributions to social reform. Harriet Tubman, a former slave who founded the Underground Railroad, went on to become active in the women's-rights movement. We know of another remarkable woman by the name of Sojourner Truth. A slave until 1827, she went on to preach emancipation and women's rights.

The evangelistic tradition also brought forth enduring literary works, such as Harriet Beecher Stowe's *Uncle Tom's Cabin* and Julia Ward Howe's lyrics to the "Battle Hymn of the Republic". Abraham Lincoln, famous for his stirring oratory, often incorporated an evangelistic style in his speeches. His second inaugural address serves as a primary example.

In our own century, evangelistic ministry has inspired both the twelve-step programs and the civil-rights movement. Few people have had as great an impact on our sociopolitical structure as Dr. Martin Luther King, Jr., a master of evangelical preaching. Even American music has been touched profoundly by evangelistic activity, especially in forms like gospel and jazz. As Pope Paul VI has said, true evangelization brings the good news "into all strata of humanity" (EN, no. 18).

In this country, evangelistic preaching is usually associated with our brothers and sisters who belong to Protestant churches. Probably the most famous evangelical preacher of our time is Billy Graham. This gifted and fearless evangelist appeals to a broad spectrum of the American people across denominational boundaries. Dr. Graham clearly and simply proclaims Jesus Christ as Lord and Savior, with the urgent need for each of us to acknowledge our sinfulness and make a decision to turn our lives over to Jesus. Thousands have accepted the altar call at the end of his crusades and become followers of Christ.

Evangelistic Preaching Is a Long-Standing Catholic Tradition as Well

It is important to remember that evangelistic preaching has been an integral part of Catholicism for centuries. Great Catholic evangelists such as St. Augustine, St. Bernard of Clairvaux, St. Peter Damien, and St. Bernardine of Siena transformed the hearts of their listeners by speaking of the dying and rising of Jesus Christ. Mendicants like St. Francis of Assisi spoke of the sacred humanity of Jesus in such vivid word-pictures that their hearers were mystically drawn to respond.

Perhaps the most articulate of all American evangelistic preachers was the unforgettable Archbishop Fulton Sheen, the very first television evangelist. He proclaimed the word of God so powerfully that he drew overflow crowds of people (including me). In fact, so many gathered to hear him conduct the seven last words service at St. Agnes Church on Good Friday that it stopped traffic around Grand Central Station in New York City.

This brings us to the techniques of evangelistic preaching in the unique Catholic style. If we keep in mind our focus on conversion and reconversion and ongoing conversion to Jesus Christ, things fall more clearly into place. We must also remember that Catholic evangelization speaks of the whole Christ, or the *totus Christus,* as St. Augustine would say, of Jesus the head of the Church in intimate and unbreakable union with his body (EN, no. 16).

We seek not only to draw people into ever-deeper communion with Jesus in his Church but also to call ourselves as members of the Church to daily reform and renewal. We are called to pray and work for our own growth in holiness as well as to work one day at a time for the ongoing reform and renewal of our country. With this overall vision before us, I offer the following suggested techniques for Catholic evangelistic preaching:

1. *Prayerfully read the Scripture passage to be preached upon, particularly the Gospel, as an encounter with the living Jesus.* Assume, for example, that we are to preach on the following passage: "I am the Good

Shepherd. I know my own and my own know me, just as the Father knows me and I know the Father. And I lay down my life for the sheep. I have other sheep that do not belong to this fold. I must bring them also, and they will listen to my voice. So there will be one flock, one Shepherd" (Jn 10:14–16).

The idea in evangelistic preaching is to read this passage several times, pray over it, and visualize Jesus shepherding and nurturing *you,* calling you by name, and bringing you home when you are lost. You might even see yourself in the arms of Jesus, with your head on his bosom, like the beloved disciple at the Last Supper.

2. *Discern the impact of this encounter on you personally. What is Jesus saying to you?* In this passage from John, for example, Jesus is saying that he calls me by name, and I am his (Is 43:1). I am important to him. I can never be far away from him, even if I try to hide or flee. He died for me, so that I and others might live. I have a Father who loves me and knows me, even though my earthly father and mother have gone to eternal life. I need not compare myself with anyone else, because Jesus calls me by my name. I am free. I am at peace.

3. *Summarize this personal encounter in a simple declarative sentence, at least for yourself. This is the message you want to communicate.* I would summarize the above in these words: Jesus shepherds me so that I may shepherd others.

4. *Illustrate this message with a contemporary person or event. Be aware of the cultural situation of the people to whom you are preaching.* One contemporary example of Jesus as shepherd is that of George De La Rosa, a member of the notorious Brown Beret gang of San Antonio. George was evangelized by his younger brother Jesse while Jesse was on death row. Jesse had fallen in love with Jesus, the Good Shepherd, who had given his life for Jesse's and our sins.

While George tried to bring drugs to him in prison, Jesse

repeatedly spoke of Jesus and the Church. Why belong to a gang if you can belong to the family of God? Jesse repeatedly asked George to take his own wife and children to Mass as well as to be a true husband and father. Finally, George gave in to Jesse's persistent request and has not missed Mass since.

At his brother's funeral, George forgave the father who had abandoned him when he was eight and the stepmother he had hated all his life—as he had promised Jesse soon before the condemned murderer's execution. Also, as part of his promise, George forgave and shook the hand of the judge he and his other brothers had vowed to assassinate.

Now, George and his wife are involved with Prison Fellowship, visiting prisoners with the Love that has loved him since before the world was created. The passage that George and his brother prayed over before Jesse was wheeled into the death chamber was that of the Good Shepherd.

We could also illustrate this message by Archbishop Oscar Romero, who gave his life for the people of El Salvador. He was truly converted when he saw to his horror how his people were cruelly murdered by the death squads. He shed his blood while he was celebrating the Precious Blood of the Eucharist.

5. *Connect this contemporary example to the life of Mary or a saint or holy person who has made an impact on the Church and whose life gives witness to your central idea. Passages from a great spiritual writer may also help to illustrate and further develop your message.* A good example here would be St. Thomas Becket, Archbishop of Canterbury, who gave his life while shepherding his flock in England.

6. *Connect your central theme to a Church teaching, document, or council. This will communicate the catholicity of your message—how your preaching relates to the Church universal.* Paragraph 754 of the *Catechism of the Catholic Church* provides a beautiful description of the Church as the flock of Jesus the Good Shepherd. Paragraph 606 of the *Catechism* speaks of the sacrifice of Jesus as "the expression of his communion of love with the Father".

7. *Communicate the impact of this message on your own life.* I could tell about how meeting George De La Rosa touched me deeply, especially when I saw how deeply he and his family touched each other. Before he left the house, this three-hundred-pound man tenderly waited for his tiny three-year-old daughter to make a sign of blessing on his forehead.

Or I could tell about how my mother nurtured me while I suffered as a child from asthma, often singing to me the reassuring hymn, "Yes, Jesus loves me, the Bible tells me so." I could go on to share how I was privileged to do the same for my mother as she lay dying of a brain tumor. I am also reminded of Mary nurturing her son Jesus.

8. *Always connect everything to Jesus. Be succinct, yet preach with passion. Show your listeners that you are in love with Jesus and with the fullness of his body, the Catholic Church.* I am a Catholic priest because I am in love with Jesus and his Church. He has been shepherding me all of my life through precious people who have nurtured me, inspiring me to do the same in my own weak way for others.

The Primary Focus of Evangelistic Preaching

Notice that evangelistic preaching, more than any other form of public speaking, represents the fruit of prayer and meditation on the word of God and on one's own spiritual life. Those who preach do not have to wonder if their message is effective or what others think of their sermons. They will be the first to know, since they themselves will be listening and feeling the impact of the proclamation while it is being delivered.

Evangelistic preaching is particularly focused on the *kerygma,* on "the initial proclamation of the gospel". To put it another way, the primary goal of missionary preaching is "to arouse faith" (CT, no. 18). With this in mind, we as preachers must be aware of our own ongoing conversion to faith in Jesus as we call others and our society to such conversion.

This particular focus of evangelistic preaching goes hand in hand with the first goal of *Go and Make Disciples: A National Plan and Strategy for Catholic Evangelization in the United States,* recently promulgated by the National Conference of Catholic Bishops. Goal I states: "To bring about in all Catholics such an enthusiasm for their faith that, in living their faith in Jesus, they freely share it with others."

Evangelistic preaching can help instill this kind of enthusiasm for the Catholic faith and the desire for daily conversion to Jesus. It can also encourage Catholics so renewed and converted to develop a welcoming attitude toward everyone, as a fulfillment of Goal II of the bishops' plan: "To invite all people in the United States, whatever their social or cultural background, to hear the message of salvation in Jesus Christ so they may come to join us in the fullness of the Catholic faith."

Finally, evangelistic preaching can challenge the Catholic community, so spiritually reformed and more welcoming, to become a leaven for the spiritual reform of our country and a return to its guiding principles. This will result in a living out of the third goal of *Go and Make Disciples:* "To foster gospel values in our society, promoting the dignity of the human person, the importance of the family, and the common good of our society so that our nation may continue to be transformed by the saving power of Jesus Christ."

May our evangelistic preaching flow from a renewed soul, and, in imitation of our Lady, serve to magnify the Lord (Lk 1:47). May our proclamation of the good news of Jesus Christ draw others into communion with her Son, particularly in the Eucharist. And may our constant calling of ourselves and of our nation to increased discipleship serve ultimately to make disciples of all nations (Mt 28:19).

Fr. Bruce Nieli, C.S.P., is Director for Evangelization of the National Conference of Catholic Bishops. Besides coordinating the activities of the NCCB Committee on Evangelization, Fr. Nieli travels throughout the United States speaking and giving workshops and retreats. For more information, contact:

> National Conference of Catholic Bishops
> Committee on Evangelization
> 3211 4th Street, N.E.
> Washington, DC 20017
> 202–541–3012

PART FOUR

Bringing the Good News to All People

13

EVANGELIZING THE POOR

Sr. Linda Koontz, S.N.J.M.

Many Catholics say to me, "I just don't know what my ministry is. I'm so confused. I've been praying for ten years to know what God wants me to do." I tell them to stop praying. God has already given us our mission and ministry in this world: it is the mission and ministry of Jesus.

When Jesus returned to Nazareth in the power of the Spirit, he went into the synagogue and stood up to read the Scripture: "The Spirit of the Lord is upon me; therefore he has anointed me. He has sent me to bring glad tidings to the poor, to proclaim liberty to captives, recovery of sight to the blind and release to prisoners, to announce a year of favor from the Lord" (Lk 4:18). Then Jesus rolled up the scroll and sat down. With all eyes fixed on him, he said, "Today this Scripture passage is fulfilled in your hearing."

When he read this passage from Isaiah 61, Jesus was talking about himself. But later on he says that he is giving that same Holy Spirit to us. Jesus came into the world not only to proclaim liberty to the captives but also to anoint each person who believes in him and who follows him with that same Holy Spirit. The Spirit of the Lord is upon *us* so that we too can bring glad tidings to the poor.

God generously gives his Holy Spirit to his sons and his daughters. He does not ration it or hold back the best gift of all. We can ask him today, "Lord, give me a double dose of the Holy Ghost. Give me the Holy Spirit so I can become the person that you meant me to be, a person who carries your good news, a person who is filled with your love and can bring that love to those who are starving."

When our Holy Father proclaimed, "Open the doors to the Redeemer", he used a word that meant to open the door so hard the hinges fall off. God wants to anoint us with his Holy Spirit, to empower us to do the works of Jesus in the midst of a world that is spiritually bankrupt and in poverty. Yet how easily we lose sight of our spiritual inheritance when we are being attacked by the enemy or being dragged down by our own low self-esteem. We need to keep reminding ourselves, "The Spirit of the Lord is upon me. He has anointed me."

Who Is Called to Serve the Poor?

Every Christian is called to serve the poor. Matthew 10:7 sums up our mission: "Go after the lost sheep of the house of Israel. Make this announcement: 'The reign of God is at hand!' Cure the sick, raise the dead, heal the lepers, expel demons. The gift you have received, give it away as a gift."

Jesus told us to "Go into the whole world and make disciples of all nations." Most Catholics seem to think he said, "Sit back and relax and let the Holy Father do it, let the bishops do it, let the priests do it." But Jesus said "Go." When we say yes, the Holy Spirit empowers us with divine energy and supernatural ability to get up and go. This is a great commission—to go into the whole world and make disciples of all nations. Yet, it is the least obeyed command of Jesus Christ.

When I was about ten years old, I had the idea that when we stood before the throne of God in the last judgment, Jesus would ask us, "Do you remember on that certain day when you had bad thoughts and you committed this sin and that sin?" And then a movie of our sins would be shown to the whole world. This idea frightened me so much that I started getting headaches!

After I surrendered my life to the Lord and experienced his forgiveness and new life in the Holy Spirit, I realized that my understanding of the last judgment was wrong. So I said, "Well, Lord, what *are* you going to ask me when I come before your judgment seat?" And I believe the answer came to me. I believe he is going to ask, "Whom did you bring with you?" As followers and disciples of Jesus bound for heaven, we have got to be taking someone along! And the Lord is going to ask each one of us, "Whom did you bring with you?"

Many of us struggle with doubts and reject our ability to be used by God. *I'm not called . . . I'm not smart enough . . . I'm not a good talker . . . I'm not attractive enough . . . I'm not the one God wants to use.* Yes, you are! You are just the one he wants to use. You are smart enough. You are not too fat. You are not too thin. You may be too busy. If you are, then you can repent today and begin to be used by the Lord Jesus.

God wants to put you to work in his kingdom. If I asked you if you think you are qualified to be an ambassador for Christ, a representative, a witness, you would most likely say, "No, I'm not. And I feel so bad about it." Fortunately, God does not call the qualified, or none of us would be called. Rather, God qualifies the ones he calls. When you answer the call to make Jesus known to the world, he qualifies you with the gifts of the Holy Spirit. He backs you up all the way. You may be the only Bible that someone will read.

Many people argue, "I'm not healed enough to serve the poor. I'm not healed enough to be a witness for Jesus." I like to say it this way, "He mends me to send me." When we begin to do the Lord's work, he will bring about the healing we need.

There are many gospels in the world today other than the good news of salvation in Jesus Christ, even in parishes, even in church circles. Only one name sets people free. If we are going to serve the poor, then we must become experts at hearing his word and doing it. We must be able to say with Paul, "I'm not ashamed of the gospel. It is the power of God for the salvation of everyone who believes" (Rom 1:16).

What the world desperately needs today is a witness—even more than it needs a cure for cancer or hunger. Why? Because men and women are dying spiritually and have never heard the only name that saves, the name of Jesus Christ. I have met young people, old people, people of every race and nation, who have said, "Why didn't someone tell me sooner? Why didn't someone tell me about Jesus Christ and his love?" If we do not bring Jesus to people, we have failed miserably. I like what one person said: "Unless we're willing to do the ridiculous, God will not do the miraculous."

A "hopeless" case. One time when I was praying with a group of people, we felt like God was saying that he wanted us to bring the gospel to people who had never heard it. So we went out into the hills of Juarez, Mexico, where the people are looked upon as downcast, outcast, with no hope. We set up a tent in the 110-degree heat and began to preach the gospel. Many who listened began weeping and giving their lives to Christ.

As we began praying with people, one of my friends went around to the back of the crowd. She handed a young man a picture of Jesus and said, "Jesus loves you." That is all she said. It is easy to say; it is the message of the gospel. That is all some people need to hear.

This young man started shaking and went home. He shook and wept the whole night. He said he felt like a surge of electricity had hit him in the stomach. He told his mother, "Jesus loves me and he wants me." His mother and his brothers laughed at him. No one on our evangelism team was aware of the fact, but this young man was a hopeless alcoholic, drug addict, and thief, with every other vice that went along with these. He had also seen his sister burn to death when he was ten years old, and from that time on he stuttered.

This young man returned the next day as we were preaching the word of God and praying for the sick and those who were oppressed. As we prayed with him, he invited the Holy Spirit to take control of his life. In that moment, God healed him. He was set free of the sickness and the heartbreak that had driven him into this life of vice. Over the next several months, God healed this man from stuttering and gave him the gift of preaching the gospel. He could not read well, he had never studied, but as he heard the word of God, he took it into his heart. That gift began to blossom, and today this former alcoholic and drug addict is preaching the gospel in the jails of Mexico. God will back up our small efforts to make his name known.

Who Are the Poor?

Who are the poor? Jesus calls us to pray for the physically sick and mentally ill, to encourage those who are weak and fainthearted, to teach the lonely that Jesus loves them and is with them, to reassure the fearful that God's power can overcome any difficulty, to tell those who feel guilty and condemned that God holds out forgiveness, to comfort the brokenhearted with the good news of Jesus Christ, to give sight to the blind, to proclaim release to prisoners, to clothe those who are in need, to share our bread with the hungry, to provide shelter for the oppressed and the homeless.

One day when I was attending a conference, we were praying to know the will of God. As I was sitting there, a thought came through my mind: *I have something against you.* When this gentle nudging would not go away, I began to think it could be the Lord—perhaps a message for some of the conference leaders I did not especially appreciate. I said, "Lord, if it's you, tell me what you want."

A line from Scripture immediately came into my mind: "If you ignore the cry of the poor, you yourself will cry out and not be heard" (Prov 21:13). I felt like I had been struck by lightning. I started weeping and pouring out my soul to God. "It's true. I don't even know who the poor are. I'm more concerned about my own comfort, my own reputation, my own security than I am about your poor. Who are they anyway, Lord? Who are the poor?"

I felt so sad because I knew that my heart had grown cold even though I was in full-time Christian work. I entered the convent in 1960. I had given my life to evangelize, and yet I was far from what the Lord wanted. But I remembered that Ezekiel tells us that if we have a hard heart, a heart of stone, Jesus can do heart surgery. He can take out our heart of stone and give us a heart of flesh, one that can feel the love of God, a heart that is interested and concerned about the plans of God.

So I said, "God, I need heart surgery. I just don't have a heart for the poor. I'm willing to change, but I can't change myself. Do something, Lord." The very next day I was invited to go into the hills of Juarez, Mexico, for an evangelization outreach. I taught geography, but I did not even know where Juarez was or where El Paso was. But I said yes because they had invited Sister Briege, a famous nun from Ireland with a healing ministry.

So in the middle of August, I found myself sitting in the desert hills with pigs running around, garbage smelling, and some of our workers falling over from heat exhaustion. I whispered to the Lord, "I'm getting out of here as fast as I can." Just then a lady leaned over and said, "I think the Lord wants you to come here and work with us."

"No way", I said. "My plane ticket is safe in my purse and I'm using it tomorrow." I told the Lord that if he really wanted me there, he would have to give me a big sign, thinking of course that he could not do that. As I tried to relax and recover from heat exhaustion, I heard another man talking about how Jesus was still in the healing business. He said, "God heals today, and we're going to pray for the sick."

Oh, no, I groaned to myself. *That's going to take about three hours because everybody here is sick.* A lady ran forward and grabbed the microphone. She began to talk in Spanish, and everyone clapped, and they were laughing, and they got excited, and she kept pointing over in my direction. I thought she was pointing at Sister Briege, but my friend said, "No she isn't! She's saying 'La gordita', the fat one, the fat one right there. She's pointing at you!"

When I asked my friend to interpret, she answered, "Well, she says she lives in a shack by the dump and that last February she was dying. She was desperate because she had no money to go to the doctor and cried out, 'Jesus!' And when she looked up, Jesus walked through the door of the shack. And she said, 'That fat one, that one right there! I know that lady! I saw her, she was right behind him.' "

I knew it must be a sign. This woman had seen me with Jesus six months before I was even there! And God began to give me other signs that he wanted me to invest my life in his mission to make his name known among the poor.

When the Poor Cry out, Jesus Sends Help

A team of us recently finished building four houses for people who had been living in shacks or had no home at all. Each house has one twelve-by-fifteen room, but those people were so grateful. One widow told me, "I spent my nights on my knees asking God for help. I never dreamed there would be help. Now I'm on my knees thanking God that there are people who love him and who will come and help those who have no one to help."

James 1:27 tells us about looking after widows and orphans in their distress and that keeping ourselves unstained from the world makes for pure worship. I began to see that genuine compassion for the poor, the helpless, and the oppressed was more important than "correct doctrine about worship". James 2:5 goes on to tell us that God chose those who are poor in the eyes of the world to be rich in faith and heirs of the kingdom. The poor gladly come and gladly receive because they know their need.

We can reach the poorest of the poor, as I discovered when I returned to Juarez some months after my first visit. We began bringing people together for lunches and having prayer meetings and proclaiming the word of God and praying with the sick and expecting Jesus to act. Five hundred people walked for miles to attend our first prayer meeting.

One woman who came said she had spent nights in prayer begging God for help because her situation was so desperate. Having been seriously ill for a number of years, this woman had no money and nowhere else to turn. In fact, she had been living in a tent. When she came forward to give her life to Jesus, she was healed and renewed in the Holy Spirit. This woman became a radiant evangelist for the Lord and began to pray for her children, all of whom were involved in prostitution, drug addiction, or other kinds of vice. By the end of the year, all of them had given their lives to Christ.

First Corinthians 2:4–5 tells us that people's lives are changed, not by nice ideas, rational arguments in favor of Christ, and lots of talk, but by a demonstration of the power of the Spirit. Where the Holy Spirit is, good things happen, and people know God is in our midst. What convinced multitudes to follow Christ is seeing men and women being healed by Jesus' mighty power and evil spirits being driven out in his name.

My first initiation into this truth came at two o'clock one morning. Another nun who did not want to go asked me if I would pray with a woman who was threatening to commit suicide. I felt Jesus urging me to get up and go. He can call on us twenty-four hours a day, and our job is to be available to him. I arrived at the woman's house to find her sitting there with a loaded gun. I was terrified. She said, "I'm going to kill myself. Nobody loves me."

This woman was an immigrant with no family. She was the poorest of the poor and had become a mean-spirited person in the midst of her poverty. I heard the Holy Spirit whisper to me, "Pray for her." So I knelt down and said the only prayer I knew up to then, but one that God answers every time: "JESUS, HELP!" And the woman fell over. I thought she'd passed out from liquor. But the Holy Spirit, God's love, had enveloped her, and she had fallen into a deep and peaceful sleep. She woke up the next morning totally sober — the first miracle.

During her sleep, Jesus came to her in a dream and touched her. I found out later that she had a ninety-year-old grandmother in Denmark, and when she used to walk by her grandmother's room, she would see the old woman kneeling down and saying, "Jesus, what about little Krista? Jesus, take little Krista into your arms."

Upon awakening, she said, "I know God loves me." Jesus had taken little Krista into his arms during the night. This woman was baptized, made her first communion, and yielded her life to the

Holy Spirit. Those who knew her were amazed at the huge changes in the personality and character of a person one friend described as "the meanest woman I ever knew". They thought it would not last, but she bore witness to Christ until she died.

Where Do You Start?

Once you believe you are called to bring good news to the poor, where do you start? Jesus said the poor you have always with you. I used to think that meant we could sit back and relax: "They're always going to be around and there's nothing we can do about it." Now I know that Jesus meant that we will always have an opportunity to serve him in the poor. The Holy Spirit will lead us to the people he wants to touch.

The poor include the materially impoverished but also the spiritually impoverished, those who do not know Jesus Christ. Because we can't reach everyone, we often use that as an excuse to reach no one. But the world is won one by one. And God is going to bring people into your path — one by one, day by day, month by month — men and women he wants *you* to love and to pray with, that God would meet their needs.

At one point I was working with refugees from Vietnam, Laos, and Cambodia. I was recuperating from hepatitis, but I learned that being weak or sick does not excuse us from being used by God. He always has us in a place and in a condition where he can use us perfectly. It was during that time that I met refugees who had been abandoned by their sponsors. So we began to do the obvious things that needed to be done. We helped them find houses, brought them blankets to ward off the cold, and taught them how to get their children into school.

While the three people on our ministry team were praying together one day, we received a prophetic word from the Lord: "It is not enough to feed them, I want to show them my power." And so we began to have a prayer meeting, a faith gathering, and developed a way to teach the gospel to these refugees, some of whom had never heard the name Jesus Christ.

We also had to overcome a language barrier. To our surprise, the Lord sent a young man from a church in Montana who spoke Vietnamese, Chinese, and English. I would give the lesson, and he would translate it into two languages. One day, as I was explaining the gift of the Holy Spirit and the new life in Christ—which I had planned would take about three months—a Chinese man said, "I want Holy Spirit! I want Holy Spirit now!" And the Holy Spirit came upon him. I saw that Jesus is the same yesterday, today, and forever, as these refugees began to come alive in the Holy Spirit.

We are called not only to do the works of mercy but also to make disciples. One distraught young refugee told us he had not been able to sleep for months, and they could not find a psychiatrist who spoke his language. His oppression was so great the person taking care of him told us he was going to have him hospitalized that week.

I said to him, "We're going to pray for you. Are you willing to accept Jesus Christ into your life?" I did not know this man had been a Buddhist monk for five years. We laid hands on him and prayed out loud, "In the name of Jesus Christ, receive healing", just as Peter had prayed. Then I had him repeat a prayer asking Jesus to touch him and fill his life, to forgive him his sin. The next week he returned, smiling and radiant. He said, "I have been sleeping." That was the first good news, and everybody clapped. Then he said, "Buddha filled my mind but Jesus filled my heart."

The Spirit anoints ordinary people like you and me to do extraordinary work in his power in order to demonstrate that Jesus is alive. I believe God wants all of us to be heroes in his kingdom. A hero is someone who has a lot of flaws but whose God is bigger than those flaws. You don't have to keep praying for the grace to evangelize. You have the grace, you have the anointing, you have the calling. Just do it!

You don't have to be perfect to share your relationship with God. You don't have to have it all figured out. You don't have to be eloquent. You need only to be in love with Jesus Christ and to be willing to share this tremendous lover with others. The Spirit of the Lord is upon you to bring good news to the poor—if you are willing to be his instrument.

ટ♠

Sr. Linda Koontz is the Director of Spirit of the Lord International Mission, an evangelistic outreach among the poor. They also provide training in this ministry. For more information, contact:

> Spirit of the Lord International Mission
> 9455 Viscount #615
> El Paso, TX 79925-7034
> 915-598-9015

14

EVANGELIZING MARRIED COUPLES

Frank and Gerry Padilla

The moral and spiritual condition of families will determine to a large degree the well-being of individuals and of nations. As Pope John Paul II asserts in his apostolic exhortation *Familiaris Consortio,* "the future of humanity passes by way of the family."

At the core of renewing marriage and family life lies the evangelization of married couples. This is not an easy task. It is hard enough to evangelize in our modern secular milieu. It is doubly hard to evangelize married couples. Why? Because we need to evangelize *two* persons and not just one. Not only that, we need to evangelize not just any two people but a particular pair.

Rather than be discouraged, we need to see the reality of what God is doing in the world today. Jesus issued the great commission to the eleven apostles: to proclaim the good news to all creation (Mk 16:15) and make disciples of all the nations (Mt 28:19). This commission is still operative today and is the task of the Church and of every Christian. In this task, we should know that Jesus is still with us, until the end of the world (Mt 28:20)!

Thus we should have faith about God's intent and God's provision. Despite the sorry condition of marriage and family life today, despite the tremendous difficulty of evangelizing married couples, God's plan is still operative: "to bring all things in the heavens and on earth into one under Christ's headship" (Eph 1:10).

Jesus, who came into the world in order to bring us salvation, "is the same yesterday, today, and forever" (Heb 13:8). His mission, entrusted by the Father, also remains the same today. We can call upon the same power of the Holy Spirit, that power conferred on Pentecost, to be witnesses unto the ends of the earth. God has done his share; we need to do ours. We need to persevere in the task. We need to give of ourselves and be willing to make sacrifices. And if we do not lose heart, then we will reap the harvest (Gal 6:9).

Rather than evangelizing in a haphazard way, we need to develop a vision for the task—a deliberate, concerted, focused, and corporate approach. There are basically three stages in evangelizing married couples: (1) attracting them; (2) converting them; and (3) keeping and growing them. (See page 186, below.)

Attracting Them

Our efforts to evangelize married couples usually come up against three problems: sin, apathy, and ignorance. There are those couples who are living lives apart from God, strongly influenced by the world and the devil. Then there are those who simply are not interested; they are busy living their lives and do not care about spiritual matters. Finally, there are those who may be fairly good people but do not realize their need for Jesus as personal Lord and Savior.

Most married couples will not seek out the Lord on their own. We need to go after them. We do this in the normal day-to-day circumstances of our lives—in our family circles, in our neighborhoods, at our jobs, with our social contacts. Notice that we do not have to be missionaries or clergy or especially mature Christians in order to evangelize. We simply reach out to people with whom we have an opportunity to interact on a regular basis.

Person-to-person. We start evangelizing by building personal relationships, by becoming friends with people. The natural context of spending chunks of time with others affords us a unique opportunity. We can bide our time. We can choose the when and the how of speaking to them about the good news.

	WHAT	BY WHOM?	HOW	WHY?
Stage 1	Attracting them	Personal (person-to-person)	Develop a personal relationship Share Christ	Need tangible witness of life Show positive effects on daily life
Stage 2	Converting them	Communal	Program-matic	Work of body of Christ Utilize different gifts in body Introduce to Christian community
Stage 3	Keeping and growing them		Follow-up Formation courses Support groups Community life and mission	Ongoing work of renewal Goal: holi-ness, maturity Bring not just to Christ but to body Learn how to serve

We do not have to throw the gospel at someone. In fact, what we want to do is to build up a wordless witness. As people interact with us, they begin to notice how things are different with us: a healthier marriage relationship, better behaved kids, a more peaceful home. They begin to notice the difference in our speech, in our attitude, in our values.

In this context, we will eventually find an opportunity to share about our life in the Lord. At that point, we stress whatever we feel would be of particular interest to them. It could be in the area of family life, or music, or Christian formation, or service to the poor, or fellowship. We should know a couple well enough to choose wisely which aspects of our renewed life would prove most attractive to them.

Converting Them

Our goal in the first stage is simply to prepare people's hearts more fully to receive the good news. Now comes the second stage: converting them. The term "conversion" is appropriate. We may be evangelizing among Catholics, but many are simply nominal or cultural Christians—in other words, "baptized pagans".

This second stage often makes use of "programmatic" evangelization. Here our Christian group or community steps into the picture. We invite those whom we have evangelized (attracted) to join a program for Christian renewal. It may be a cursillo, or a Life in the Spirit seminar, or a Christian Life Program, or some other group evangelistic effort. Whatever program is utilized, it should basically contain two important elements: (1) an effective means of proclaiming the gospel; and (2) an environment that can attract them.

Proclaiming the good news. Proclaiming the gospel is done through a combination of teachings, discussions, and personal witnessing. All three are important and reinforce one another. We must use authentic, clear, and orthodox teaching to impart the meaning of the good news of Jesus Christ. Small group discussions allow a greater retention of what is heard in these teachings. Personal witnessing gives life and particular relevance to what is taught and discussed.

These tools become even more effective when done by married lay people. Program participants can relate better to the program resource persons and identify more easily with the practical life implications of what is taught. It is not theology but a practical living out of the good news.

It is also preferable, perhaps even crucial, that the program not be a one-shot affair, e.g., a one-day Life in the Spirit seminar or a one-evening evangelization rally. Solid conversion and growth need continuing proclamation and care. One of the more effective programs currently being utilized is the Christian Life Program of Couples for Christ, which extends over thirteen weeks.

Finally, a successful program should include not only a presentation of the basic truths of the Christian faith but also a clear call to repentance, a positive response to the Lordship of Jesus, and a prayer for empowerment (baptism in the Holy Spirit).

An effective environment. Many people can be attracted through person-to-person evangelization, attracted enough to agree to go to the formal program. At that point the challenge is to move from mere attraction to actual conversion.

During the program, the evil one will be working more intently to deter married couples from pursuing a new life in Christ through this particular program. One of our jobs is to help them in deciding to come back week after week. Thus our program should have a number of appealing features. And since each couple differs in personality, needs, desires, and expectations, our program should be multifaceted.

The first feature of attraction should be having an equal number of men and women comprise the team, a feature so simple yet so effective. A disproportionate number of women in groups and activities often deters men who may be searching for answers in the Church. A significant obstacle in men's spiritual lives can be thinking that spiritual activities are mainly for women.

The second feature of attraction involves having men assume the primary role of leadership. It is hard enough to get men involved in spiritual activities, but often when they are attracted and then join a group led by women, their interest wanes. When they see other men taking leadership in the group, they tend to stay. And so God can continue to work in their lives through the Church.

Male leadership in a group of married couples can present challenges. In the usual situation where the woman is the more spiritual of the two, her husband often holds back and finds it difficult to become more involved. But if the man is given an opportunity to move on, without being spiritually overshadowed by his wife, chances are he will "overtake" his wife and ultimately assume spiritual leadership in their married life—an outcome all wives would welcome.

A third feature of attraction is encouraging warm fellowship. The most effective atmosphere for evangelization is not somber or formal or "churchy", but more like a social gathering. The team members strive to be warm, friendly, caring, always reaching out. Newcomers experience a powerful magnet when they see total strangers welcoming them like friends, when they receive service with a warm smile. Lively music and less formal prayer offer other aids to warm fellowship.

Our goal in this second stage of evangelizing married couples is to bring the program participants to repentance and conversion, to the point of accepting Jesus as their personal Lord and Savior, to receiving the empowerment of the Holy Spirit, and to being integrated into the Christian group or community.

Keeping and Growing Them

Now we come to the third stage. Our aim in evangelization is renewal. Our goal is for the good news of Jesus Christ to be lived out in the lives of people. Our desire is for people to experience salvation now, leading to salvation in the hereafter. Thus we cannot stop at the initial conversion of couples during the organized program. Otherwise many of them will fall back into their old lifestyle. This lack of follow-up or follow-through is a major shortcoming of many good programs in the Church today.

Evangelization is an ongoing work. We do not stop at initial conversion but move on to implantation: planting people in the church in general and in a Christian group or parish in particular. Then we do not stop at implantation but move on to helping people in being formed and growing to Christian maturity. This growth process extends for the rest of a person's life. Furthermore, those evangelized have to move on and become evangelizers themselves, which is how the cycle of renewal continues in ever-widening circles.

The Christian community. Thus we recognize a need for the evangelized couple to join a committed community of Christians. This could be the parish community, if it is structured to support Christians in their everyday lives, or it could be a lay group operating within the parish.

For such a community to continue effectively the task of evangelizing married couples, several elements should be present. First, commitments need to be clearly spelled out. Real community is not a matter of being included in the membership rolls but of faithfully living out the life of the community. Important areas of commitment would include regular personal prayer, Bible reading, and attendance at meetings. We are called on in faithfulness in such areas by making a clear commitment to the Lord and to one another.

Second, there should be "cell groups". These are small support groups comprised of five to seven couples who meet regularly. These cell groups provide opportunities to grow in real friendships and to care for one another more intimately, thus addressing the common problem of anonymity in a large group.

Third, there should be weekly meetings. People involved in

church groups may be used to meeting only monthly or fort-nightly. But this sort of schedule leaves a couple too long in the world between meetings. For the couples to realize the impor-tance of the spiritual dimension of their lives, they need to come together with their brothers and sisters in Christ on a more regular basis.

Other elements which need to be offered by the Christian community are ongoing formation, a corporate life and identity, opportunities for service, a sense of mission, and a clear vision for the group regarding its place in God's plan.

The task of evangelizing married couples is crucial for God's plan for the family to come to pass, for societies to have and live out Christian values, for the Church to be strengthened, for disciples to be made of all the nations. We all need to apply ourselves to this task. We need to develop a vision for this work. Then we need to give of our time, our talent, and our treasure. In all of this, we must have the confidence that God is with us and will empower us with his Holy Spirit.

ৰ

Frank and Gerry Padilla are leaders in Couples for Christ, a movement that focuses on renewing family life with specific ministries to couples, children, young adults, single men and women, and widows. For more information, contact:

> Couples for Christ Global Mission Foundation, Inc.
> 15/F Strata 200
> Emerald Avenue
> Ortigas Center
> Pasig, Metro Manila
> PHILIPPINES
> 63–2–633–2781
> 63–2–635–2780 (FAX)

In the United States contact:
> Couples for Christ
> 3137 N. Oleander
> Chicago, IL 60635
> 312–637–4750

EVANGELIZING TEENAGERS

Frank Mercadante

How can we effectively reach adolescents with the good news of Jesus Christ? Perhaps no other age group presents so many tough challenges.

Misconceptions about God and apprehensions about his desires can prevent teenagers from embracing the faith of their parents and enjoying the adventure of following Christ. Some of these misconceptions originate from the Church herself, perhaps sermons that depict Jesus as heavy-hearted, serious, and sad. Adolescents may conclude that such a person offers no excitement and has no relevance to their lives. Young people naturally want to experience life as an adventure, not a funeral wake. They decide to set aside church until they grow older and more accustomed to the "mundane things in life".

My own faith adventure began in my senior year of high school when some friends invited me to a parish retreat. I heard other students describe a Jesus unknown to me. They sounded like they knew him personally, almost as if they had had lunch with him earlier that day! By the end of the first night, I too had met Jesus in a personal way and experienced his love. That weekend altered the course of my life. I went on to spend fourteen years in full-time parish youth ministry.

Our ministry grew from a meager beginning with fourteen students to a multifaceted outreach that involved over five hundred young people. Over fifty student evangelists would meet before school on Tuesday mornings at six o'clock to pray and organize themselves to share the gospel with peers. Jesus wants to send out many workers to gather young people into his kingdom. With this mandate, let's consider some fundamental principles of youth evangelization.

Why Should We Evangelize Teenagers?

Our young people are restless, searching among an overwhelming number of options for something to believe in. We are obligated by love to share with them the only name worthy of their allegiance. Some of us might feel insecure because we do not want to be rejected. It certainly can be intimidating when approaching adolescents. But this mission is too important to be stymied by any barriers, real or imagined. Christ can take us beyond our fears and deficiencies, help us to know that the Holy Spirit will guide us and supply whatever we need. Unusual and exciting encounters will follow. Let me suggest three reasons we should evangelize teenagers.

First, young people face a crisis of identity. One question looms large: *Who am I?* Developmentally, adolescence is a pivotal period in a person's journey. Many critical decisions will have lifelong consequences. If the Church is not there to offer answers, then peers or modern culture will. Most often the answer they will hear is "You're nobody unless you have. . . ." Our consumer society tells us that we need things to be satisfied. Attaining the American dream is all that matters. If you have a three-car garage and a summer home, you are somebody. The gospel tells us that we are "somebody" because God created us for a purpose and even died for us. We do not have to do anything or have anything to earn this love. God loves us for who we are.

Second, young people are dealing with questions of purpose. *Why do I exist? What is the purpose of my life? What direction will my life take? What is my life all about?* Again, contemporary culture stands ready with answers: Life is all about accumulating things, being popular, being attractive. Scripture teaches us much more profound values: Life is about loving, giving, and serving.

Third, we need to evangelize adolescents so that we can benefit from their enthusiasm and idealism. Their emotions are not all straightened out and under control yet, but their zeal can be contagious and inspiring. Once young people have caught fire for the Lord, they can live out the Scriptures in an idealistic way that reminds us of the raw power of love. Resolving relationship difficulties inflamed by hormones can be a huge challenge, but even in that arena their enthusiasm makes for rich rewards.

Effective Youth Ministry Is Based on Building Relationships

Jesus' style of interpersonal evangelization illustrates some solid principles about evangelization. Instead of having a standard or "canned" approach, we need to identify an individual's need and then share the good news in a way that speaks to that need. Implementing this approach requires a knowledge of the Scriptures. We also need to be in touch with the Holy Spirit. Evangelism is not merely a human interaction. Conversion never happens apart from God.

Enter the world of the adolescent. Adolescents need to see us as approachable, credible, caring, and worthy of trust. Relational youth ministry involves a willingness to be personally present to youth, to go where teens spend time, to venture forth into their world and walk alongside them. We should not embrace their culture without restraint but seek to understand it and be able to converse with them about it. Youth will take us seriously only when we take them and their experiences and perspectives seriously. A good rule of thumb is to *listen and learn first* and earn the right to be heard.

Move from being program-centered to being person-centered. A program-centered model attempts to reach youth with only content. A people-centered model reaches them with the "content" of our love and through our relationship with them. Interesting presentations will bring young people to a program a few times, but if these young people do not develop any significant relationships, they will not continue to come. We do not want to become so absorbed in *doing* the "right things" at meetings that we miss *being* present and expressing love.

Share your life and faith. After making contact and developing a relationship with a young person, we have a natural context in which to share God's action in our lives. They usually become interested and begin asking questions about our faith. It is also important to invite them to respond to the good news. If they are open, pray with them and for their needs. Let them know that a "new life" is possible for them as well through a personal relationship with Christ.

Be sure to follow through. After bringing teenagers to a relationship with Christ, we need to help them grow in their relationship with Christ, teach them how to pray, and explain the relevance of Scripture. Do your best to connect them with others who can help them grow as well. Try to incorporate them into the life of the youth and parish community. Introduce them to other students who can support them spiritually. Our ultimate destination is to make "apostles" of young people, so that they can embrace the mission of the Church and be sent out to proclaim the gospel to others.

Relational outreach never conforms itself to a "neat and tidy" plan. Getting involved in other people's lives and letting them become part of ours entails vulnerability, opening ourselves up to feeling rejected. We need to push through our initial feelings of reluctance. By establishing relationships with young people we will become a credible and significant influence in their lives. When the going gets tough, God will give us strength and grace to persevere.

Large-Group Evangelization

Much of the focus up to this point has centered on relational and interpersonal evangelization of youth. You may be in a position to develop a group program that could expand your opportunities for reaching young people with the gospel. What goes into large-group evangelization?

A large-group gathering does not provide a lot of intimacy or deep sharing but does offer more excitement with lots of other teens. Young people typically attend events because of who will be there. They want to meet new people and build friendships with each other and with caring adults.

First, we need to schedule a regular event for a particular day, time, and location, and often enough to maintain some momentum. Consistency helps young people establish some element of routine in their busy lives and also cuts down on our need to publicize an event. If at all possible, we should give names to our programs that actually publicize for us. For instance, a group of young people meet in downtown Chicago for an event called "Second Saturday".

Second, we need to design quality events that carry an attractive and appealing image. Many young people assume a church-sponsored event will be boring. We need to develop innovative, fast-paced, and high-energy programming that can successfully compete for a young person's time and energy. Youth meetings need to use a variety of methods to convey the gospel and move quickly from one activity to another before boredom sets in, perhaps a ten-minute skit, a ten-minute youth sharing, a short talk by an adult, and end with a slide show that carries the same theme.

Large-group events need to breed a sense of enthusiasm and excitement. Young people typically have lots of energy and need physical activity. One of their highest priorities is to have fun. A successful large-group meeting is one young people consider "the place to be". They are looking for opportunities to gather. What better place than the church?

Young people will attend a large-group evangelistic meeting

because it meets their perceived needs. Once we convey our love and concern in this way, we can more readily address their deeper need for spiritual conversion. Teens may sense something missing in their lives or experience a longing for more, yet few would be able to express their need for God. A roomful of teens who are experiencing a good time is not enough. If we fail to invite them to Jesus and a deeper conversion of heart, we have fallen short of our goal. Each meeting should highlight the person and teachings of Christ.

Extending a warm and enthusiastic welcome as people arrive weighs more heavily in the minds of young people than the content or activities. After a brief, official welcome, the meeting can begin with a short and simple prayer that avoids theological language or sober imagery. After using humor or a fun activity to put people at ease, we should proclaim the gospel in a relevant and creative manner, with content rooted in the Scriptures and Church teaching.

After closing the meeting, we do not want to give students the impression they have to rush away because the program is over and we "old people" are tired. Providing refreshments encourages them to hang around so that we can talk and interact with one another. This is where real ministry occurs, especially in one-to-one interactions that solicit their response to the meeting.

Large-group evangelization will attract the largest cross-section of young people, but it will not touch everyone. We need to go beyond attracting just the interested and focus on unreached adolescents in our community. This may include jocks, troubled teens, or unchurched kids. This kind of outreach requires innovative thinking. First we must identify those students who are not being reached by our present efforts. Second, we need to find a common ground for meeting these groups. What might interest or attract them?

Once we find a point of contact, we need to develop a program, event, activity, or relationship. We need to think carefully and consider all the details. If we wanted to reach the athletes in our community, we might sponsor a city-wide slam-dunk contest and specifically invite varsity basketball players. We would publicize the event throughout the city, inviting everyone else to come as spectators.

No matter what the program, we need to keep in mind our ultimate purpose, the sharing of the gospel. Our planning process should include some way to help break down barriers to faith and pave the way to a closer relationship with Christ. Sometimes building and creating a positive awareness and experience will suffice, the kind of experiences we can build on later. Or we may pursue more direct evangelization.

The youth of our nation will be evangelized. The question is: by whom or what? Will it be the Church? Or will it be the contemporary American culture that packages its message with slick sophistication and catchy media?

I believe it is a myth that today's teens are not interested in spiritual things. We would not have such a problem with drugs, alcohol, sex, and the occult if they were not spiritually hungry. Unfortunately, they are trying to fill deep spiritual needs with artificial substitutes. The Church has the answer: Jesus Christ. Let's commit ourselves to applying excellence to our task by living and proclaiming the gospel in a relevant and creative way.

Frank Mercadante is the Executive Director of Cultivation Ministries, which helps parishes develop their own youth ministries to evangelize teenagers. For more information, contact:

Cultivation Ministries
P.O. Box 662
St. Charles, IL 60174
708–513–8222

16

EVANGELIZING IN
BUSINESS AND GOVERNMENT

Michael Timmis

Eleven years ago I had everything that the world tells us brings happiness: a wife, two handsome children, a successful career, wealth, and stature in the community. Yet, I was lonely, miserable, self-righteous, and critical.

As my material wealth increased, I became spiritually impoverished. I felt empty inside. I expressed my mounting frustrations by being critical and demanding of those around me. My son viewed me as an adversary and was gradually retreating from me, and the only woman I have ever loved was becoming quieter and quieter in our marriage.

I would go to church each Sunday, receive Communion, and pray that somehow I could bridge the gap between God and myself. While I totally believed in Jesus Christ and knew without doubt that he was my Lord and Savior, I did not have or feel any personal relationship with him. Feeling more and more distant from God allowed me to adopt an indifferent approach to my faith. I convinced myself that I really didn't sin because I didn't commit adultery, I didn't cheat in business, I went to church faithfully, and kept up the requirements of being a so-called "good Christian".

Then my wife asked me to attend a dinner with her at a local country club. When I asked her what the dinner was about, she told me that there would be a discussion on religion. Well, I had absolutely no desire to hear about religion! Having studied more philosophy and theology than most people, I thought I had heard it all, and I did not want to be preached to. Somehow my wife prevailed, and we went to the dinner.

That evening changed my life. I did not hear anything about religion, but I heard a lot about a person I really didn't know very well, the person of Jesus Christ. I listened to a professional athlete and his wife who had come all the way from Dallas to share their faith. They described how their marriage had been falling apart but how Christ intervened. They developed a personal relationship with him that saved their marriage and finally brought them true happiness. I also heard a local businessman talk about his personal relationship with God. I could identify with him because he seemed to have the same kind of problems I had, yet his love for Christ was totally transparent.

At the end of the dinner, I said a simple prayer and committed my life to Jesus Christ and accepted him as my personal Savior. It is difficult for me to describe the incredible inner joy of what Jesus did in my heart that night. Some of my friends call it "being born again", others call it "being renewed", and still others say "committed to Jesus Christ". Whatever you call it, I began to understand that the whole purpose of my life is to love Jesus Christ with all of my heart, soul, mind, and strength, and to learn how to love others for the love of him.

Becoming an Effective Advocate for Christ

My experience was so transforming that my children and many of my friends thought I had gone through some sort of mental change, and it frightened them. I remember going to a priest friend and explaining to him what had happened. I received no encouragement, no understanding, and, quite frankly, no interest. I mention this detail because many of us think evangelizing in the marketplace includes reaching out to a social-economic group that is predominantly Catholic. When our efforts are met with suspicion or objection, it makes it doubly hard, and often the spirit of evangelism is snuffed out.

God was gracious to me and made it clear that he did not want me to join another denomination but rather follow the scriptural instruction to stay exactly where I was, continuing as I was when he called me (1 Cor 7:17). As I began to be renewed in all aspects of my spiritual life, I also began to be renewed in my Catholicism. I read the Vatican II documents, where it states that ignorance of the Scriptures is ignorance of Christ and that all Scripture is God-breathed or divinely inspired for our instruction.

As a lawyer and businessman, I had executed literally hundreds of contracts, all of which I had read personally because they affected me. Yet I had never read the most basic of all contracts, the New Testament, the New Covenant between God and the human race. I realized how ignorant I was of the "contract" that God had made with me through my religious experience in the Church and through the Scriptures, that it was something on which I could rely on a daily basis. I began to understand the absolute necessity of knowing God's word, as best described by an anonymous, fourteenth-century monk who authored a book called *The Cloud of Unknowing:*

> God's Word written or spoken is like a mirror. Reason is your spiritual eye and conscience your spiritual reflection. And just as you use a mirror to detect a blemish in your physical appearance—and without a mirror or someone to tell you where the blemish is, you would not discover it—so it is spiritually. Without reading or hearing God's Word, a man who is spiritually blind on account of habitual sin is simply unable to see the foul stain on his conscience.

Reading Scripture convicted me of my responsibility to share with others what God was giving to me, first with my wife and children and then with my friends. I made the common mistake of becoming overzealous, preachy, and all-knowing and very easily fell back into many of the traits that I had acquired before my rebirth in Christ. I discovered through painful experience that without someone to check you, advise you, lead you, and make you accountable in evangelism, most likely you will end up being totally self-righteous, narrow, and ineffective.

As a lawyer, I am a trained advocate, but in reality most businessmen and women are also advocates. A good advocate can be very effective in so-called evangelism, in presenting facts about Jesus Christ, but that is not the same as presenting the person of Jesus Christ. When I think of evangelism, I think of *changed lives,* not people saying "I do", "I will", raising their hands, or coming forward at a crusade or altar call. Interestingly, Billy Graham has estimated that 90 percent of the people who come forward at one of his rallies are not living their new faith a year later.

Evangelism for me changed substantially when I began to *live* the life of Christ rather than *talk about* the life of Christ. A good friend of mine said to me early on: "You have been successful as a lawyer; you have been successful as a businessman; I am sure you will be successful in religion." And I would suspect that was a common feeling among the people who knew me.

One of the most profound experiences came approximately one year after this transformation. I met a man who ultimately became my spiritual mentor (and who still is today). He told me that if I wanted to be involved in evangelism, *I should first go home and learn how to love my wife and children and wait upon the Lord.* This is one of the best pieces of advice I have ever received; I encourage you to take it to heart for yourself.

I began to realize that evangelism means *being available* to the Lord as opposed to deciding "this is what God should do" and then dragging him into my project. True evangelism is like being an usher at a theater. An *usher* brings people in, sits them down, and facilitates their watching the play—the central figure in the play being Jesus Christ. However, if I think of myself as the *major actor* in that play, I will not let the Christ in me evangelize those I am trying to serve.

To me, evangelism has become basically representing Jesus Christ where I am. Many years ago my spiritual mentor told me that if I would be a light *where I am,* other people would be attracted to the light and thus to the word of God. I found that to be true. We usually think of evangelism as "going". I believe evangelism in the main is "staying" and being consistent.

Where Was God Calling Me to Proclaim the Good News?

As I started to change, I began to receive numerous invitations to speak about that change (early on those invitations came mostly from Protestant Evangelical organizations). I began to speak publicly about my relationship with Jesus Christ. When a businessman does that, he begins to set himself apart to some degree. As a friend told me many years ago, people are watching you to see if this is for real. And if you fall, you take many others with you. That helped instill discipline in me, because the one person I did not want to let down was Jesus Christ.

God called my wife, Nancy, and me to evangelize in several different arenas. These may suggest some ways in which you can share the good news with others in the business world. As I mentioned earlier, I met the person of Jesus Christ at an outreach dinner. A group of us put on a number of dinners in our community, where, after dinner, average people, homemakers, business leaders, professionals, and political leaders would talk about Jesus Christ coming into their lives and making them the kind of people he wants them to be. We make these dinners a pleasant social experience and hold them primarily in homes. We ask people to bring their friends and sponsor a table by bringing their own china and silverware, etc., so they can feel like an integral part of the event.

The Lord led Nancy and me to look around our community of Grosse Pointe, Michigan, and ask certain couples (covering the spectrum of local denominations) to come together and pray monthly to lift up Christ in our area. After nine years, this group of eight couples is still together. Notwithstanding the fact that the group includes Protestant Evangelicals who have been following Christ for decades, they look to me as their leader—which proves that God does not call the qualified, he qualifies the called.

With this small prayer group as a starting point, we started Bible studies and prayer groups as well as other activities. Each of us decided that we would support the work undertaken by the others. Out of the prayers of our community group has come a fellowship program in Christ that reaches over 150 high-school and middle-school students each week, again including all the denominations of our area. We also put on an annual seminar which brings together approximately 135 people for a weekend of fellowship in Jesus Christ, where we bring speakers from around the country—Catholic and Protestant—to lift up Jesus Christ.

Two of us from the group volunteered to put on a mayor's prayer breakfast in our community, which became a regular event. Approximately five hundred people attended the most recent one. When you are willing to do the necessary footwork, you can select speakers who make the breakfast a meaningful event rather than a "feel good" event, an event that really lifts up the person of Jesus Christ as opposed to an event that accomplishes virtually nothing.

I regularly meet with two groups of men. One group is comprised of men my age who have met together for nine years. We started out with just three of us, and now there are approximately twenty. When they first came, none of these men had a personal relationship with Jesus Christ, but all were hungry. Through the years all of them have been personally transformed and have transformed their marriages and families. Most of their wives have joined some form of prayer group or Bible study as well.

As a business leader, I am often asked to speak in secular settings about different topics, e.g., the free-enterprise system, politics, or ethics. I always take advantage of these settings to make it clear that I represent the King of kings, that I owe any success I have to the Lord, and that success to me begins with being a man of God. Even though I am not bringing what might be called an evangelistic message per se, I believe this is a very important part of evangelism. I have talked to many mixed groups of Christians and non-Christians and never once has anyone told me they were offended. That is because I keep my remarks limited solely to the Jesus Christ I know personally.

Together with a young man who has been working with me for the past couple of years, we decided to hold a weekend and invite college students from Michigan campuses to meet in the Spirit of Jesus Christ at a local suburban hotel. We patterned this weekend after a program we saw in Washington, D.C., called the

National Student Leadership Conference. For the last two years we have had over one hundred young college students from diverse backgrounds, different denominations, races, etc., meet solely around the person of Jesus Christ.

For each four students, there is one older mentor. For example, a husband and wife would be responsible for eight students. We schedule a number of events during the weekend, and the mentors stay with their group for the entire time. Three events highlight each weekend: a breakfast where political leaders speak to the group (this year we had the lieutenant governor of Michigan); a work project with the poor on Saturday afternoon; and a dinner for the students at private homes around the metroplex which affords the opportunity for more adults to mix with the college students.

Last but not least, my wife, Nancy, and I feel that Christ has called us to lift him up to the poor. We do this in the city of Detroit through a number of projects. For example, we mentor African Americans in conjunction with public and parochial schools, and we work with Cornerstone Schools, which are three Christ-centered inner-city schools formed in 1991. In addition, God has called us to work in Third World countries. We work with other believers in Latin America and Africa (where our son has lived for six years). The whole thrust of these activities is to lift up the person of Jesus Christ and to offer his love through self-help projects.

Reaching out to Government Leaders

Another aspect of my life in Christ involves evangelizing government leaders. After traveling to over eighty countries in the last six years, I have observed several basic consistencies among these world leaders. Whatever their religion, color, or degree of power, all are lonely, depressed, distrustful, concerned, face difficulty in their personal lives, and have no close friends. In short, they are all hungry for the good news of Jesus Christ.

In literally hundreds of meetings with political leaders (representing Christians, Jews, Hindus, Moslems, Buddhists, and others), I have never once had an unpleasant experience. When we have talked about Jesus Christ and his message of reconciliation, I have never had a disagreement; I have never had anyone tell me that he was offended; and I have never had anyone say "I do not believe you." The most common response was that we had told them about a Jesus Christ they had never heard of before.

I want to underscore a principle that I think is critical to evangelism: when I lift up Jesus Christ to someone, I do not lift up anything else. I do not lift up Christianity or any "isms" or any methodologies. I prayerfully concentrate on sharing the love Jesus Christ has given to me. I believe that this is the only biblical and effective form of evangelism that leads to changed lives, that opens the door so that Jesus can come into the lives of our listeners.

My first evangelistic trip was to Poland in 1987—before the fall of communism—where I had been asked to talk to Polish communist leaders about Jesus Christ. This struck me as quite preposterous, but the Spirit led me forward even though I knew very little about Poland and have no ethnic connection. I frankly did not believe that an ordinary person who is basically an unknown outside of his own community could be an effective witness to world government leaders.

To make a long story short, over the course of that trip I met with the vice president of Poland, most of the cabinet members, and the head of the Polish KGB. All I did was share my experiences about Jesus Christ and his love. The reception I received was overwhelming. The day I left, my picture appeared on the front page of the Warsaw daily newspaper, showing me shaking hands with the vice president with the headline, "American Businessman Comes to Discuss Jesus Christ with the Vice President."

This experience proved to me that when Jesus Christ is lifted up, he is irresistible to all men and women, whoever they may be. While I continue to be called to evangelize government leaders around the world, I have found that these same principles hold true on the local scene—with judges, with mayors, with members of the legislature, with the governor.

Evangelism as a Way of Life

What I have described to you is not a methodology, not a recorded series of projects, but rather a description of evangelism as a way of life. This way of life begins with taking Jesus Christ to the four corners of my mind before I take him to the four corners of the world. The four corners of my mind are: (1) my personal relationship with Jesus Christ; (2) my relationship with my wife, family, and friends; (3) my relationship as it pertains to my human sexuality—my manhood; and (4) my career, which includes my wealth and my ego.

I have found that the area of career, wealth, and ego is the most difficult for every business, professional, or political person to face. Taking Jesus into this corner means realizing that I can only evangelize others if I first evangelize *myself*. Of course, that is an ongoing process, one which allows me to look back and evaluate how well I am doing only this morning or this afternoon.

I believe evangelism is not possible without daily prayer, and by that I mean praying for myself and others and meditative prayer. The older and busier I become, the more I realize how absolutely critical it is to spend a portion of each day in prayer *without fail*. On those few days when I let my day get away from me because of meetings from morning to night, I never go to bed until I finish a quality time of prayer. That takes personal commitment.

Second, Scripture is an integral part of every day. It is a time when I believe God conveys to me his thoughts, his encouragement, his advice, and his admonition. Third, I try to go to Mass on a daily basis.

When I was wrestling with what God wanted me to do with my life, he made it clear to me that he wanted me to devote a portion of my life to evangelization in the Catholic Church. I thought the best way I could do that was by becoming an exemplary Catholic, and so I started going to Mass every day—with the view that people then would not doubt my Catholic credentials when I talked to them about Christ.

That reason quickly became totally irrelevant. Through the

beauty of worshipping at Mass, I discovered an even deeper intimacy with Jesus Christ through the sacrifice of the Mass and by receiving the Eucharist. On the days I find it impossible to get to Mass, I feel a deep sense of incompleteness. Now I plan my day around Mass, and if I miss it in the morning, I try to get there at noon.

Fourth, as I said earlier, accountability is critical. I need to be accountable to someone—a person who is a good enough friend and a brother in Christ—who will tell me exactly what he sees in me: the good, the bad, and the ugly.

What Is Our Call?

In closing, I would like to share three quotes from the Vatican II documents that provide a framework for evangelism in the marketplace.

> Between the members of this body there exists, further, such a unity and solidarity that a member who does not work at the growth of the body to the extent of his possibilities must be considered useless both to the Church and to himself (AA, no. 2).

> This witness of life, however, is not the sole element in the apostolate: the true apostle is on the lookout for occasions of announcing Christ by word, either to unbelievers to draw them toward the faith, or to the faithful to instruct them, strengthen them, incite them to a more fervent life (AA, no. 6).

> The apostolate in one's social environment endeavors to infuse the Christian spirit into the mentality and behavior, laws, and structures of the community in which one lives. To such a degree it is the special work and responsibility of lay people, that no one else can ever properly supply for them. In this area laymen and women can conduct the apostolate of like toward like. There the witness of their life is completed by the witness of their word (AA, no. 13).

I can tell you that in all my years of attending Mass, I have heard only one homily on these principles, and that was given by

Fr. Bodhan Kosicki of St. Lucy's Church in St. Clair Shores, Michigan. I suggest that less than 1 percent of Catholics know these principles, yet they are critical to our call to share the good news with others. Before the laity can meet its responsibility in evangelism, we must understand the critical importance of evangelism to the average Catholic.

In the final analysis, each of us has to figure out the best way to proceed in evangelizing both ourselves and others. While we are all called to the same question, we are called to different answers. I hope my experience has at least stimulated your own thinking about how you can bring the good news to those around you.

17

EVANGELIZING HISPANIC AMERICANS

Pepe Alonso

North American society is comprised of many ethnic groups with different cultures, languages, and life styles. The Christian ideal is to achieve unity within this diversity, but we must not confuse integration with assimilation.

In the *National Pastoral Plan for the Hispanic Ministry* (NPPHM), issued in November 1987, the American bishops explain the difference between assimilation and integration:

> Through the policy of assimilation, new immigrants are forced to give up their language, culture, values, and traditions and adopt a form of life and worship foreign to them in order to be accepted as parish members. This attitude alienates new Catholic immigrants from the church and makes them vulnerable to sects and other denominations.
>
> By integration, we mean that our Hispanic people are to be welcomed to our church institutions at all levels. They are to be served in their language when possible, and their cultural values and religious traditions are to be respected (NPPHM, no. 4).

Taking the oath for United States citizenship in no way requires a person to renounce his cultural identity. In just the same way, our efforts to bring people into the Church must not infringe on their ethnic heritage. Unless we take into consideration the multicultural dimension of our society, our efforts to bring others to Christ will fail. We cannot evangelize with the mentality of stirring everyone into one big melting pot.

St. Paul offers one of the clearest examples of effective multi-cultural evangelization:

> Although I am free in regard to all, I have made myself a slave to all so as to win over as many as possible. To the Jews I became like a Jew to win over Jews; to those under the law I became like one under the law—though I myself am not under the law—to win over those under the law. To those outside the law I became like one outside the law—though I am not outside God's law but within the law of Christ—to win over those outside the law. To the weak I became weak, to win over the weak. I have become all things to all, to save at least some (1 Cor 9:19–22).

In *Evangelii Nuntiandi,* Pope Paul VI emphasizes this same principle: "Evangelization loses much of its force and effectiveness if it does not take into consideration the actual people to whom it is addressed, if it does not use their language, their signs and symbols, if it does not answer the questions they ask, and if it does not have impact on their concrete life" (EN, no. 63).

A Difficult Balancing Act

Hispanics are fast becoming the largest minority in the United States. Their continued resistance to giving up their language and culture offers clear evidence of the pride they take in their cultural heritage. The primary goal of Hispanics has been to participate in American society without being assimilated by it—an extremely difficult balancing act.

Certain historical factors help us to understand why Hispanics have not followed the same pattern of assimilation as other large immigrant groups. For one thing, people of Spanish ancestry already occupied much of the United States well before other Europeans came to take possession of these lands. Mexicans were the first to colonize Arizona, Nevada, New Mexico, California, and Texas.

Puerto Ricans possess American citizenship by birth, but the majority do not consider themselves "gringos". Cubans, who came for political not economic reasons, arrived in large numbers and established concentrated Cuban communities. They live their own lives and maintain their own culture so well that they have never made irreversible changes. The majority of Hispanics have not become separated from their homelands by vast oceans. Their countries are so close that they constantly travel back and forth, nourishing their roots in a way that allows their traditions not only to survive but even to thrive.

The term "Hispanic" is not applied exclusively to those born in one country but is a generic term applied to people from Argentina, Chile, Paraguay, Uruguay, Peru, Bolivia, Ecuador, Colombia, Venezuela, Panama, Costa Rica, Nicaragua, Honduras, El Salvador, Guatemala, Mexico, Cuba, Puerto Rico, Dominican Republic, Spain, and the United States. In fact, according to the 1990 census, Hispanics from the United States make up the *fifth largest* Hispanic population in the world. America's twenty-five million is topped only by Mexico (87.7), Spain (38.6), Colombia (34.3), and Argentina (33.1).

Even though each one of these countries boasts a separate and well-established culture, not only a common language but also a similar value system is shared. According to the American bishops, values common to Hispanics include "a profound respect for the dignity of the person, a profound and respectful love for the family life, a marvelous sense of community, a fond thankfulness for life itself—a gift from God, and an authentic and solid devotion to Mary." The bishops go on to say that for Hispanic Catholics, "the culture has become a way to live the faith and transmit it" (NPPHM, no. 10).

The Signs of the Times

In terms of the Hispanic presence in the United States and in the Catholic Church, certain statistics can help us read the signs of the time in which we live. To disregard these signs when planning our evangelistic efforts would be a tragic error.

The 1990 census reports twenty-five million Hispanics, which I believe to be a very conservative figure. The projected number of Hispanics by the year 2000 is thirty-one million, almost 12 percent of the projected U.S. population. The projection for the year 2020 is forty-nine million, or 15.2 percent of the total population. In 1950, there were less than four million Hispanics; in 1980, there were fifteen million, nine million of whom were Mexican. From 1950 to 1980, the population of the United States grew by 50 percent, while the Hispanic segment increased a whopping 270 percent!

The three largest Hispanic groups in the United States, according to the 1990 census, are Mexican Americans (almost 13.5 million), Puerto Ricans (over 2.7 million), and Cubans (over one million). Others totaled over five million more.

The three metropolitan areas with the most Hispanics are Los Angeles (over 4.7 million), New York (over 2.8 million), and Miami (over one million). Other cities with a large Hispanic population include San Francisco, Chicago, Houston, San Antonio, Dallas, El Paso, and Fresno. Five metropolitan areas in Texas have a large percentage of Hispanics: Laredo (93.9 percent), McAllen (85.2 percent), Brownsville (81.9 percent), El Paso (69.6 percent), and San Antonio (47.4 percent). Miami, Los Angeles, and Fresno, California, have about one-third Hispanics out of their total population.

Catholics and Hispanics in the United States. It is estimated that there are some 58,267,424 Catholics in the United States, of which 24,099,406 (41.36 percent) are Hispanic. This percentage is rising much faster than other non-Hispanic groups. It is estimated that by the turn of the century, Hispanics will make up 50 percent of the Catholic Church. That means one of every two Catholics in the United States will be Hispanic.

Yet we see a huge disproportion in the pastoral leadership of the American church. Consider the following current statistics: out of ten cardinals, only one is Hispanic (Cardinal Aponte from Puerto Rico); out of forty-five archbishops, only two are Hispanic; out of 352 bishops, fifteen are Hispanic (five of whom are in

Puerto Rico); and out of 52,277 priests, only 3,908 are Hispanic (7.47 percent).

How can we analyze these statistics? Perhaps the projections based on the 1990 census came up short due to the large number of illegal aliens, approximately 10 percent more than government records indicate. Although this group is not reflected by any official statistics, it cannot be ignored. These are real people who place significant demands on the Catholic Church.

The rate of growth among Hispanics in the United States is enormous and appears to be increasing. We do not believe the pastoral resources of the Church are capable of caring for this rapidly growing segment of the population, which may explain why certain sects such as Jehovah's Witnesses are winning thousands and thousands of Hispanics every month.

Because of the shortage of pastoral leadership, I believe it is the hour of the laity. Together with Hispanics and in communion with the hierarchy of the Church, I pray that we lay people will wake up to the real needs before us. Only then can we carry out the mission of the Church: evangelization.

Reevangelizing the Baptized: Kerygma *vs.* Catechesis

In their analysis of the pastoral situation of Hispanics in the United States, the American bishops recognized the following: "It is more important than ever that Hispanics recover their identity and their Catholicism, be reevangelized with the Word of the Lord, and join together in a necessary union with all of the other Hispanics who have come from all over the world where Spanish is spoken" (NPPHM, no. 12).

Later in the same pastoral plan, they state: "The great majority of Hispanics feel left out of the Catholic Church. Evangelization has been limited to the Sunday Liturgy and a sacramental preparation which has not focused on the kind of profound conversion which brings together all the dimensions of the faith, spiritual growth, and justice to transform society" (NPPHM, no. 37).

What the bishops are saying is that the Church has taught Hispanics the catechism, made them Catholic, but has not given them the basic fundamentals. We have not presented them the good news; we have not led them to a personal relationship with Jesus. We have catechized them but left out the first step: the *kerygma,* which is the proclamation of the gospel.

Many Catholics do not make any distinction between *kerygma* and catechesis. Consequently, they carry out an enormous number of activities labeled "evangelization" which in fact are something else. If our evangelization of Hispanics is to be effective, we need to examine the fundamental differences between *kerygma* and catechesis—even though the dividing line is thin and difficult to discern.

It is possible to say that *every action of the Church is evangelization,* that there are different stages and levels of evangelization, and that this activity never terminates. Nonetheless, for clarity of understanding, I would like to define "evangelization" more narrowly within this particular context as the first stage, or the *kerygmatic* evangelization, or the first proclamation of the gospel.

Etymology: The Greek word *kerygma* comes from the verb *keryssein,* which means to proclaim or shout. The word "catechesis" stems from the Greek word *katechein,* which means to teach or retain.

Objectives: The general objective of *kerygma* is to be born again, to have life. The objective of catechesis is to grow in Christ, to have an abundant life.

Content: The content of *kerygma* is one person, Jesus, who died, rose from the dead, and was glorified. Christ is Savior, Lord, Messiah. The content of catechesis is the doctrine of the faith: morality, dogma, biblical study, etc.

Methodology: The methodology of *kerygma* consists of proclaiming Jesus as the good news. *Kerygma* addresses the will and is typically accompanied by personal testimony. The methodology of catechesis consists of teaching in an orderly and progressive manner. Catechesis addresses the understanding and is accompanied by the faith of the whole Church.

Agent: The agent in *kerygma* is the evangelist, a witness full of the Holy Spirit. The agent of catechesis is the person doing the catechizing, a teacher filled with the Holy Spirit.

Goals: The specific goals of *kerygma* concerning a person being evangelized are the following: an experience of the love of God and of one's own state of sin; a personal encounter with Jesus through faith and conversion; the acceptance of Jesus as personal Savior and Lord; the reception of the gift of the Holy Spirit; and integration into the Church community. The goals of catechesis are more limited: an encounter with the body of Christ which is the Church; growth in the holiness of the people of God.

Response: The response to *kerygma* is personal: *my* Savior, *my* Lord, *my* Messiah. The response to catechesis is communitarian and social: *our* Savior, *our* Lord, *our* Messiah.

Time frame: The time frame for *kerygma* is *now.* The time frame for catechism is sometime soon. Catechesis must be *preceded* by *kerygma.*

Hispanics Must Be Integrated into Parish Life

The *kerygma* consists of six basic topics: God loves us unconditionally; sin has ruptured this relationship; Jesus is the only hope of salvation from the consequence of sin, which is death; we need to have a personal experience of Jesus the Savior through faith and conversion; Jesus promises to send the Holy Spirit to enable us to live this new life in Christ; we can maintain this new life only by joining together with our brothers and sisters in Christ.

These six points of proclamation set the stage for effective catechesis and integration into the life of the Church, where Christians can best grow in their personal faith. Every instance of evangelization should focus on fleshing out these central ideas in a personal way, adapting the presentation to the situation. However, in no circumstances should the basic message of the *kerygma* be altered.

Many Hispanics live in poverty, especially in Central and South American countries and in the Caribbean islands. While the Church needs to be concerned with the material needs of mankind, we cannot neglect the primary importance of spiritual poverty. The "theology of liberation" as taught and practiced over the last generation has focused attention on how best to meet these needs. Clearly the Church must oppose unjust and oppressive social structures as part of her service to the poor, but our methods must be in accordance with the teachings of Jesus.

In evangelizing Hispanics, it is of singular importance that the process not stop with the acceptance of the gospel in the heart of the convert. That person's spiritual growth must be watched over and guided within the Church and particularly drawn into the life of the local parish.

However, there is a big difference between Latin American parishes and the typical American parish. The American bishops make this observation: "The Hispanic community recognizes that the parish is, historically and ecclesiastically, the basic organizational unit of the church in the United States and will continue being so" (NPPHM, no. 37). Recognizing the importance of the parish to the Hispanic, the bishops propose that it is necessary "to create an inviting atmosphere which among other things will recognize the culture of those on the fringe" (NPPHM, no. 45).

This proposal gives rise to obvious challenges. First, a parish that does not welcome Hispanics paves the way for competing gospels. Of particular danger are the various "sects" that cater to the Hispanic and lure away thousands of our brothers and sisters to sometimes misguided heresies. Second, a parish that does not have a pastoral plan to include Hispanics will fail in its evangelization efforts. The Hispanic will not be content to be a mere spectator of the show: he wants to be an integral part of it. Third, the parish that evangelizes Hispanics must make a special effort to know and understand these diverse cultures, since each one contains valuable elements and traditions which can enrich parish life.

If a parish truly wishes to evangelize and welcome Hispanics, it must change from being simply an administrative unit to being a highly pastoral parish. Hispanics cannot continue being just another number on our weekly envelopes and in our computers. Because of their deeply rooted cultural values, they must experience being welcomed and accepted as valued human beings, given pastoral opportunities to grow in holiness, and given the opportunity to share their talents in the life of the parish.

In order to achieve this goal, the American bishops propose a vehicle that fits well with the Hispanic cultural tendency: *communities.* "At the same time it is recognized that their conversion and the sense of being church is experienced best in small communities, within the parish, which are more personal and make the members feel more like participants" (NPPHM, no. 37).

They further recommend that our efforts of evangelization to Hispanics make a priority of these goals:

> Recognize, develop, accompany, and support the small ecclesiastical communities and other groups within the church (Cursillos de Cristiandad, Emmaus, Family Christian Movement, Renew, Charismatic Movement, prayer groups, etc.) which together with the bishop are effective instruments of evangelization for the Hispanic. These small ecclesiastical communities and other groups within the parish framework promote faith experiences and conversion, the missionary movement, interpersonal relations, fraternal love, prophetic questioning and pro-justice movements. These communities are a prophetic challenge to the renewal of the church and to the humanization of our society (NPPHM, no. 40).

The *National Pastoral Plan for the Hispanic Ministry* proposes as a next step the formation of Hispanics as agents of evangelization: "To prepare visitation teams to be proclaimers of the Word and of the Love of God and to form communities with the families visited and thus create a 'bridge' between the fringe members and the church" (NPPHM, no. 48). I see three primary implications from the bishops' proposal:

1. The Hispanic should not only visit other Hispanics on the fringe of the Church but should also evangelize them.
2. In order for this to take place, it is necessary to prepare or train Hispanics. The evangelist is not born but made. Evangelization schools are necessary in our Catholic world

since the majority of us have been trained to catechize but rarely trained to evangelize.

3. The Hispanic is the best agent to be the bridge to other Hispanics.

The American bishops call on the great Hispanic people of the United States to commit themselves to this missionary vision. We can accomplish the evangelization of the Hispanic world only with God's help and through the instrumentality of the Church.

❧

Jose (Pepe) Alonso is the Mission Director of Kerigma Asociacion Misionera Hispana, which promotes evangelization of Hispanics in the United States, especially through evangelization schools and rallies. For more information, contact:

> Kerigma Asociacion Misionera Hispana
> P.O. Box 557206
> Miami, FL 33255
> 305-661-0590

PART FIVE

Evangelizing as a Parish

18

THE STORY OF AN EVANGELIZING PARISH

Fr. Marc Montminy

Five years ago, Ste. Marie's in Manchester, New Hampshire, was a struggling inner-city, Franco-American parish: five hundred thousand dollars in debt and rising; funerals far outnumbering baptisms and marriages combined; and a church with a two-hundred-fifty-foot brick spire towering above a rectory, school, and convent, all looking tired and worn.

Today, Ste. Marie's shines as a humble beacon of renewal: a staff committed to evangelization and praying for a deeper release of the Holy Spirit; a Sunday renewal liturgy grown ten times over; more than five hundred attending ongoing Scripture study groups, Cursillo groups, contemplative prayer groups, and charismatic prayer groups; and a shrinking debt of just over one hundred thousand dollars with renovations happening in every corner.

How did all this come about?

God Knows How to Put All the Pieces in Place

Eleven years ago, I was appointed liaison to the Catholic charismatic renewal and cursillo movement in the diocese of Manchester. At first, my position seemed reasonably effective. Cursillo weekends were being held, people were being converted, and ultreya groups were flourishing. I would visit twenty to thirty prayer groups each year, hold leaders' conferences, and direct diocesan-wide events.

As time went on, however, I noticed that young adults and men were missing from the picture. Prayer moved me to seek new directions for renewal. I felt the need to expand renewal so that it could become all things to all people. Limiting ourselves to charismatic prayer groups had become an obstacle for many. New models were needed.

We began to offer retreats for men and women, couples' retreats, young-adult weekends, family weekends, men's and women's breakfasts, high-school retreats, days of renewal, and healing services. People started coming out of the woodwork. One hundred thirty men at a retreat, thirty couples at another, two hundred forty people at a family weekend.

Within five years, two young men were added to the staff as full-time associates. The name of our office was changed to Spiritual Renewal Services (SRS) to reflect a broader vision: to bring a deeper release of the Holy Spirit to as many people as possible in a variety of ways. The vision for renewal burned in my heart and in the hearts of those with whom I collaborated.

Eleven years later, the renewal office was financially sound, with over $58,000 being contributed by monthly donors and through scheduled events. Sixty healing services were being conducted a year, eight parish missions, over twenty weekend retreats, monthly days of renewal, and eight parish missions a year. With this model, we were able to reach clergy and laity in fifty-two parishes, well over a third of the total number in our area.

A center for spiritual direction was established during this period. A staff of ten religious and priests began doing part-time spiritual direction for well over 130 people. A young-adult ministry was established in the diocese to help people familiarize themselves with the teachings and traditions of the Church and give them a greater sense of self-worth as members of the body of Christ.

In the meantime, on June 15, 1988, much to my surprise, the bishop appointed me pastor of this large and struggling inner-city parish. Although I had been living in the rectory and doing part-time ministry at Ste. Marie's on a limited basis, I had never been able to implement the vision that I felt could change the face of this flock. My new assignment meant that I could bring that vision to the people of God to whom I had been sent as shepherd.

Having given you an overview of this scenario, I would like to communicate some important components that have helped this parish renewal to succeed.

Prayer

Jesus tells us to pray always. Becoming even more convinced of this as I began shepherding this large debt-ridden parish, my associate and I began praying at least three mornings a week for one hour, petitioning the Lord to confirm and strengthen the vision.

We were not alone. In 1987, I had opened an old convent on the property as a house of contemplative prayer. A sister who was hired to direct this ministry began to pray daily for the renewal of the parish. I then asked the existing staff to join me in prayer and pleaded with parish organizations, prayer groups, and individuals to join me in this most important task.

Within a matter of months, we could see the power of God moving within and beyond the parish. I remember one morning pleading with the Lord for an evangelist. The parish had no means of supporting such a person, but I knew in my heart that this was a missing link in our efforts at renewal. The following day, the parish received a check for twenty thousand dollars from an anonymous donor, who asked that this money be used for whatever purpose we deemed necessary.

On Christmas eve of that same year, the parish staff met at ten o'clock at night to pray before the crib that had been set up in the church. We came together to plead for a greater outpouring of the Holy Spirit on the entire parish community. Twelve hundred people attended midnight Mass that night, one being an elderly woman who donated seventeen thousand dollars to be applied to the parish debt. I began to see lives changing, people returning to the sacraments, and an empty church once again being filled with living stones.

I had started a young-adult prayer group in 1983 and also begged these young people to pray with me for the renewal of the entire parish community. At times, over one hundred of them would show up on Wednesday evenings to worship God and to intercede for a fresh outpouring of the Holy Spirit.

George Curran, who served as codirector of SRS, had envisioned households for single young adults. Four of these households existed in the parish when I became pastor. These twenty-five young people met with me and my associate pastor five days a week for daily prayer. The time: six o'clock in the morning. A widowed woman who felt called to a new lifestyle moved into the house of prayer and began to intercede throughout the night for a new Pentecost. The main priority of the staff and of parish members became prayer.

Vision and Mission

Without a vision, a people perish. Prayer should always lead us to a vision. When I became pastor of Ste. Marie, the pastoral council was doing what most councils do: they decided on the purchase of new boilers, concerned themselves with the debt, decided which roof to fix next, and were often burdened with issues that really belonged to the realm of other competent staff.

During my first month as pastor, I met with the pastoral council and asked them to pray and to dream with me. For the next five months, our meetings consisted of an hour of prayer and an hour of sharing our dreams of what we would like the parish to look like in the next five to ten years. Our deacon, who works for a large government firm, gave a workshop on vision and shared with the members of the council the importance of visionary people in the history of civilization.

With a solid foundation of prayer and vision, the pastoral council wrote a mission statement, in collaboration with every existing committee, society, and organization in the parish. A town meeting was held to ask parishioners to share their own hopes and dreams for this parish. One man became so excited about the prospects for growth that he donated three huge spotlights to illuminate our church building, which happens to stand on one of the highest points in the city. The lighted church can now be seen from the highway and from every bridge in the city.

Appropriately enough, our vision statement is based on Matthew 5:14, 16: "You are the light of the world. A city set on a hill cannot be hidden. . . . In the same way, your light must shine before all so that they may see goodness in your acts and give praise to your heavenly Father." Our mission statement reads as follows:

As we look back on the rich heritage of the community of Sainte Marie, we see a community that sought to bring dignity and hope to an immigrant people by being a beacon of light shining in the darkness.

Over one hundred years ago, Monsignor Hevey raised up a vision that gathered and empowered a community of French Canadian Catholic immigrants to establish a church, hospital, orphanage, schools, convents, cemetery, and credit union. These signs of their commitment stand tall among us today as a monument to them and a challenge to us.

We remember with joy and are grateful for all that God has done in and through the community of Ste. Marie. We are proud of our heritage and are rooted in it; and we are convinced that God continues to work among us today. He makes present his kingdom among us as we evangelize, celebrate the sacraments, and provide pastoral care and religious education. Through these means, God is forming us into one body, a community of disciples, gifted by his Spirit and sensitive to the needs of all who are near.

God's call to our community today remains the same: to proclaim Jesus Christ in word and deed! This is a call to renew our baptismal commitment where we pledge to live for God, and to be his light in the world.

We feel a particular urgency to live this call today in the midst of a disintegrating society marked by such manifestations of darkness as alienation, loneliness, and despair. Only the light of Christ can overcome this darkness; only his love can bring life out of death.

As we continue our journey with God, we will keep our eyes on the cross of Christ, our ears attentive to his word, and our hearts docile to his Spirit. In that same Spirit we offer what follows as means through which we will fulfill God's plan for our community today:

— By providing a eucharistic liturgy marked by living faith, prophetic preaching, and inspiring music, in the midst of a welcoming environment.

— By developing and nurturing small faith communities where individuals can experience spiritual and personal growth and form supportive relationships of brotherhood and sisterhood with others in the group.

— By offering diverse catechetical programs for community members of all ages which will lead them to a deepened understanding of our faith.

— By promoting social justice as a community through financial means and personal sacrifice and through community programs.

— By being an evangelizing community, who reaches out with the gospel to families, friends, and co-workers, and welcomes into our midst all those who seek Jesus: the Way, the Truth and the Life.

As an extension of our mission statement, every staff group, organization, and society was asked to write a statement with clear goals and objectives that would complement the greater parish mission. The results were quite helpful. Since the mission statement was written in 1988, the five objectives mentioned at the end of the statement have come to fruition. The parish now has four Sunday Eucharists, each appealing to a different group while maintaining sound liturgical principles.

As people enter the church, they are warmly welcomed by teams of greeters who make them feel at home and loved by God. Competent musicians who have been touched by God's presence lead the assembly in song. Lectors, extraordinary ministers, and servers abound. Communion under both species has become a part of weekday celebrations as well as on Sunday. Prayer teams are available after Sunday Masses to pray with people who may have a variety of needs. Over thirty men and women bring Communion to the homebound and to the sick at the local hospital as an extension of our celebration. Twelve men visit the state prison on a weekly basis, sharing the power of the Holy Spirit and imparting a greater hope in God.

Through the work of a full-time evangelist, small faith communities have been established. At present, over 180 parishioners meet weekly in homes to share and pray the Scriptures. Over 120 adults meet weekly at a charismatic prayer meeting. Over one hundred people meet in group reunions and a quarterly ultreya group.

Young families and young adults have formed support groups to meet the needs of a growing population who want to be connected more deeply to the church. Three years ago, we instituted an annual Family Day, featuring teachings, games, athletics, historical walks, dinner, dance, and a card game for the elderly — with over five hundred people in attendance.

"Experiencing New Life Seminars" are held twice a year to introduce more and more people to the power of the Holy Spirit. For those who may be at a different point in their spiritual lives, the parish has organized a variety of ministries which allow for diversity while at the same time creating a greater sense of unity.

As a result of our mission statement, the pastoral staff and pastoral council have felt a great urgency to introduce the parishioners to solid Catholic teaching. We have opened a parish bookstore, offered catechetical programs on basic Church teachings, and held parish seminars in apologetics featuring speakers such as Peter Kreeft, Scott and Kimberly Hahn, Francis Martin, Dr. Thomas Howard, Ann Shields, John Bertolucci, and Michael Scanlan.

At present, the parish is conducting, in conjunction with the RCIA process, a Sunday morning catechesis on fundamentals of Roman Catholicism. Family-based catechesis is on the horizon as we begin, this year, with Advent and Lenten days of renewal. An organization to foster the involvement of young men as shepherds of their families has been extremely successful. Over forty men now make up the "Men of Joseph", a group which fosters weekly family prayer time, Sunday Eucharist as a family, reconciliation twice a year, and attendance at a weekday Mass every three weeks.

In 1989, the parish hired a full-time youth minister, whose office presently coordinates all junior-high, high-school, and confirmation activities. Over twenty-six adult advisors share their talents. A total youth-ministry program has evolved in which our young people lead prayer services, journey to shrines, go to conferences in Steubenville, attend diocesan and parish retreats, participate in work camps, and work with the poor. Recently, through New Hampshire Catholic Charities, the youth office has initiated Rainbows for All God's Children, a support group for children and teenagers who have experienced the pain of separation, divorce, or death within their families.

The parish also tries to reach out to others in need. An active Vincentian community visits the sick and the poor, bringing them not only the good news but the basics needed for human existence: food, clothes, furnishings, and a listening ear.

Our vision is to be a parish community bringing the light of Christ to a people. It is not a matter of everyone's being at the same level of spiritual maturity or even of everyone's being faithful. It is a matter of growing into Christ, by all the tortuous routes that human beings take. We see ourselves as a people called to faith and love.

Developing a sense of community is at the center of our parish vision. We are not simply seekers after the truth; we have been called to share a life together, life with each other in Christ. Jesus did not die on the Cross or send his Spirit just so that we could be nice to each other or organize a lot of parish activities or commission groups who would take care of the needs of the poor. He died and rose and sent the Holy Spirit primarily so that we would know him, and through him love the Father with all our hearts and souls and minds—and love each other with the overflow of his love in us.

The best of parishes will never be without its problems: its addicted and rebellious youth, its broken marriages, its forgotten lonely, and people losing their first fervor of conversion. Part of our vision is that in the midst of the many people who are hurting will be parish members who are alive in the Spirit, mature, settled, and convinced of the deep love that God has for all of us. The vision is that everyone will receive the care and attention that they need.

Servant-Leadership

Leadership is a crucial component not only in establishing the vision but also in carrying it out. A pastor is called above all to be a servant, to wash the feet of his people. Rather than an exercise in futility, leadership is based on the belief that there is a greater power at work within us. A priest has received extraordinary strength to capture the vision and to live the vision which is the kingdom of God. Paul sums up these vast resources in his prayer for the budding community at Ephesus:

> May he enlighten your innermost vision that you may know the great hope to which he has called you, the wealth of his glorious heritage to be distributed among the members of the church, and the immeasurable scope of his power in us who believe. It is like the strength he showed in raising Christ from the dead and seating him at his right hand in heaven, high above every principality, power, virtue, domination, and name that can be given in this age or in the age to come (Eph 1:18–21).

The world in which we live is alien to that call. It often mocks, degrades, and confuses the role of a priest. Because of this, many priests have become confused in their role, many times living like bachelors rather than celibate priests. If a priest is confused about his role, imagine how the rest of the community feels.

A priest will not be renewed or empowered simply by taking more time off, delving more deeply into self, attending continuing education classes or convocations. A priest who strives for servant-leadership will discover his true identity only by entering into the heart of Christ, the Christ who prays to the Father, who admits his vulnerability, and who is empowered by the Spirit to bring forth the kingdom of God. If a priest is to be a servant-leader, he must embark on that same journey and teach others by example that the kingdom of God is in our midst.

Regardless of the number of talented people who may be available, if a pastor is not present to his people as one who washes feet, a parish cannot grow. It has been my experience over many years of diocesan work that priestly leadership is vital for the spiritual and physical renewal of any parish community.

A pastor in servant-leadership must believe in his staff, affirm them, and be willing to trust in their gifts. He must work closely with his pastoral council, challenging them to help him in carrying out the vision that God has given the parish. He must shepherd his extended staff: the maintenance staff, the secretaries, the teachers in the school, the housekeeping staff, the volunteers. He must challenge them to spiritual growth and be with them in their pain and in their joy. A pastor, then, is called to *ignite* the hearts and souls of the people placed in his care.

Parish Spirituality

Spirituality is a particular style or method of following Christ. It has elements and a pattern to help people develop a deeper life in the Spirit. For centuries many thought the only way to holiness lay in monastic life or in religious orders, which often adapted monastic spirituality. The word is out: Jesus wants everyone to be holy. Spiritual growth is for everyone, which means that the ordinariness of everyday life is meant to be caught up in the vision of Jesus and the power of the Holy Spirit. For that to happen, each one of us must hear the good news and respond.

But growing into the magnificent people God created us to be is more or less chancy and filled with obstacles and dangers. The parable of the farmer and the seed in Luke 8:5–8 tells us that sometimes the word reaches us when we are like rock or at the side of the road. Most of the time, we fail to recognize the weeds and thorns in ourselves that can choke the life within us.

From time to time, God brings forth men and women who are outstanding in holiness, who not only yield a hundredfold but often help others avoid dangers and cultivate their own hearts to yield the fruit of the Spirit. Holiness is all around us. One of the joys of shepherding a parish is discovering the many saints around us and learning how to tap into the richness of their spirituality.

Twice a year, we have an evening for young married couples. Usually thirty to forty couples will come to hear a husband and wife who have been together a lot longer witness the pains and the joys of married life. On one occasion, a couple who had been married sixty-five years shared how they had never missed their evening prayer with the exception of a few trips that required the husband to leave town. The young couples were moved and began asking them more about prayer.

On another occasion, a couple who had been married for twenty-five years shared their regret at having used birth control as a means of avoiding pregnancy. To my great amazement, the younger couples began asking questions and relating their own discomfort at often taking on the values of the world rather than the values of the kingdom.

Parish spirituality means being open and alive to the present moment. The adult converts who assemble around the font at the Easter vigil are immersed in the baptismal waters of new life. The community gathers at the cemetery to pray with a young couple who recently lost their three-month-old baby. A group of women bake for the families who mourn their loved ones and then serve them after every funeral liturgy. This is all an integral part of parish spirituality.

The renewed parish seeks to help people discover God in all the ordinary events of daily life. We come together to celebrate our life in Christ at Sunday Eucharist—with all the messiness that such a communal gathering entails: the families walking in late, the babies crying during the homily, the altar servers who fight in the sanctuary, and the lector who arrives one minute before Mass. Spirituality means learning how to follow Christ in the midst of the very ordinary turbulence of human life.

A Deeper Release of the Holy Spirit

Another important element of parish renewal has been the development of the Catholic understanding of the baptism in the Holy Spirit. At times, charismatics have unnecessarily alienated themselves from the mainstream of parish life by defining this experience too narrowly. For example, many deeply spiritual priests, bishops, and laity have not been considered "Spirit-filled" if they have not completed a Life in the Spirit seminar and spoken in tongues.

Unfortunately, this narrow view can quickly divide noncharismatics from those charismatics who believe they alone possess the fullness of the Holy Spirit. Power struggles often follow, with charismatics being pushed to the fringe.

I have come to believe that baptism in the Holy Spirit is a process of being totally immersed in the life of Christ. Our parish currently has three charismatic prayer groups: one adult group made up of about 130 people; a young-adult prayer group consisting of about fifty to sixty young adults; and a French-speaking prayer group with twenty adults. The overall number of charismatics is small when compared to the sixteen hundred registered families, who total about forty-five hundred people.

Charismatic prayer groups cannot be clubs for the "spiritually mature". They must be a part of God's great plan for his Church. Their role is not to safeguard the spiritual gifts or to make the parish charismatic but to bring as many people as possible to a deeper love of Christ through the baptism of the Holy Spirit. Theirs is only a training ground.

It is my belief that there are many other ways within the parish community by which people can experience a deeper release of the Holy Spirit. Ste. Marie's offers Experiencing New Life seminars three times a year. They usually take place on a weekend and are conducted by the Office of Evangelization. Hundreds have gone through these seminars and have been deeply blessed and touched by the power of God.

Another model we have used for seven years is a novena to the Holy Spirit. For nine evenings, we invite parishioners to attend a prayer service, during which lay persons witness to their lives in the Holy Spirit. Each novena is concluded by a Pentecost celebration, attended by well over one thousand people. We have seen noticeable fruit from novenas.

Praying for the release of the Holy Spirit has become commonplace in our liturgical assembly. Often parishioners are invited to be prayed with after Sunday liturgy. The Prayer of the Faithful often includes petitions asking for a greater release of the Spirit.

At Sunday liturgies the priest reminds the parishioners who are coming forward to receive the Body and Blood of Christ of their call to ongoing conversion: to accept Jesus Christ as Lord and Savior of their whole lives, and to seek greater wisdom, power, healing, and strength through the power of the Holy Spirit.

The priest or deacon must use every opportunity to evangelize and catechize, whether it be at the time of baptism, a small group meeting, marriage preparation, or homily. Parish renewal comes about only through hard work, committed prayer, and belief in a power greater than one's own. I hope our experience at Ste. Marie's proves helpful in your own efforts toward renewal. These observations are simply a feeble attempt to put on paper what I have come to believe so deeply in my heart, that parish life is not only necessary but more than ever vital for the people of our generation.

19

DOING EVANGELIZATION AS A PARISH

David Thorp

Becoming an evangelical parish does not equate with doing evangelical activities. In fact, it is possible to have a committed core of parishioners who are busily engaged in a variety of evangelical efforts—home visitation, leading Bible studies, welcoming newcomers—and yet not have an evangelical parish.

Herein lies the great temptation and, in the long run, the death of evangelization: to segregate evangelical activities and those involved in them. Other members of the parish praise their efforts by exclaiming, "We are grateful for all that you're doing! We are so fortunate that you are such good evangelizers." Translation: "Boy are we glad that *you* are doing the evangelizing, because that means we're off the hook!"

If evangelization is just another "what", just another activity that we do, and not the "how" and "why" in every dimension of our corporate life, then a parish can easily remain essentially unchanged. Having parishioners involved as evangelizers is vital, but even more important is the need to articulate and implement a vision for the evangelizing parish.

Soon after assuming my role as director of the Office for Evangelization for the Archdiocese of Boston, I had a conversation with the head of the Evangelistic Association of New England. When I told him that I felt a little daunted by the work ahead of me, he said, "I envy your position. You Catholics have so many things in place: parishes in every neighborhood or town, schools, social service agencies, hospitals. . . . If you could ever mobilize those structures with an evangelical vision, it would be incredible."

To use my words, "If the people within these structures could catch a vision for evangelization that they lived out in all their activities, it would be incredible." How can we cultivate a vision for evangelization? And how can we begin to live out this vision in a parish setting?

Why Evangelize?

An Anglican named Dr. David Barrett conducted a research project for the Southern Baptist Mission Board. In the course of his research, he discovered more than *seven hundred* definitions of the word "evangelization" in print. Some were highly theological, others more colloquial. Many overlapped, while some seemed contradictory. One conclusion I drew from Dr. Barrett's study is that we need to look at evangelization from a variety of angles so that we can catch (or, more properly, be caught up by) the widest possible understanding of the Lord's call to us as his disciples.

Vision is the starting point for action. I may not be able to articulate the vision all the time, but unless I am grasped by it—if only in a "I-can-feel-it-in-my-guts" way—then I probably will not be involved in action. But, once I have been grasped, there is no stopping me.

Before I picture evangelization with a wide-angle lens, I would like to challenge you to ask yourself two questions: *Why do I evangelize? Why do I see evangelization as important to my life and to the life of my parish?* Your answers will bear some similarity to those of others but will also be stamped with your unique relationship with the Lord Jesus Christ and with your own set of human relationships.

Here are a few general reasons why we evangelize. We do so first of all because Jesus commanded us to. He gave the Church, on the day of Ascension, "the unending task of evangelizing as a restless power, to stir and to stimulate all its actions until all nations have heard his good news and until every person has become his disciple" (Mt 28:18–20).[1]

Second, we evangelize because we have become convinced that what we have to share is *good* news—indeed, the *best*. We echo the words of Peter when many disciples of Jesus no longer followed him: "Lord, to whom else shall we go? You have the words of eternal life; and we have believed, and have come to know, that you are the Holy One of God" (Jn 6:8–9). We share the gospel with others because salvation is offered to every person in Jesus Christ, because in him people can be brought enlightenment and be lifted from error, because he bears a unique message.[2]

Third, we evangelize because we are surrounded by people who are hungering, thirsting, and literally dying for the good news. While they may not express their need in such direct fashion, many are undoubtedly wondering to themselves: *Is anyone there? Does anyone care? Is there hope? Is there any sense and meaning to life? Is life possible?* When we have the answer for their questions, to withhold the Way, the Truth, and the Life is to violate the rights of others and to place ourselves in peril, as Pope Paul VI points out so well in *Evangelii Nuntiandi* (no. 80).

Fourth, we evangelize because of love for others. "Because we have experienced the love of Christ, we want to share it. The gifts God has given to us are not gifts for ourselves. . . . Our faith makes our hearts abound with a love-filled desire to bring all people to Jesus' gospel and to the table of the Eucharist."[3]

Viewing Evangelization with a Wide-Angle Lens

Evangelization is growth up and out: *up* because it attempts to help those who are already Christians to make progress in the spiritual life; *out* because the Church must reach beyond her

---

[1] *Go and Make Disciples: A National Plan and Strategy for Catholic Evangelization in the United States* (Washington, D.C.: USCC Office for Publishing and Promotion Services, 1993), p. 4, col. 2.

[2] Ibid., p. 5, col. 1.

[3] Ibid., p. 5, col. 2.

existing membership and seek to add members to the body of Christ. Those who have begun with the Lord need to renew their life in him in an ongoing way lest they grow stale. In the Christian life, there is always *more*. Having experienced conversion once, we must be converted continually lest we become just "tired old believers".[4]

However, evangelization is not just for the sake of renewing the Church or adding muscle to her own life. We seek renewal so that the Church can grow out. A congregation of one hundred should be praying about and planning ways of adding twenty-five new members; a parish with five hundred families should be looking for ways of having six hundred. While we are not the lords of the harvest and cannot control the results, we can set our sights on steady growth. We do so not merely to add to our numbers and so become *bigger;* we do so in obedience to God, and so that he may be honored more fully by the people for whom Jesus Christ died and rose.

When we think in terms of those whom the Church is trying to reach, evangelization means *inspiration, invitation,* and *perspiration.* The parish is trying to *inspire* its active Catholics to live fully the life into which they have been grafted through the confession of faith and their baptism. Many may be "simmering" in the Christian life, not allowing themselves to be grasped fully by the power of the word and Spirit, settling for less than the Lord offers. There needs to be a "fanning into flame" of the Holy Spirit in their lives.

The parish is also trying to reach out to inactive members, who for many different reasons no longer participate in the congregation's life of worship, teaching, and service. Many adults send their children for religious instruction even though neither they nor their children worship with any regularity. We need to find ways of establishing contact with these people so that we can *invite* them into full life with the community of faith. In reaching out, we need to listen to their stories: how they neglected their life of

[4] Benedict Groeschel, "On-going Conversion: The Challenge and the Chore", *New Catholic World* 229, no. 1370 (March/April 1986): 57–60.

faith, how they were neglected by the community, how they walked away, and how some believe they were driven away.

Then, too, the parish is trying to reach the increasing number of men and women who have no church community to call their own, who have no religious tradition, or who profess non-Christian religions. Such outreach will cause us to *perspire.* If we are not willing to dedicate ourselves to the "hard work" of being faithful over a long period of time, even when we see little fruit, we will have a short life span as individual evangelizers or as an evangelizing community. One lay evangelizer sums it up this way: "If you want to evangelize, throw away your watch and stop counting heads."

Helping Others to See with an Evangelical Lens

To quote a pastoral worker who attended a meeting about evangelization: "I hate that word." Many in our pews are put off or confused about evangelization. While we should not give up the word, we can talk about evangelizing activity without ever using it. With this in mind, how can we point out ways in which evangelization is occurring and clearly name an activity as evangelistic?

One way to draw attention to this essential ministry is through the weekly parish bulletin. A number of brief pamphlets that describe evangelization can be used as inserts.[5] Another way is to plant seeds in people's minds through a brief column in the weekly bulletin, something like "Sharing Your Faith" or "Reaching out to Those Around You". One parish has developed twenty-six brief statements about evangelization. Along with notices about specific outreach activities, a different statement appears in each week's bulletin. Evangelization can become part of the weekly public prayer of the congregation. Have people begin to pray

[5] Among the brochures that can be recommended are: "Sharing Our Catholic Faith: How We Can . . . " (Franciscan Communications); "Catholic Evangelization", a series of five pamphlets (Paulist National Catholic Evangelization Association); "Twenty Little Thoughts about Evangelization", an article by Fr. Tom Forrest, C.Ss.R., which appeared in *New Evangelization 2000.* (Evangelization 2000 grants permission for the reprinting of articles.)

specifically for individuals with whom they are in regular contact, that the Lord will bring them to a conversion of mind and heart.

Such methods raise people's consciousness about evangelization, reminding them that the life they have received is meant to be shared freely and generously with others. Challenge the worshipping congregation to look for opportunities to invite others to hear the gospel and be touched by the grace of God. Most people will not say on their own initiative, "This is a great parish. I think I'll tell others about it and look for ways to help them meet the Lord here as I have." They need to keep hearing this call and receive hints on how to talk to others about the Lord and his Church.

A catalyst for parish action. In my family it is everyone's responsibility to make sure that the house stays clean. But we all know what happens when something is everyone's job: no one does it because we are all waiting for the "other guy" to do it. However, with the right catalyst (almost always my wife or me), everyone gets to work.

Evangelization is the privilege and the duty of every Christian. But without a catalyst to help move a parish to action—specifically to pray and think about evangelization, to plan for evangelization, to recruit evangelizers, to help carry out special projects, to develop an evangelical attitude in every ministry—very little evangelization will be sustained in the life of the whole parish.

A parish evangelization committee can be the kind of catalyst that helps move vision into specific actions. Recruit basically friendly people with these characteristics: an interest in parish renewal and growth; a personal conviction about the gospel message (you cannot share what you do not have); a conviction that they have something of great value to share with others; a desire to share faith; a conviction that life in Christ as a parish member will enrich and bless others; a concern about inactive or alienated Catholics and the unchurched.

Print notices in the weekly bulletin about the formation of an evangelization committee and extend a broad invitation to become part of the committee. Also be sure to issue a personal invitation (a phone call, a hand-written letter, a face-to-face conversation) to those who have the interest and the gifts from God in this area. Such contacts themselves provide wonderful opportunities for evangelism: to affirm people in their gifts, to call forth these gifts, to establish and deepen a relationship with an individual.

Thinking Smart: Developing a Plan That Works

A plan is a guide that includes the goals and objectives of a parish, an assessment of current and future conditions, and specific strategies and tactics for reaching those goals. A plan is a blueprint of how we can get from where we are today to where God wants us to be in the future. Some people think that planning and walking in the Spirit are diametrically opposed. They argue, "We want to be open to the movement of the Spirit in all that we do. We don't want to rely on merely human wisdom to dictate our actions."

People filled with the power of the Holy Spirit sometimes want to explode with that power. Explosions certainly create a sensation, but after the big bang the power may be all spent. What if we allowed the power to be channeled through a plan that allowed for a sustained—yet no less powerful—burn? Having a plan is akin to taking fire and placing it in a fireplace. The fire's glow and warmth, contained in the right place, are not diminished but are actually increased.

A plan identifies and clarifies the problems that can prevent you from growing and the methods that can be used to produce growth. Until we clearly understand our situation, we cannot respond to problems in an intelligent and creative way or take advantage of available opportunities. A plan transforms the dream into reality; a plan gives "legs" to the vision. You can inspire people to great things, but unless you give them the tools to implement that vision, nothing will be done.

A plan helps to prioritize the ministry objectives. Formulating a plan means that we are willing to say: Here are the strengths, the gifts we have received from the Lord; here are our weaknesses, the areas in which God has much work to do with us; these are the opportunities the Lord has given us to witness to and share the gospel; these are our present resources; these are the resources we need in order to accomplish God's plan for us; here is what we can do and cannot do at this time; here is what we must and must not do at this time.

Of course, if we had unlimited resources and unlimited time, planning would be unnecessary. Most of us, however, have obvious limits. We need to maximize the resources we do have, harnessing them for the service of the Lord and his kingdom. Planning helps us to reduce any waste of precious gifts: the grace God offers us; the talents he has placed in our care; the opportunities he has given to us; the goodwill and the assets of others who want to join us in reaching out to others.

Planning establishes responsibility and accountability. We take time to identify people who will help accomplish the plan, and we call them to move ahead in dynamic and creative ways. Giving them specific responsibilities also means that they can be made accountable.

How Can We Develop an Effective Evangelistic Strategy?

Developing an evangelistic strategy involves responding to the question: *What does God want us to do now?* Let's examine each of the four main elements of this question: *God, us, to do,* and *now.*

God. Since the call to evangelize comes from God, we need continually to seek his plan for outreach in a particular parish. The question is not so much "What do *we* want to do?" as it is "What does *God* want us to do?" In responding to God's call to us, we need to discern *carefully* what God is already doing to call individuals to himself. Like Jesus, we want to see and hear what the Father is doing and then join in that work (Jn 5:19–30). We need to move *confidently,* out of an awareness that God anoints with his grace all whom he appoints to a task.

Since God desires that others know the good news through our efforts, he will grace us abundantly to share it with others. We need to avoid becoming so task-oriented that we neglect praying together and sharing with one another the good things God has done for us.

Us. Since God is calling *us,* we need to know who we are, how we have been gifted, what God has established in the parish at this time. Each person and parish is different. Congregations vary in size, age, history, finances, resources, leadership. Because of these differences, no two parishes have exactly the same experience of church life.

In order to come to a clearer understanding of our current parish situation, we need to focus on the positive elements in our shared life. These strengths form the foundation from which we reach out; these are the resources which God will use to bring others into a deeper relationship with himself and his people. God is not looking for *perfect* parishes and parishioners; none is to be found. He is looking for *willing* parishes and parishioners. If we waited until we were perfect, we would never even begin to evangelize. God simply asks us to place who we are and what we have been given at his disposal.

This aspect of the planning process need not be overwhelming. Much of this information is readily available or can be obtained with a minimum of research or a few "interviews" with staff members. You will be amazed to discover how many parishioners— even those who are serving on an evangelization commission or otherwise committed to sharing the good news—remain unaware of the nature of the parish and what resources are available.

Understanding *us* could mean many things: taking a look at existing programs or resources; taking a look at parish priorities, examining how we make use of our time and money, or how we employ our key people and our energies; taking a look at the parish's overall schedule year in terms of busy times, times with less activity, or annual events.

Specific questions can also be directed toward resources and possible avenues for evangelism. For example, what spiritual gifts are found within our parish, and how can they be used for evangelization? What existing structures within the parish can be utilized as entry points into the life of the parish? What vehicles do we have for reaching out to inactive and alienated Catholics and to those who are without any church family to call their own? What natural contacts exist by virtue of kinship, occupation, and ethnic background that might provide bridges for sharing the gospel and the life of the community with those outside of our parish?

The New Testament describes a common way of bringing people into the kingdom, one that could be called *oikos evangelization*. *Oikos* is the Greek word for "household". When one member of the family hears and responds to the good news, often the whole family is brought into the faith community. If we view this concept in a more expanded way, we could consider others with whom we share our lives: those who live on my street or in my neighborhood; those with whom I work; those in my extended family; those who enjoy the same things I enjoy.

We could also take a closer look at the area the parish serves. How large is it geographically? Does it encompass neighborhoods, defined areas, or subsections? Are there higher or lower concentrations of housing? Do we have a way to touch all parts of the parish? Realistically, what areas are possible to reach or more easily reached than others?

What is the total number of people living within the geographical boundaries of our parish? Has there been any notable change in the population: rapid influx, steady growth, or decline? Has there been any significant new construction of single-family homes, apartments, or condominiums?

What are the characteristics of the population in terms of ethnic groups, race, religious heritage, national origin, age? How has this changed over the past five, ten, fifteen or more years? How does the registered Catholic population compare to the general population: Is it the same or very different? What points of commonality can be identified? How do those who actively participate in the parish compare with those who are simply registered members?

What are the socioeconomic characteristics of the population: How are people employed, what is the employment level, what is the extent of formal education? What churches and synagogues exist within the area? Who have they reached? How? Why? What other evangelizing efforts are being made?

To do. When trying to discern where we should begin, there are a number of questions to consider. Our answers should be based on experience, either past or present. We cannot plan adequately if we remain within cloistered walls, behind rectory doors, within the church's meeting rooms. We will fail to help people see the importance of the gospel for their lives unless our planning is based on reality.

Of all the groups in our parish, which ones can we reach at this time? No one church can reach every group within a city or town. Certain churches are better equipped to touch some people than others. Keep this simple principle in mind: when launching a new outreach venture, target your efforts to those whose backgrounds are most similar to your own. Match up the parish profile and the community profile. It is easiest to reach those with whom you have the most points of contact.

Perhaps a parish could begin with a concentrated outreach to Catholics who are baptized but not actively participating in the life of the faith community. Perhaps an ethnic or racial link between parish members and the unchurched who live in the area may make this kind of outreach possible. Try to understand the level of resistance or receptivity of these groups to the gospel message. Why are Catholics separated from the parish community? How could they be invited to reconsider the message and life of the Church?

Since the good news is not just abstract doctrine but a real response to real people, it would be good to know more about their felt needs, concerns, and aspirations. What are the pressure points in this group, and how does Christianity address them?

Their needs may be *physical* (food, clothing, housing), *psychological* (to be loved, accepted, supported, welcomed), *spiritual* (hope, mercy, forgiveness, understanding Christianity or the Church), or *social* (a place to belong or gather). What hopes and desires motivate this group, and how does Christianity fulfill or bring about the realization of that dream? How can we capture their attention?

In thinking about how we can communicate effectively with our target group, we may want to examine the dominant social dynamics and structures. In what sorts of groups do people tend to gather? Is the group we are trying to contact best reached by large meetings (parish missions, feast-day celebrations, healing services, celebrations of popular piety), through small groups (prayer groups, discussion or adult-education studies, neighborhood Bible studies), or one-to-one conversations?

What methods of communication would be the most effective? Is this group apt to be reached by print (mail, posters, newspaper, bulletins, brochures), by electronic media (radio, TV), or by personal contact (telephone, face-to-face)? Do people react more favorably to informal or casual invitations or to more formal contacts? What has worked in the past as we sought to make our message and our programs known to others?

Now. The best goals, objectives, and action steps are those that are SMART: *Specific, Measurable, Achievable, Reviewable,* and *Time-defined.* *Specific* means that we know who is going to be doing what, and when they are going to do it. *Measurable* means that we have an idea of what we are trying to accomplish in some way that can be quantified, e.g., we are going to visit fifty homes in the Green Street area.

Achievable means that we do not seek to reach beyond our resources—leaving room of course for God to do wondrous things with those resources and our willingness to reach out to others. "Our parish will reach the world for Christ" is not an achievable goal. *Reviewable* means that we are able to analyze and learn from our outreach so that we can expand our efforts.

Time-defined means that our plan has a beginning and an end. If not, we may never get started at all. Having an end does not mean we will be finished with evangelization at some point but that we are able to finish one particular project and then move on to the next activity as God directs.

Every parish is called to be an evangelical parish. However, this does not happen overnight or even over a few months. Your evangelical parish will not be a carbon copy of the one in the next town. God wants to use every parish to reach all its people—and beyond. If we are *willing* to be messengers of the good news, God will send us to those who hunger and thirst for the Word of Life. If we are purposeful and deliberate without being in a rush, if we are zealous without being frantic, our parish can be transformed into an evangelical parish.

20

TRANSFORMING THE PARISH INTO
AN EVANGELIZING COMMUNITY

Ernesto Elizondo

The parish is the fundamental structure for the pastoral ministry of the Church and one of the primary places where people can learn and embrace the Christian faith. We urgently need to rediscover the importance of evangelizing at the parish level.

The pope's call to a new evangelization urges each congregation to seek for new ways to *be* the church and to fulfill the mission of the Church in its entirety. When we meditate on the Church's mission, we are focusing on the mission of the people of God, *our* mission. The Church is not only the bishops or the priests, nor is she the building in which we meet. The Church is the people of God, the body of Christ, the mystery and sacrament of communion, communion in the Holy Spirit.

We know that there is but one mission, *the mission of Jesus Christ* to bring the good news to all people. We are ambassadors of the mission that Jesus himself left us. Ambassadors do not go to other countries to fulfill their own personal agenda. Every ambassador represents a particular government. As ambassadors of Christ, we are called to continue his mission.

Jesus is our example. He did not weigh all the options and personally choose what to say or do. His attitude was clearly one of submission to his heavenly Father: "My food is to do the will of the one who sent me" (Jn 4:34); "I always do what pleases my Father" (Jn 8:29). Jesus, in turn, says to his disciples, "As my Father has sent me, I send you, go" (Jn 20:21). Jesus Christ has left us a specific mission to fulfill. While we can distinguish within this single mission a diversity of ministries, we do not have the right to choose our own mission or adjust it to suit ourselves.

We as the people of God also need to view our call in an *integral* manner. We cannot fragmentize the mission and pick and choose the part that we like the best. We are called to the *whole* mission of Christ. The Holy Spirit has been given to empower us to continue that mission.

We need to foster the vision of transforming each parish into an *evangelizing community* and all of our parishes into a *communion of communities,* or, as Pope John Paul II described it, a *"family of families".*

What Is Evangelization?

Many Catholics lack a clear and precise understanding of what *evangelization* means. Without this clarity, we cannot respond fully to the pope's exhortation. We can distinguish four aspects of evangelization which are meant to follow one after another:

1. *Kerygma:* The first missionary announcement proclaims the good news of salvation as a free gift through the death and Resurrection of Jesus Christ. "This has as its purpose the arousing of the beginnings of faith so that men will adhere to the word of God" (*General Catechetical Directory,* no. 17).
2. *Ministry of the Word:* Besides the *kerygma,* this includes catechesis, liturgical homilies, and theology.
3. *Development of the Church's ministries:* The mission of the church manifests itself in four dimensions of ministry: ministry of the word, ministry of communion (i.e., building community), liturgical ministry, and social action.
4. *Social transformation:* This means to build and establish the kingdom of God by transforming the unfair structures of society by the power of the Holy Spirit.

When evangelizing, we need to provide each of these elements and in this order. They are not alternative choices. The Church's mission of evangelization needs to be accomplished in its entirety. It is not enough to provide sacraments, not enough to catechize children, not enough to build small communities, not enough to engage in social transformation. All of these are important and necessary, but all are based on the foundation of the *kerygma.*

The primary goal of evangelization is to bring the good news, the *kerygma,* to others at every opportunity. It is not a matter of waiting for the people to come to the parish but of going out in search of those who have left the Church or of those who have no church.

Sacred Scripture challenges each and every one of us: "How can they hear without someone to preach? And how can people preach unless they are sent? As it is written, 'How beautiful are the feet of those who bring the good news!'" (Rom 10:14–15). It is important that all parishioners actively go out and share their faith, motivated and empowered by the Holy Spirit.

To whom are we going to bring the good news? Jesus said, "Go into the whole world and proclaim the gospel to every creature" (Mk 16:15). Within the scope of each individual parish, the "whole world" especially includes every person within the geographical boundaries of that parish. An evangelizing community should view these people as the primary recipients of their gospel message.

Go to All!

The concept of *integral evangelization* means, first of all, that we need to bring the good news to *all* people. We must begin by going out to all Catholics within the parish boundaries and inviting them to join the parish family. Statistics tell us that out of the approximately sixty million Catholics within the United States, more than half miss Sunday Mass. That means we need to bring back to the Church those thirty million or more Catholics who do not regularly participate in the parish community.

Jesus tells us in the parable of the Good Shepherd that when one sheep was lost, the Good Shepherd left the ninety-nine and went in search of the one who was lost. When he found that sheep, he healed it and brought it back to the flock. Within our parishes, it is often the other way around. In some parishes, time is spent with one sheep, caring for it and pampering it while the ninety-nine are lost. Each one of us is called to go out in search for each and every lost sheep.

In the majority of our parishes, people come to church when they choose to and when they can. Many come with the idea of receiving a "service" and experience the parish as a "religious service station" at which they can quickly refill their spiritual gas tanks. They want to attend a parish where they can receive the best and fastest service: where the homily is shortest; where requirements for baptism are minimal; where the best choir sings.

In a word, many parishioners lack any sense of commitment and belonging. Many people attend the parish with the same mentality that can be found at a country club where people pay a fee to receive certain benefits of membership. In our efforts to promote evangelization, we must bring Catholics to an awareness of the necessity for personal commitment to the parish.

Give Them All!

People will ask, "What does the parish offer me if I return to the Catholic Church?" We need to *give them all,* every dimension of the mission of the Church. When we were baptized as children, we became members of Christ in his roles as Prophet, Priest, and King. This fact tells us that the three main dimensions of the Church's mission are the *prophetic* ministry, the *priestly* ministry, and the *kingly* ministry. Every Catholic needs to be spiritually nourished through all of these ministries.

The prophetic ministry. Jesus the Prophet spoke in the name of his Father. The prophetic ministry of Jesus includes *kerygma* (announcing the good news of salvation), a systematic and progressive catechesis, homilies, and theology.

The priestly ministry. Jesus the Priest practices his priestly ministry primarily through the liturgy and the sacraments. Jesus offered sacrifices to the Father, the ultimate sacrifice being his life. The sacraments and every other aspect of our worship celebrations define this dimension of the Church's mission.

Unfortunately, the majority of our parishes are primarily liturgical and sacramental parishes. Their strength lies in providing this liturgical dimension of the total mission of the Catholic Church, but to a certain extent they neglect the other dimensions. Clearly the sacraments are vital and a necessary treasure for us as Catholics. The Eucharist alone is the summit and source of the Christian's life. However, we also need to emphasize the importance of the other dimensions of the mission of the Church.

The kingly ministry. Jesus the Good Shepherd also exercises part of his *kingly* ministry, when we gather as a parish community, by uniting and congregating his sheep. Community, or *koinonia* in Greek, does not automatically and immediately come into existence. Of paramount importance in our mission as followers of Christ is our duty to *build* community, day by day, day in and day out.

The fact that we attend Mass at the same parish and hold hands to pray the Our Father does not mean that we are community. There needs to be a sharing of our lives on a deep level with our brothers and sisters in Christ. The experience of the first Christian communities as recorded in the New Testament offers a clear example.

Jesus also exercises his kingly ministry through *social action, diakonia* in Greek. As Christians, we build a kingdom of justice and peace through serving the needs of others. This is clearly a desire within the heart of Jesus, as exemplified in his washing the apostles' feet at the Last Supper. Jesus came to serve, not to be served.

Through social action, a genuine liberation can come into being, with communities living new models of life, where a new world is built in fraternal solidarity. We as Catholics need to state and demonstrate a clear preferential option for the poor. We need to work toward the elimination of need, oppression, and exploitation. This can be accomplished only by fostering gospel values within our society.

Involving All

For centuries, we have believed that priests and religious were the only ones responsible for fulfilling the mission of the Church. However, Pope John Paul II's call to a new evangelization has reminded us that sharing the good news is the mission of the whole Church. We need to be guided and led by the Church's pastoral leadership, but every member of the Church needs to participate actively. Our mission, as the people of God and the body of Christ, is to evangelize.

Each parishioner has gifts and charisms for the building of the kingdom of God. Some are called to be evangelizers, some prophets, some pastors, some teachers (Eph 4:11). What is important is that each of us discern and actively use these gifts. It is important that we give not only our talents but also a tithe of our money and time toward our primary mission of evangelization. If you spend forty hours at your job, a tithe or one-tenth of that time would mean committing a minimum of four hours a week to extend the kingdom of God or perhaps one week per year to participate in an evangelization outreach effort.

We also need to help other members of the parish become more aware of the importance of our mission. We are called to be apostles of Christ not because of a shortage of priests and religious. Even if we enjoyed an abundance of priests and religious, the laity would need to participate actively in the mission of the Church. Evangelization is both a duty and a privilege.

Each and every one who has been evangelized is also called to become involved in the mission of the Church. Pope Paul VI said, "Finally, the person who has been evangelized goes on to evangelize others. Here lies the test of truth, the touchstone of evangelization: it is unthinkable that a person should accept the Word and give himself to the kingdom without becoming a person who bears witness to it and proclaims it in his turn" (EN, no. 24).

Transforming the Parish

In order to fulfill the mission of the Church in its totality, parishes need a well-organized and systematic plan. Below is the Systematic Integral New Evangelization (SINE) pastoral process, which was initiated by Fr. Alfonso Navarro, M.Sp.S.C. It is now being implemented in sixteen countries around the world. In the United States, over ninety parishes in seventeen different dioceses are using this plan at the current time, and over twelve hundred small communities have been formed as a response to the challenge of transforming our parishes into evangelizing communities.

This pastoral plan is not designed for a particular type of parish—rural or urban, rich or poor—or for a particular country or culture or language. Since it presents the essential mission of the Church, this plan can be implemented by any parish in any continent or country.

This pastoral plan begins with the experience of a kerygmatic retreat for people who are ready to listen and respond to Jesus' invitation to salvation and new life in him. At the end of the retreat, all are called to continue in their spiritual growth both as *disciples* and as *apostles.*

Parishioners choose to live as *disciples* of Christ by participating in small Christian communities and by receiving a systematic catechesis that they apply to their lives. The fruit they experience from encountering Christ in these ways is a renewed sacramental life.

The call to be *apostles* is also emphasized. Those who continue in their small communities are invited to discover their gifts and to use them within the evangelizing parish. They are invited to be apostles by giving both a witness of word and deed and by committing themselves to mission in the parish.

Some may feel called to host meetings in their homes. For a

month before kerygmatic retreats or parish missions, home meetings take place to prepare new people to encounter the *kerygma*. Others serve on home-visitation teams which visit inactive people in their geographical area and invite them to the home meetings or other evangelistic activities.

Once a year all who have accepted the call to the apostolate join in an intensive visitation of as many people within the geographical bounds of the parish as possible. To facilitate this, the parish territory is divided into smaller sectors. The "apostles" invite those they speak with to come to a mission held at the parish during the evenings that week.

If this pastoral plan has the full support of the pastor and is implemented in the name of the parish, it can succeed.

Ernesto Elizondo is the National Coordinator of SINE in the United States, an organization that promotes the implementation of a holistic model for transforming the parish into an evangelizing community. For more information, contact:

SINE National Office
4401 Highcrest Road
Rockford, IL 61107
815–227–1639
815–227–1840 FAX

PART SIX

Evangelization and Christian Unity

21

ECUMENICAL ISSUES IN EVANGELIZATION

Fr. Peter Hocken

We might wonder if evangelization is a promising field for ecumenical collaboration, given the fact that the Christian world seems to be polarized between two camps: mainline denominations, for which evangelization has not been a high priority, and the "nonsacramental" streams, for which evangelism has been a high priority and church has not. These latter streams include Evangelicals, Holiness Christians, Pentecostals, and independent charismatics.

Positive relationships have been hindered by mutual disdain. Members of mainline denominations easily regard the evangelistic streams as bastions of "conservative fundamentalism", while the latter typically perceive mainliners as lost in "lifeless liberalism". Ecumenical relationships are further complicated by widespread anti-Catholic sentiments inherited by the "nonsacramental" streams, for whom the Church of Rome symbolizes the triumph of outward religion and thus "the false church".

You can see why evangelization is a difficult ecumenical issue. The Catholic Church has dialogued the most with mainline denominations that are not currently strong on evangelization, while the evangelistic streams have been suspicious of the ecumenical movement. The latter also tend to group Catholics along with non-Christians as targets for evangelism. Meanwhile, Catholics often see them as "sects" to be fought rather than as potential allies of any kind.

How can we cooperate in evangelization across this major

divide? Is there an ecumenical alternative to squaring off for a war of polemics between the Catholic Church and "the sects"? I want to suggest that significant collaboration is possible; indeed it is already happening in a few places.[1]

Why Does Catholic Evangelization Have an Ecumenical Component?

First, Vatican II's acceptance of the ecumenical movement as a work of the Holy Spirit has affected all areas of church life. Evangelization necessarily has an ecumenical dimension, because ecumenism is a dimension of everything Christian and ecclesial.

Second, the rise of the charismatic renewal has made possible new forms of collaboration across the church-stream divide. The charismatic renewal has an inherently evangelistic thrust. Through it, God has given vast numbers of ordinary Catholics an inner power and motivation to proclaim their faith in Christ to others. This inner equipping was not the result of any training program but flowed from the baptism in the Spirit. Evangelistic zeal was not so much the grace sought as the natural concomitant of a transformed relationship to God and to Jesus.

This current of renewal has affected virtually all church traditions, with the same grace being poured out on all. Charismatics quickly discovered that the new life they had in common could be exercised together. Not only could they pray together and share their witness together, they could speak together about Jesus to others. Thus the rise of shared evangelism has been as spontaneous as the desire to evangelize itself.

This ecumenical cooperation in evangelization typically has taken three forms. The first is the ordinary evangelistic outreach of ecumenical communities. The second is Catholic participation in interdenominational agencies. Youth with a Mission is a prominent example of an evangelistic organization that

---

[1] For the full text of this paper, see *One in Christ* 31 (January 1995).

has been rethinking its attitudes to the Catholic Church and often now desires to help Catholics become effective evangelists.[2]

A third pattern is the formation of ecumenical teams for evangelistic work. These may be one-time events, perhaps organized by councils of churches, or they may be the work of more permanent teams, such as La Tente de l'Unité in France. Catholics have sometimes participated in Billy Graham's campaigns, though this is generally limited to having Catholic counselors who can refer Catholic "converts" to Catholic parishes. This is really evangelical evangelism with an ecumenical follow-up.

Theological Issues

I believe that the ecumenical sharing that has been developing in recent years is not an aberration to be corrected but a response to the Spirit of God. However, theological reflection on these developments is needed. I will try to identify the major theological issues involved.

The distinctiveness of the kerygma. Theologians and catechists today commonly acknowledge that Christian formation involves distinct phases, which I would like to describe as follows: (1) the initial proclamation to the unconvinced; (2) the preparation of the convinced for baptism and reception into the community of faith; and (3) postbaptismal formation. The greatest potential for ecumenical sharing is found at the first stage.

The New Testament indicates a basic initial proclamation of salvation in Christ (*kerygma*), often called the gospel or the good news. The basic preaching of the apostles and disciples included these essential elements: the advent of the kingdom of God; the mighty saving deeds of God in history, reaching their climax in the Passion, death, Resurrection, and Ascension of Jesus; the return of Christ for judgment at the end of the age. This proclamation seeks to bring the hearer to repentance and faith. Those who

[2] See also P. Hocken, "Youth with a Mission", *Pneuma* 16 (1994): 265–70.

accept the good news of salvation in Christ are baptized. They receive the forgiveness of sins and the gift of the Holy Spirit.

The twentieth-century renewal of the Catholic Church centered on Vatican II has involved a recovery of the distinct phases in Christian formation and thus a recovery also, though more gradual, of the *kerygma*. The stages in the RCIA are the most obvious example. The distinction of the basic *kerygma* from subsequent catechetical teaching is clearer in John Paul II's *Catechesi Tradendae* (no. 25) than it had been in Paul VI's *Evangelii Nuntiandi* (no. 22).

Both documents reflect the Catholic concern to bring the gospel to bear on all aspects of life, and so they mean by "evangelization" something much wider than what most Protestants mean by "evangelism". However, both papal documents recognize that there is an initial proclamation that is necessary and distinctive. *Catechesi Tradendae* indicates that this initial proclamation is ordered to conversion and precedes catechesis (nos. 19, 25).

The recovery of the *kerygma* is not simply a work of theological research but an action of the Holy Spirit in the Church. The Spirit is using the movements of spiritual renewal to recover the *kerygma,* not simply in theory but in action.

First, the Holy Spirit teaches the Christian inwardly of the truths expressed outwardly in the word of God and the teaching of the Church. The gift of the Holy Spirit, consciously received, both clarifies the content of the message to be preached and internally equips the Christian for evangelism. It is the Holy Spirit within the Christian who gives the desire and the capacity to evangelize. Only as the gospel message is brought to life within the Christian can he proclaim that gospel with faith and power. This is why exhortations to evangelize to people who have no personal testimony to conversion will have no effect.

Second, the *kerygma* proclaimed with faith has the power to elicit interior conversion of heart in others. The differentiation of the *kerygma* from subsequent catechesis holds the key to effective evangelization. The Christian evangelist is a herald (*kerux*) who announces a death and Resurrection that has the power to produce the hearer's conversion — itself a death and resurrection.

The basis for joint proclamation of the kerygma. The degree of faith-agreement necessary for jointly proclaiming the gospel will vary according to the nature of the collaboration: less would be needed for unofficial efforts, like the spontaneous initiative of a neighborhood group; more would be needed for official, institutionalized, and ongoing collaboration, like an interconfessional missionary society.

For a more official outreach, we could take as the necessary content of the *kerygma* what Pope Paul VI described as "the foundation, center and at the same time summit of its dynamism", that is, "a clear proclamation that, in Jesus Christ, the Son of God made man, who died and rose from the dead, salvation is offered to all men, as a gift of God's grace and mercy" (EN, no. 27).

The recently issued statement *Evangelicals and Catholics Together* at least implies that joint proclamation of the gospel is possible.[3] The authors affirm together the contents of the Apostles' Creed. At the same time, they include a statement of the conditional nature of this agreement, one which could be used by all participating bodies in formal patterns of joint evangelism: "These differing beliefs about the relationship between baptism, new birth, and membership in the church should be honestly presented to the Christian who has undergone conversion."

Such joint proclamation is not possible with all Protestants: for example, with those of very liberal tendencies who deny central elements in the *kerygma* or with those who hold doctrines that deviate from the basic gospel message. Catholics are more united with Evangelicals and Pentecostals on the *kerygma,* where our characteristic differences of emphasis are complementary rather than inherently opposed. An obvious example is the Evangelical emphasis on the "substitutionary atonement" (Christ died in our place) and the Catholic preference for the language of "representation" and "solidarity" (Christ represents all humanity before the Father). One without the other leads to imbalance.

An ecumenical approach can help us as Catholics to see the

[3] "Evangelicals and Catholics Together: The Christian Mission in the Third Millennium", *First Things* 43 (May 1994): 15–23.

links between doctrinal emphasis and evangelistic impact. In particular, it can help us to view more positively the evangelical accent on conversion as a critical rupture with the past. Catholics need to recognize the necessity for a radical turning to God, one which takes seriously the New Testament teaching that spiritual rebirth entails a death to the old life and a resurrection to a new life of the Spirit (see Rom 6:3–11, 8:13; Gal 5:24; Col 2:11–12, 3:3).

In fact, this death to the old life is at the heart of the sacramental symbolism of baptism and is expressed in the threefold renunciation of Satan and sin. Only converts who have experienced this spiritual death and resurrection and a radically changed life in Jesus Christ will have a personal testimony with the power to evangelize others.

The relationship between evangelization and Church. Here is where we meet the most difficult theological questions. The Catholic Church is concerned with affirming the full ecclesial instrumentality and context for the work of evangelization as well as the unique relationship of the Catholic Church to the one Church of Jesus Christ.

In the Catholic understanding, the gospel is proclaimed by the Church so that new life may be generated within the Church for the Church. This view affirms the maternal role of the Church, formed and moved by the Holy Spirit. The evangelized thus have a Spirit-formed mother as well as a life-giving Father.

Perhaps the most crucial theological issue concerns the Catholic sense of the total inner coherence of divine revelation. Thus, for the Catholic Church, the divinely revealed good news of salvation in Christ necessarily bears an inner orientation to the whole mystery of the Church. Thus any deficiencies in faith concerning the full mystery of the Church inevitably weaken our grasp of the basic gospel message. This concern for the inner coherence of all revealed truth was evident in the Vatican *Instruction on the Church as Communion,* particularly the observations on the relationship of papal primacy to ecclesial communion.[4]

The basis for anything separated Christians do in common is what they share of the Spirit in Christ: Catholic documents on ecumenism have emphasized the basis for this sharing in our common baptism. In the Catholic understanding, this sharing in divine things is to be understood not in an individualistic way but in an ecclesial framework. That is to say, Christians act as members of churches or ecclesial communities, and their acts of sharing are instances of "partial communion" between separated churches or ecclesial communities.

Catholic participation in joint evangelistic ventures need not be seen as positing an initial nonecclesial stage of joint evangelism followed by a stage of separate ecclesial initiation. It can be practiced as a "partial communion" between ecclesial communities, leading to converts being received into "partially separated" churches and ecclesial communities. However, joint proclamation at the official level requires some agreement on these two points: evangelization is an expression of the Church; and no impediments should be placed in the way of converts choosing the full Catholic process of initiation.

The coherence of the whole Catholic faith has important ecumenical consequences. This works both ways, for evil and for good. On the one hand, objective error, defects in faith, and prejudice would operate to weaken and subvert an individual's faith, whether Catholic or Protestant. On the other hand, the authentic presence of Christ and the Spirit of God always works to increase the truth and life by which one is possessed.

On this basis, we could propose a complementary principle: Wherever the Holy Spirit is at work in other Christians, and the reality of salvation in the God-man is confessed, there exists an inner orientation to the fullness of Christ. Such a perspective

---

[4] The Congregation for the Doctrine of the Faith, "Letter to the Bishops of the Catholic Church on Some Aspects of the Church Understood as Communion", dated June 15, 1992.

underlines the gravity of all prejudice and the grace required to overcome it. Allowing the Holy Spirit to accomplish this work of grace moves us farther along the path from sectarianism to full catholicity.

Ecumenical collaboration in evangelization represents an abandonment of competition as well as of attitudes of hostility and prejudice between the churches. As stated in *Evangelicals and Catholics Together,* "We do know that existing patterns of distrustful polemic and conflict are not the way" (no. 2).

We must also recognize, however, that ecumenical cooperation founded on a theology of partial communion more obviously applies to mainline Protestant denominations than to the Evangelical and Pentecostal sectors. The potential for collaboration could be evaluated by asking potential Protestant partners a key question: Do they understand that evangelization essentially means bringing a person into a local church as an expression of the body of Christ?

Here we need to take note of some significant stirrings in parts of the Evangelical and Pentecostal world in relation to church. Spurred partly by an awareness of the debilitating spiritual effects of rampant individualism and partly by the "church growth" movement, strategies of "church planting" have been developing throughout the Evangelical world. One of the fastest-growing sectors is the independent charismatics, sometimes called "non-denominationals", who generally place a stronger emphasis on the covenantal character of the local church as the body of Christ than do most Pentecostals and Evangelicals. While this new emphasis on church is still far from the Catholic sacramental-liturgical understanding, it nonetheless marks an important trend that could favor increased ecumenical cooperation.

Joint evangelism expresses in a visible way the reconciling power of the gospel being proclaimed. This proclamation is weakened and contradicted by competitive and polemical evangelism. Like any other ecumenical activity, joint evangelism brings to fuller expression the "imperfect" unity between our churches and ecclesial communities. Each expression of "partial communion" inevitably deepens that partial communion and helps move us toward full reconciliation and full communion.

Ecumenical learning is a two-way street. Working with Catholics who have a strong sense of church can help other Christians to consider with greater seriousness the church and the corporate character of Christian life. However, the growing Evangelical and charismatic focus on building the body of Christ can invigorate Catholics, whose emphasis on church can often be more external— whether institutional or sacramental. We all need to be reminded of the importance of living together in love, of team leadership, and of reaching a common mind in Christ.

Toward an Ecumenical Strategy

An ecumenical strategy for world evangelization would have two thrusts: (1) a policy of developing positive relationships with the most evangelistic non-Catholic Christians, helping them to become not less evangelistic but more ecumenical; (2) the firm rooting of Catholic evangelization in church renewal, of which ecumenism is an intrinsic dimension. Such a strategy would help to encourage and develop ecumenical attitudes within the Evangelical, Pentecostal, and charismatic streams.

Most lasting changes in attitude begin through personal contact. At Vatican II, the daily interaction between the bishops and the non-Catholic observers changed many hearts. Youth with a Mission's changing attitudes to the Catholic Church began through meetings between its Protestant leaders and charismatic Catholics. Other impetus for closer contact has come from collaboration on pro-life and other moral issues.

We cannot control or organize such openness to the Catholic Church on the part of Protestant or parachurch bodies, but we can help the process by our prayers, our friendship, and our assistance when invited. We as Catholics also have much to learn in order to collaborate with the Evangelical and Pentecostal streams. We need to be as well informed about what is happening in this dynamic sector as our ecumenical specialists are in regard to the "mainline" denominations. This is not easy, because their world is more fluid and changes more rapidly.

Finally, only a renewed Church can evangelize. Only a renewed

Church will have the desire to evangelize. The only way that the Catholic Church can stem the hemorrhage of baptized Catholics to other churches is through our own renewal. Only when Catholics preach a message that is as life-giving as that of other preachers and evangelists will the major motive for leaving be removed. Unfortunately, division has led us to oppose and reject elements that belong to the full Catholic and biblical heritage. A heart for renewal means a heart open to all the biblical truth and life found among other parts of the body of Christ.

At first glance, what appears to be a problem turns out to be a grace and an opportunity. Vatican II intuitively grasped this essential link between renewal of the Church and ecumenism: that each tradition, including the Roman Catholic, needs the witness of the Spirit in other traditions for its own full vitality and vigor.

An essential element in this renewal is repentance for our failings in the past and the present. As a Church, we score more highly in modern times for rethinking our theology and adapting our structures than we do for publicly admitting our failures. This has important spiritual repercussions. Because an authentic renewal requires a change of heart before God, becoming an effective evangelizing Church may require a corporate humbling before the Lord, along with the confession of our weaknesses and failings in this area.

This radical link between ecumenism and renewal, between authentic ecumenism and authentic renewal, suggests that the Holy Spirit is challenging the Catholic Church to trust in the power of the truth given by the Lord. In a context of deep renewal, ecumenical collaboration will lead, not to the frequently lamented evils of confusion and false irenicism, but to a greater sharing in revealed truth. Together, we can make major strides toward the realization of the prayer of Jesus that "all may be one".

22

STRIVING SIDE BY SIDE FOR THE GOSPEL IN A POST–CHRISTIAN CULTURE

Charles Colson

As the principal drafters of *Evangelicals and Catholics Together,* Richard Neuhaus and I labored alongside many others to record the gospel truths jointly professed by Evangelicals and Catholics. We consider it critical for all true Christians to make a common stand in defense of truth, of our historic confession of belief, and of a Christian worldview against the forces of pantheism, atheism, and secularism that threaten to roll over us like a flood.

When the apostles preached the gospel in Jerusalem, they had a very simple and direct message: "The Messiah has come. He has been raised from the dead. He lives." The Jews understood this message because they had studied the Scriptures and knew there was going to be a Messiah.

When Paul preached in Athens, he presented a very different message. Because the Greeks had no prior knowledge of God's plan to save the human race, he had to explain what the Jews took for granted. He had to give them the basic fundamentals of our faith, from the beginning when God had created the world. Paul finally introduced the true God in a way they could understand by referring to their temple to the unknown gods.

God calls all Christians to join together in proclaiming the good news of salvation in Christ. But we cannot understand what it means to evangelize the world until we know the world in which we are called to evangelize. In fact, we are talking to a world that no longer knows Jesus, or the historical background, or even the most basic biblical knowledge. We can no longer preach the gospel as if we were in Jerusalem. We live in Athens. We live in a world surrounded by temples to unknown gods. Clearly we live in a post-Christian culture.

America's Rapid Decline into Paganism

Let me give you a few statistics that illustrate how our nation has become a post-Christian culture. In 1963, 65 percent of Americans believed the Bible to be literally true. In 1982, nineteen years later, only 32 percent believed the Bible to be literally true.

One-half of all Americans today believe that all roads lead to heaven. One-half believe in ESP. One-quarter believe in reincarnation. You do not think the New Age is a threat, even inside our churches? One out of three Americans says he has communicated with the dead! A sin before God!

Eighty percent of all Americans today say there are no moral absolutes binding in every situation. Eighty-one percent believe you can find your own religious truth apart from a relationship to a church or synagogue. Eighty-one percent do not believe they need us, the body of Christ. They do not understand the gospel. America is a pagan culture.

Actually, the analogy of Athens fails somewhat because Athens was a *pre*-Christian culture. We are a *post*-Christian culture, but pagan nonetheless. Just look at our textbooks. Consider the fact that prayer has been eliminated from public places by a Supreme Court that seems determined to eradicate religious values. Look at the media coverage. Peter Berger, a sociologist at Boston University, once observed that the most religious nation in the world is India, and the most irreligious nation is Sweden. And, Berger added, "America is a country of Indians ruled by Swedes."

How did this happen so quickly? We live in a pagan culture. If we are serious about evangelism, if we are serious about building the church, if we are serious about witnessing the kingdom of God in the world today, the most critical question is "Why did this happen? What are the root causes?"

Understanding the reasons is essential, because Evangelicals and Pentecostals and Roman Catholics and moral conservatives of every stripe are running around putting out fires here, there, everywhere. Meanwhile, somebody is sitting in the background lighting them all, and we cannot tell why all these fires keep breaking out. We exhaust our energy fighting all the battles without understanding the strategy of the war.

There is a war going on—a war for the hearts and the minds of people. And it is being waged by cultural elites in America. This war has profound implications for the Church. Most Christians never stop to think about it because they are busy attacking particular problems. We may lose one battle and win the next, but meanwhile we are losing the war.

How did America, over a period of just thirty years, lose its Christian roots? Why are we no longer living in Jerusalem? Why do we live in Athens? Since ancient times, mankind has believed in certain transcendent truths and values. The Torah, the Jewish law, was based upon absolute truth, absolute values. Certain things were true because they were true, not because they were *thought* to be true, but because they *were* true, because they were absolutes.

The Greeks approached absolutes in exactly the same way. Their culture assumed the existence of truth, beauty, and justice. Justice determined how they would live together as a people, which Plato took as the topic of *The Republic.* The Greeks perceived the world as being made up of four material essences—earth, air, water, and fire—with the *quintessential* intellectual inquiry involving the *fifth* essence, the spiritual essence that would hold them all together.

In fact, intellectuals throughout history have considered theology the queen of sciences, believing that matter made sense only in view of a spiritual dimension of absolutes. After the Greeks came the Romans, who believed, as Cicero said, that without God there could be no concord or harmony or justice in society. And then the Christian influence burst forth on the world. For fifteen centuries of Western civilization, Judeo-Christian revelation by and large established the absolute values by which we would live together as a people.

A mere couple of hundred years ago, the Age of Reason began, also known as the Enlightenment. Intellectuals, particularly in Europe, began to hypothesize the creation of the universe without God. That meant that moral values could be established apart from God, through the human mind. Philosophers began to argue that through reason alone, human beings could achieve the Greek absolutes: truth, beauty, justice, meaning, and moral behavior.

This shift in thinking soon traveled to America. Paul Johnson, a British historian and brilliant scholar, wrote *The History of Christianity* and *Modern Times* to explain what he thought happened in Western culture. Johnson identified as pivotal the year 1919, when Einstein proposed the theory of relativity. The general population soon confused *relativity* in the physical sciences with *relativism* in the field of ideas.

Relativism began to invade popular culture gradually through the 1920s. Then Freud came along with his therapeutic notion of life, that people are just repressed by their neuroses. As Freudian theories became fashionable, Americans lost any sense of individual accountability.

The most profound shift took place in the sixties, when a social revolution blazed through America. From France came the writings of existentialists by the names of Camus and Sartre: "God is dead! Life has no meaning, so overcome the nothingness of life by your own heroic individualism." This was the message of the sixties. And the younger generation believed what they were taught on campus. They flaunted life's meaninglessness by a sort of communal individualism in the form of letting their hair grow, wearing tie-dyed clothes and long beads, enjoying cheap drugs and free sex.

I happened to be working in the White House during those years and witnessed that ugly period in American life from a national perspective. With division on the campuses and the whole country split right down the middle over our involvement in

Vietnam, it was like a civil war. And we thought it was simply a temporary aberration. It was not. It was a fundamental change in how we view life and reality.

In the seventies, we emerged from that ugly decade and breathed a collective sigh of relief, thinking to ourselves, *Whew! That's behind us!* It wasn't. The kids simply shaved off their long hair, got rid of their tie-dyes, turned in their beads for three-piece pin-striped suits, graduated from cheap drugs to cocaine, and went to New York and became Yuppies.

Today, from the White House through the Congress, through the newsrooms of America, through the universities, the values of the sixties have become mainstream values. "God is dead; life has no meaning; live for the moment." It used to take a century for the ideas of intellectuals to filter down to the public and change how people think. Television and modern media now make it happen instantaneously. We thus embraced the values of the sixties almost overnight.

"There Is No Truth"

We are living in an era that is gradually being recognized as the postmodern era, not just *post-Christian,* but *postmodern.* The thinkers of the modern era believed, unlike the Christians and the Jews, that you could find truth through reason. But the *postmodernist* says not only can you not find truth through Judeo-Christian revelation (because that could not possibly be true), but neither can you find it through reason. Thus the postmodernist concludes: there is no truth.

Stanley Fish is a professor at Duke with enormous influence in academia today. He says, in effect, that all *principles* are *preferences,* which means that our job is to see that others do not impose their views on us; rather we impose our views on them! As you can imagine, this sort of approach to truth produces an enormous struggle for power in society.

Academic circles refer to the consequences as "deconstruction-ism". Simply put, history no longer has any meaning. When

Christians say, "The Bible is true; Jesus Christ actually died on the Cross for your sins", many people simply shrug their shoulders. They say, "History has no meaning. It is only subjective, only how I view it."

When Christians invest a certain value in cultural traditions, the postmodern thinker says, "There are no values except those which a culture adopts for itself." Intellectuals call this "multiculturalism". I call it "tribalism". If no culture can claim any objective truth, then all cultures are equal. If cultural values are simply the result of people's subjective evaluations, we cannot claim that our culture is superior to that of Brazil, where beating wives and girlfriends is commonly accepted as a reasonable response to displeasure. Americans are horrified by it. But the multiculturalist says we have to respect all cultures since they are all equal.

Christian apologist Ravi Zacharias captures the absurdity of this view. He notes that in some cultures, neighbors *love* one another, and in others they *eat* one another. Which one do you *prefer?* Yet multiculturalism is at the heart of the politically correct movement on campuses.

If there are no shared values by which we live together, then we begin to reduce people to their lowest common denominator of identity. We may filter down through women minorities, and through all the subgroups currently contending for power in this politicized structure. After working hard and long to find a group with whom to identify someone totally, a person may end up reduced to membership in the group of left-handed, blue-eyed transvestites!

Stanley Fish, one of the leaders in deconstructionism, wrote a book called *There's No Such Thing as Free Speech, and It's a Good Thing, Too.* According to the predominant moral view, you cannot talk openly and freely in a politically correct culture because you are liable to offend one of these subgroups, which is now the only way we can establish our identity, since we cannot have a common culture.

Cultural relativism makes reasonable moral discourse impossible. Try debating with a friend on the right to life, as I recently did.

Basically, what the debate boils down to is "I prefer that you not kill babies", while the other side says, "I prefer that you do." If there is no truth, then we have no objective yardstick by which to measure our actions. There is only what I subjectively apprehend. Political debate degenerates into an endless tug-of-war. Alistair McIntire, the noted moral theologian at Notre Dame, says that politics today is simply a civil war carried on by other means.

I encourage you to read a threshold case in the Supreme Court, *Casey v. Planned Parenthood*, a legal ruling that marked a major turning point in American life, where values dramatically changed in the law. The case was brought by Planned Parenthood against Governor Casey of Pennsylvania to oppose all restrictions on abortion. The Court declared: "At the heart of liberty is the right to define one's own concept of existence, of meaning, of the universe, of the mystery of human life."

Everybody can act upon their beliefs in the mystery of human life in their own way! That is the culture of death! We confuse freedom of conscience—the belief that we hold about the mystery of life— with our ability to act upon it. Such a position totally deconstructs the political structures in America. We no longer enjoy a political consensus in this country. There cannot be any consensus! There is no truth.

Recently a judge in the state of Washington struck down a statute banning assisted suicide that had been passed by the voters. Her precedent? She read from the *Casey v. Planned Parenthood* decision. This pivotal case denies the existence of any objective standards. We will never win the abortion debate—not as long as the prevailing cultural attitude in America is reflected in that Supreme Court decision.

What inevitably follows, of course, is moral chaos. Crime has increased 560 *percent* in the last thirty years in America. It is out of control. Dostoyevsky was right: If there is no God, everything is permissible. All of this is simply the result of postmodern thought that there are no values, reflected in the Supreme Court's decision that the mystery of life is dependent upon the subjective determination of every single human being.

Will Durant, the famous historian, says that no society in

human history has ever survived without a strong moral code, nor has there been a case in which that moral code has not been informed by religious truth. If he is right, then our society is absolutely bound, not for deconstruction, but for *destruction.* And that is the environment in which we have to evangelize.

A recent Barna poll reported 71 percent of the American people as saying there is no such thing as truth. We Christians follow a man who says "I am the truth", yet 40 percent of the Evangelicals who responded to that same poll said there is no such thing as truth. They are no better off than the pagans.

How can we possibly convince somebody that Jesus Christ is *the* truth if people do not believe there is any such thing as truth? Before we can begin to evangelize, we have got to do what Paul did at Mars Hill: educate people on the current cultural crisis and teach them that there *is* truth. And that Jesus Christ embodies that truth.

Being the Church

I have painted a pretty bleak picture, but just when we reach the point of utter despair, God has a wonderful way of opening a little window of opportunity. And many people seem to be reaching that point of despair. Various polls indicate that a majority of Americans (71 percent, according to the *Times Mirror*) are dissatisfied with the way things are going. During President Clinton's campaign we heard, "It's the economy, stupid!" Just one year later, only a small percentage rated the economy as their major concern, while 50 percent cited crime, drugs, and even family values.

Despite the fact that the cultural elite is brainwashing us, the American people know something is not right. And their concerns focus on the very things upon which we stand to make common witness to the world. We must begin to witness to the kingdom while people are hungering inside to see the truth.

President Clinton recently held a one-hour press conference with the MTV generation. One student asked him about his underpants: Did he wear boxers or briefs? And of course the press zeroed in on that sensational topic. But a seventeen-year-old asked the most revealing question I have heard in a long time. Dahlia Schweitzer of Bethesda, Maryland, asked: "Mr. President, it seems to me that Kurt Cobain's recent suicide exemplified the emptiness that many in our generation feel. How do you propose to teach our youth how important life is?"

Young Dahlia Schweitzer got right to the heart of the issue. According to the *New York Times* report, Mr. Clinton did not seem to have a legislative solution at hand. Thank God! Are we going to pass a meaning-of-life bill? He could have acknowledged that the killing of babies fails to venerate life in our culture; he did not. Instead he answered that self-esteem is important; you have got to feel important and good about yourself. More therapeutic psycho-babble!

But Clinton is the wrong person to ask. *Where is there meaning in life?* The president cannot do anything to meet this need; politics will never solve that problem. That question is being asked of *us,* the followers of Jesus Christ. And the only way that we can give a credible answer is by *being* the Church. The answer wells up from within a society when true believers live out their faith. And that is the challenge we face today.

It has never been more crucial for the Church to be the Church. Catholic historian Christopher Dawson said, "Being precedes doing." Christians have a tendency to follow the ways of the world. We join a movement or try to change the whole world through organized crusades. It does not work that way. Every time the Church has done that, she has failed.

Our first priority is to *be* the people of God: holy, righteous communities exemplifying the kingdom yet to come, equipping one another, loving one another, working together. Being the Church means *showing the love of God,* not just attending a service to have our ears tickled and to feel good about ourselves. The job of the Church is not to make people *happy;* it is to make them *holy and equipped,* able to live out their faith in the world! That is the call upon the Church.

When we get our priorities mixed up and try to change the

world, we fail and discredit the gospel. It has happened throughout the two thousand years of Christianity—from liberation theology on the left to all the triumphalistic movements on the right,
most notably the Moral Majority in the eighties.

I am not saying we should not go out and try to fight these
battles. We had better be out on the front lines, whether they put
us in jail or not. God bless the people who stand in front of
abortion clinics. Yes, we are called to bring justice and righteousness
into public places, but only as it flows out of our *being* a holy
community. Being precedes doing. Until we *are* the people of
God, we cannot make a difference in the world, no matter how
well intentioned our efforts may be.

Standing Together for the Cause of Christ

I am absolutely convinced that a new alignment is taking place
among those who share a common belief in the historic confession
of orthodoxy, in the Apostles' Creed, in the Nicene Creed. I do
not mean to minimize our theological differences, reducing them
to some watered-down ecumenism, but at the heart of the gospel
our core beliefs are the same. We have got to be able to stand
together on this common truth. Otherwise we cannot succeed in
evangelizing the world. Unity is a prerequisite. As Jesus said in his
high-priestly prayer, "Father, let them be one with one another as I
am one with you, in order that the world will know that you did
send me."

The precondition to evangelism is that the world begin to see
us together. The Church consists of 1.8 billion Christians who are
splintered all over the lot into different confessions and different
groups, and all fighting with one another. Meanwhile, we face
one billion well-organized Muslims, 430 million New Age, occult,
and neo-Hindus invading every area, and a myriad of committed
secularists who are determined to eliminate Christianity because
we represent truth—which in their minds does not exist.

Regardless of the confession from which we come, regardless
of the tradition, regardless of our view of the Church and the

sacraments, true believers must come together on the deity of Christ and on the fact that he died on the Cross for our sins, that he was bodily raised from the dead, that he is coming again, that the Scripture is infallible—as our document *Evangelicals and Catholics Together* confirms.

If we cannot stand together on these grounds and relate those truths to a common worldview, then we have no hope. We must do so in order to bring these truths about the public good into the public square. Those of us who share a common confession of orthodox Christian belief must stand tall—whether we be Methodists, or Baptists, or Episcopalians, or Roman Catholics, or Orthodox. The fact of the matter is that if we cannot stand together, we will be overrun by the forces arrayed against us.

The time has come for true believers to reach out their hands across five hundred years of division and say, "I love you, brother. I love you, sister." John Wesley put it so wonderfully when he said, "If your heart beats as mine, if you believe as I do that Jesus Christ was raised from the dead and died on the Cross for my sins, then I extend the right hand of fellowship to you." Our common faith must unify us. Truly to be the Church, we must stand together and be one.

Richard Neuhaus and I and several others worked on such a statement for two years. Since publishing *Evangelicals and Catholics Together,* I have discovered a very interesting thing. If I had to judge Christianity by the loving nature of the letters I receive, I would become a Buddhist. And some of the angriest letters have come from liberal Catholics. The *National Catholic Reporter* excoriated us, labeling us a right-wing movement in disguise. And conservative Protestants tell me that I have absolutely sold out the heritage of the Reformation, that I am a traitor.

But we do not judge Christianity by letters like this, but rather by the historic truth upon which we base our common faith: that Jesus Christ bodily rose from the dead and that we are saved by his blood. I believe we should be willing to give our lives in defense of the cause of Christ. We must stand together as the body of Christ and *be* the Church.

Defending the Truth

The second thing we have got to do is to defend the truth, which means having a common worldview. We no longer can say, "I'm saved, Jesus in me, hallelujah, I'm in church, I've been blessed, I have been anointed with the Holy Spirit, I have the power of God in my life, oh wonderful!" The Christian's earliest baptismal confession was simply "Jesus is Lord!"

If Jesus is Lord, then he is Lord of all of creation, and we must look at all of the world through the eyes of Scripture. When we do that, then we begin to discern all that is happening in the world today. We begin to look at all of life through Christian eyes, through a Christian mind, through a biblically-informed view of reality.

If we are informed about biblical truth as expressed in our own society, we can make wonderful arguments in today's debate. Who brought hospitals to America? Christians. Who brought schools and universities to America? Christians. Who formed the vanguard in abolishing slavery? Christians. Every humane social reform has come about through the influence of Christians.

I say to my secular friends, "You want to be tolerant, you want to get rid of the Christian influence, you don't want us pushing our agenda down your throat. That's fine, but where are you going to get the compassionate people who go out and do good, who go into the prisons and hug these guys who are dying with AIDS? Where are you going to get the people who have a sense of virtue, who believe that there are standards of righteousness by which we live? It comes from Christians!"

An absolute prerequisite for evangelism today is presenting this sort of cultural apologetic, intelligently and thoughtfully defending the role of Christianity in society. I am not saying that the word of God will not convict, but if you walk up to a man and say, "Hey, brother, *the Bible says . . .* ", immediately he will think, *I don't believe what this guy is about to read to me.* But if you can begin to explain to him the historic truth of Christianity and its influence in society, suddenly you have opened him up just a little bit.

Christian influence has a powerful effect in every area of life.

Recent studies at the National Institute of Health indicate that Christians live longer and healthier lives. What a great argument for faith! You can say to your friends, "Did you know that medical reports name a Christian way of life as the single most important ingredient in health and longevity? That living by Christian standards and values respects the dignity of the body that God has given us? Don't you realize what that means to the public good?" And you will see their eyes begin to open.

Be prepared to defend the truth and expose the bankruptcy of modern thought. Don't back away; don't be shy. Even though you are in a minority, go out and tell people why Christianity is so vital to our society. And you will suddenly hear your secular neighbors asking questions, because they are all like Dahlia Schweitzer. They have been soaked in this culture, and yet they are saying "There's something missing, there's got to be a deeper meaning of life. Where is it?" And if they do not find the answer, it is because we failed to give it to them.

Demonstrating the Truth

Third, it is absolutely critical that we demonstrate Christian living. Remember that the gospel is proclamation, revealed propositional truth. People have got to hear it with their ears, but they also need to see it with their eyes. Take Angel Tree®, the Prison Fellowship program closest to my heart. Hundreds of thousands of kids have a mommy or daddy in prison, and many of these families are absolutely destitute, with nowhere to turn. But last year we reached more than 363,000 kids with Christmas gifts.

Prison inmates fill out a form with their children's addresses. Then church volunteers call the families and find out what the children want, purchase the gifts, and deliver them along with a gospel activity book and illustrated Bibles. Every year my wife and I deliver some of these gifts, and we love taking our grandchildren along. It is a wonderful program.

This year we drew the name of a child in a public housing project. The police warned us that we should not go there without a police escort. But we said, "No way are we going to deliver Christmas gifts to a child with a police escort." Halfway through the projects, after seeing all these teenagers standing on street corners and staring at us, I must admit I started to think, *Maybe the police were right.*

We made it safely to this little corner unit and knocked on the door. A young lad answered the door—the cutest little kid—and he took us inside. We got there a few minutes earlier than expected, so his mother was not home from work yet, but his sister was there. The only things in the room were a couple of big chairs with the stuffing coming out and a bare Christmas tree leaning against the wall. And I said, "Here are some presents from your daddy." And this little kid says, "I knew my daddy wouldn't forget me!"

After we brought these gifts in and put them under the undecorated tree, I asked the boy his name. He said, "Emmanuel". "Do you know what Emmanuel means?" I asked. And I got out my Bible and showed him that Emmanuel means "God is with us." About two minutes later his mother came in the door. Emmanuel ran over and grabbed her around the legs and said, "Mommy, Mommy, do you know what my name means? God is with us!" In that dreary little place in the projects, God is with them. That family is in church today, worshipping God.

We have to take the gospel out so people can see it and feel it and touch it. Inner-city problems alone are immense. According to a 1992 study by the National Center on Institutions and Alternatives, fifty-six percent of the black male population of inner-city Baltimore between the ages of 18 and 35 are in jail, on bond awaiting trial, on probation, on parole or under warrant for arrest. [1] And a city is finished if it has no leadership. Somehow Christians like us have simply got to go into those areas and let them know God is with us. That is what will bring them to Christ.

[1] *St. Petersburg Times,* September 8, 1992, p. A-12.

Overcoming Evil with Good

Last fall I was visited by the Holy Spirit in a powerful way and given a message that I know I am to share with the world—something that has happened only five or six times in my life. I was in Poland to mark the charter of the fifty-eighth country in Prison Fellowship International. The head of our Polish ministry, Fr. Jan Sikorski, is the chaplain general of the Polish prison system. He had decided to hold the service to commission Prison Fellowship Poland in the church courtyard where Fr. Jerzy Popieluszko used to preach.

Fr. Jerzy was a young, frail priest who used to stand on the balcony of this church and preach at Sunday Mass. A hundred thousand people would come and listen. This little guy with a bold, booming voice would preach two messages: Defend the truth, and overcome evil with good. Sunday after Sunday he would preach those same messages during the early eighties. A polished granite tombstone in the shape of a cross stands in the center of the church courtyard to mark Fr. Jerzy's grave. And in the tree next to his monument is carved a crucifix.

As Polish television crews recorded the event, Fr. Sikorski began to speak to the crowd: "We're here today because Jerzy Popieluszko would be so thrilled that the prisoners of Poland have been set free, and this ministry is coming to set prisoners free." As I looked up at that balcony, I was struck by the moment, by the sense of history, by what God had done in that place—that little, frail man standing up there preaching: "Defend the truth! Overcome evil with good!"

Fr. Sikorski went on to tell the story, how Jerzy Popieluszko would preach that message week after week in the early eighties. Of course the communist oppressors could not stand it, so they would send agents to break into his apartment and ransack it. They ran him off the road a few times. They had him arrested on false charges. Fr. Jerzy continued to preach, and he continued to practice what he preached. During the holidays in Poland, he would go out into the snow-covered streets and hand out Polish

Christmas cookies to the hated communist troops and say, "Jesus loves you."

Then Fr. Jerzy disappeared. People knelt on factory floors to pray for his safe return. Work almost stopped in Gdansk and Krakow and Warsaw. Churches were filled with people praying for Fr. Jerzy. Four days later they found his body floating in the Vistula River. His fingernails were torn out, his eyes were gouged out. He had been tortured.

The people filled the churches to mourn the loss of this holy man, and then they came marching out of the churches. The communists had moved in tanks and troops to deal with the confrontation. But Fr. Jerzy had taught them well. Tens of thousands of people marched through the streets of Warsaw and Krakow and Gdansk, carrying huge banners and chanting, "We forgive, we forgive, we forgive." How remarkable, yet that is the simple gospel message. A few years later that monstrous communist system fell from its own weight, because evil cannot stand against good.

I was given a rare opportunity in that Polish courtyard, a place that was usually fenced off. But they took the fence down for this special occasion, and the head of chaplains, a Monsignor from the Vatican, and I were given the privilege of placing flowers on the grave. I felt shivers as I laid the flowers at the tombstone. I turned around and looked again at the balcony from which that frail little priest had preached his message: "Defend the truth! Overcome evil with good!"

And I thought about how lax we Americans are in defending the truth. I thought about how we are so caught up with fighting the enemy, the cultural opposition, that we punch them in the eyes with our fingers instead of giving them the essence of the gospel: God sent his Son—perfect good enrobed in human flesh—to die on the Cross to overcome an evil world. And I looked up to the balcony that day and I heard the message ringing out to the Church all around the world: "Defend the truth! Overcome evil with good."

Let Dahlia Schweitzer's question haunt you every day: *Where is the meaning in life?* And let the answer that comes from our God ring in your ears and in your mouths: "Defend the truth! Overcome evil with good." Amen.

તે

Prison Fellowship is an international organization that spreads God's message of hope to prisoners and their families. For more information, contact:

> Prison Fellowship
> P.O. Box 17500
> Washington, D.C. 20041–0500
> 703–478–0100

INDEX